NOTARY

HOME

STUDY

COURSE

Notary Home Study Course

The Most Complete and Helpful
Self-Education Program for Notaries

ELEVENTH EDITION

NATIONAL NOTARY ASSOCIATION

Published by:

National Notary Association Press
9350 De Soto Avenue, P.O. Box 2402
Chatsworth, CA 91313-2402
(818) 739-4000
Fax: (818) 700-0920

www.NationalNotary.org
e-mail: nna@nationalnotary.org

Eleventh Edition
First Edition © 1985

ISBN Number: 1-59767-048-0
LOC Number: 2005928943

Dedicated to the memory of
Raymond C. Rothman (1922–1995),
National Notary Association founder
and pioneer Notary educator.

Table of Contents

PREFACE

Milton G. Valera

Learning is not attained by chance,
it must be sought for with ardor
and attended to with diligence.

Those are the words of Abigail Adams, wife of second U.S. President John Adams. She wrote them to her son, John Quincy, then only thirteen. It proved to be excellent advice, as John Quincy Adams led a long and productive career in government service as diplomat, Senator, Congressman, Secretary of State and the sixth U.S. President.

More than 200 years later, the wisdom in those words remains undeniable: Acquiring knowledge and skill takes effort.

One does not become proficient in a deceptively complex field such as notarization merely by completing an application, paying a fee and proclaiming, "I am a Notary." Though being a Notary is seldom one's full-time vocation — it is usually an adjunct to another career — holding the office of Notary Public requires a full-time professional commitment to mastering the practices, procedures and customs of the office.

The apparent simplicity of the Notary Public's duties belies the enormous responsibility the Notary carries as society's impartial witness. Without the Notary Public, the workings of commerce and law simply would grind to a halt. Document fraud would proliferate and our courts would become more burdened than ever with challenges to document signatures that were forged, coerced or incompetently made.

Today, business transactions between strangers are common, and we rely on the Notary to verify that the signers of documents are who they claim to be and not impostors trying to cheat an innocent victim out of valuable rights or property through a phony document. Our society trusts Notaries as official witnesses in the everyday business of government and private enterprise. We have important expectations regarding the documents they notarize, and we rely heavily on the Notary to perform every notarial act with the utmost integrity and professionalism.

This will be even more the case in the future, as we put the technology of electronic documents into everyday use. Where once it was unthinkable to conduct business without meeting face to face, in just a few years, transactions between widely separated strangers who sign electronic documents in cyberspace will be commonplace. The speed of transactions will accelerate substantially, with documents prepared at the touch of a computer key. And more than ever, our society will need someone to verify the authenticity of document signatures. That person is the Notary Public — *the* official, impartial witness of our society.

I urge you to rise to and exceed these expectations. I urge you to take pride in your Notary career. And I urge you to keep the promise of the future.

You are to be commended for taking the initial step — obtaining this *Notary Home Study Course*. By doing so, you have shown that you are a conscientious Notary or Notary-to-be, and that you recognize the importance of learning and fully understanding your official responsibilities.

The *Notary Home Study Course* was developed by the staff of the National Notary Association to be your resource to achieve understanding of the many and varied notarial procedures. It will explain all the important aspects of lawful, prudent and ethical practice. And it will be an invaluable reference throughout your Notary career.

Whether you are a longtime Notary or about to be commissioned for the first time, I am confident the *Notary Home Study Course* will provide you with new insight and understanding. Your improved comprehension of notarial practices and procedures will result in greater proficiency as a Notary Public.

Milton G. Valera

President

National Notary Association

FOREWORD

Allen J.
Beermann

As a former state official who commissioned Notaries, as an attorney who understands the importance of a notarial act, and as a Notary Public, myself, I wish to express my gratitude personally and on behalf of Notaries everywhere to the National Notary Association for its extraordinary efforts in preparing and publishing the *Notary Home Study Course*.

I am very excited about this marvelous educational opportunity for you, the new or renewing Notary.

For many years, conscientious Notaries, citizens, attorneys and governmental officials have been concerned about the lack of educational programs for those persons preparing to hold the office of Notary. Yet, for too long, the prevailing attitude in official circles about improving education for Notaries has been "do not disturb." Now, the National Notary Association has taken action, and there is a comprehensive educational program available to every Notary in every state who wishes to mold himself or herself into a true professional.

Now in its fifth decade of service to the American Notary, the National Notary Association has sought to bring professionalism to the office of Notary Public. The Association always has believed that, while integrity and dedication are essential qualities to ensure success in any professional field, the key to the attainment of professional status is *education*. The most sincere and dedicated individual cannot succeed without proper training. That is the overriding premise of the *Notary Home Study Course*.

In addition to explaining the principles of notarization and setting guidelines for performing notarial acts, the *Notary Home Study Course* addresses special duties and documents and carefully delineates what constitutes notarial misconduct. Of critical importance is the part explaining professional responsibility and notarial ethics and outlining the unofficial standards of practice that mark the professional.

The *Notary Home Study Course* has been the most important tool available for improving the standards of Notaries and of notarial acts in this country. In fact, I must conclude that this *Notary Home Study Course* is not only recommended or desirable, it is *imperative* for every commissioned Notary in these United States.

But let me remind you as a student that the dictionary is the only place where "success" comes before "work." It is one thing to begin the *Notary Home Study Course* with the best intentions; it is quite another to persevere through its 24 chapters and fully reap its benefits. Success never just happens — it is caused. You cannot control the length of your life, but you can have something to say about its width and depth. I encourage you to study and master the important notarial concepts in the *Notary Home Study Course* and to use this book as a reference throughout your notarial career.

To get by in this world, there are two ways we can do something: we can do it right, or we can do it over. The *Notary Home Study Course* is your opportunity as a Notary, once and for all, to learn how to do it right. The time you spend studying now will pay dividends in time saved in the future.

I am honored that the National Notary Association has given me this opportunity to offer you an encouraging word as you begin an important educational experience. I am convinced that you and all others who conscientiously complete this *Notary Home Study Course* and use it as a guide in solving practical notarial problems will enjoy success as true professional Notaries.

Allen J. Beermann
Secretary of State of Nebraska
1970–1994

INTRODUCTION

About This Course

The *Notary Home Study Course* teaches Notaries and would-be Notaries how to perform notarial acts. It provides the information necessary to develop the skills and confidence to perform virtually any notarial act. A learn-by-doing program, the *Notary Home Study Course* proceeds at a pace and place determined by the comfort of the student.

We have arranged the *Notary Home Study Course* into six parts to lead the student logically from an understanding of the basic concepts of notarization (Part I), through comprehension of the various notarial acts (Part III), to an appreciation of the subtleties of the Notary's professional responsibilities (Part VI).

Each chapter concludes with a summary and a list of important terms to help the reader review and understand key concepts. These definitions of important terms emphasize their application to notarial duties, rather than their usage outside the scope of notarization. Also, at the end of each chapter is a brief test. In many chapters, the tests pose true-to-life situations that require the student to complete notarial certificates and make journal entries as if for actual notarial acts. This offers the student invaluable hands-on experience. Correct responses for the tests can be found in Appendix 4.

Since laws governing Notaries differ from state to state, the *Notary Home Study Course* describes common statutory requirements. Notarial certificate wordings cited are typical examples and not necessarily prescribed by law in any given state. Where appropriate, unique or unusual notarial laws are pointed out. In addition, Appendix 2 lists several key Notary law provisions for each state and U.S. territory, as well as the address and phone number of each state's Notary regulating official.

When state laws are vague or incomplete in defining the modern Notary's duties — as is often the case — the Notary should follow rules of prudence and common sense. The *Notary Home Study Course* points out procedures that are dictated by custom, common sense and good business practice. We also have included the latest draft of the National Notary Association's *Notary Public Code of Professional Responsibility* (Appendix 1) in its entirety. The Code defines standards of conduct for ethical and professionally responsible Notaries Public. These standards have the dual aim of maximizing the public's protection while minimizing the Notary's liability.

The *Notary Home Study Course* is the most comprehensive and practical self-education tool ever developed for Notaries. Its drafts and revisions have been critiqued by experienced attorneys, business and surety executives, teachers and Notary-regulating officials from around the nation. And its final form reflects their invaluable expertise. This eleventh edition has been completely revised to make the detailed concepts easier than ever to understand, and includes more vital information on specific Notary practices and procedures.

Overwhelmingly, though, the *Notary Home Study Course* reflects the National Notary Association's unequalled five decades of experience educating and serving Notaries Public. Since its founding in 1957 by Raymond C. Rothman and its subsequent stewardship by current president Milton G. Valera, the NNA has educated, trained and informed hundreds of thousands of Notaries throughout the United States.

While it serves as a comprehensive nuts-and-bolts guide to learning and understanding notarization, the *Notary Home Study Course* is not intended to take the place of an attorney or state official in resolving varying interpretations of notarial law or regulation. It must be complemented by careful study of other state-specific materials often provided by a state's commissioning official. In fact, the *Course* is particularly useful in illuminating the often technical wording in such official literature.

By allowing convenient study and review of important concepts, the *Notary Home Study Course* also complements educational seminars and other classroom programs for Notaries.

The *Notary Home Study Course* also includes a take-at-home Comprehensive Examination issued and evaluated by the NNA's Educational Services Department. Upon completion of all the chapters, the student may opt to take the Exam by mailing the card at the back of the book. Those who earn a passing score will be awarded the National Notary Association's Certificate of Excellence, recognition of the new skills the student has attained.

By completing the 24 chapters of the *Notary Home Study Course* and passing the Comprehensive Examination, students demonstrate an uncommon degree of professional dedication. As knowledgeable public servants, *Notary Home Study Course* graduates are ready to perform in the vital and varying role of official impartial witnesses with legal, technical and ethical accuracy. ■

PART I: PRINCIPLES OF NOTARIZATION

CHAPTER 1

What Is a Notary Public?

Ask the average person to explain what a Notary Public is, and the answer is likely to be vague or, perhaps, even dead wrong. Typical responses might be, "It's someone who handles real estate papers," or, "It's someone who legalizes documents," or, "It's someone who stamps and signs important papers." All substantially miss the mark.

Most people do not have a clear idea of the Notary's function, and there are many misconceptions. These vague and incorrect ideas cause many improper requests to be made of Notaries.

IMPARTIAL WITNESS

The basic function of a Notary Public is simple: A Notary is a person of proven integrity commissioned by the state to serve the public as an official, impartial witness. In the most basic of terms, the Notary has the power to witness the signing of documents and to administer oaths. Most often, the Notary's duties involve signed documents and require the Notary to ensure a signer's identity and willingness to sign.

Anyone, of course, can serve as a witness, but Notaries are *impartial* witnesses. That is, Notaries must not have a financial or beneficial

The Notary Public serves the public as an impartial witness.

interest in the transactions they observe; they may neither gain nor lose as a result of the transaction. Adhering to this principle of impartiality is the basis of notarial ethics and places the Notary's motives above suspicion.

In addition, because Notaries are state-appointed officials, the witnessing acts they perform — called *notarial acts* or *notarizations* — carry the sanction and authority of their state.

STATE NOTARY LAWS VARY

While the general principles of notarization are common throughout the United States, each of the 50 states, the District of Columbia and other U.S. jurisdictions enact their own laws that specify the duties of Notaries. These laws vary from state to state and define the office of Notary Public — from the minimum age for Notary applicants to the type of official seal that must be used in performing a notarial act. (See Appendix 2, "State Notary Officials and Key Law Provisions," page 363.)

Notaries must carefully obey the laws of their particular state (or *jurisdiction*), regardless of where a particular document may have been prepared or may be filed.

A Notary's authority to serve as an official witness comes through a written authorization called a *commission* or *appointment*. Depending on state law, the Notary commission is issued by the Governor, Secretary of State, Attorney General or another official such as a local judge. (Again, see Appendix 2, page 363.)

The jurisdiction and term of office of Notaries also will vary from state to state. Most empower Notaries to act anywhere within the state borders, although a few restrict the authority of certain Notaries to their counties of residence. Most states set a four-year term of office, but terms do range from two years to life.

SERVE THE PUBLIC

As public officials, Notaries are commissioned to serve all persons in their jurisdictions. In this respect, they are similar to elected representatives, such as senators and members of state assemblies. In fact, Notaries in some states are "elected" in the sense that their integrity must be endorsed by legislators, county officials or registered voters before they can be commissioned.

Although Notaries are commissioned to serve the public, they owe primary allegiance to the laws of their respective states. This allegiance to law may cause a conflict, since the Notary is also a private individual with obligations to an employer, customers, friends and family. Inevitably, in order to adhere to state statutes and good conduct, Notaries sometimes must displease employers, customers, friends or family members who request an improper notarial act. For instance, an employer might instruct an employee to notarize only for clients — a violation of the Notary's duty to serve all persons making reasonable and lawful requests for notarial acts.

MINISTERIAL OFFICIALS

Notaries are classified as *ministerial* officials, as distinguished from *judicial* officials. Theoretically, ministerial officials follow simple, written rules without having to use significant judgment or *discretion*. In contrast, judicial officials are expected to exercise considerable judgment and discretion in the daily execution of their duties.

But what works neatly in theory does not always hold in practice. Notaries constantly must rely on their own resources in following written rules (notarial laws) that are often vague or incomplete and fail to provide guidelines on many vital matters. For example, laws may require Notaries to identify a document signer without indicating what constitutes proof of identity, leaving the Notary to decide.

Many questions must be resolved without official guidance — from where to place the official Notary seal when there is no room on the document to how to know a person is not being forced to sign a document against his or her will.

Yet, the Notary's discretion is exercised within narrow limits and applies only to his or her own actions. Acting outside these limits, the Notary risks prosecution for the *unauthorized practice of law*. A Notary has no authority to advise others unless the Notary is also an attorney or

Notaries may not help signers draft, prepare, select or understand documents.

a certified expert in a pertinent field — for example, an expert in real estate, escrow or a similar field. The notarial commission does not authorize the Notary to help other persons draft, prepare, complete, select or understand a document. As ministerial officials, Notaries may not even determine what type of notarial act to perform, since this decision has important legal ramifications.

RESPONSIBLE FOR INDIVIDUAL ACTIONS

Notaries who act irresponsibly may be sued for damages caused by their misconduct.

While Notaries have limited authority, their personal financial responsibility for their official acts may be limitless. A Notary who performs his or her duties improperly may be subject to a civil lawsuit to recover financial damages caused by the error.

Most states require Notaries to obtain surety bonds as a guarantee that the public will be protected from any financial loss due to a Notary's improper actions. The bond will pay claims up to the bond value — from $500 to $15,000 — but it does not free the Notary from financial responsibility. The bonding company will attempt to recover its loss from the Notary, but should a claim exceed the bond amount, the Notary will also be held liable for the difference.

To best protect the public and themselves, Notaries must always remember that their commissions belong to them alone. Accordingly, every Notary must exercise *reasonable care*, that degree of concern and attentiveness that a person of normal intelligence and responsibility would exhibit. A Notary's responsibility cannot be shared. An employer, for example, may have paid for a Notary's commissioning fees and notarial supplies, but the employer cannot dictate that the Notary's commission be used improperly. The ultimate responsibility for a Notary's improper act lies with the Notary.

Although Notaries also may be employees when performing notarial acts, they are first public officials who owe primary allegiance to the state's laws and people.

SUMMARY

The Notary Public serves as an official, impartial witness with the power to witness the signing of documents and to administer oaths. Notaries may not benefit from the transactions they witness and, as state-appointed officials, they act with the authority of the state.

Each state's Notary laws vary, so Notaries must carefully obey the laws of their particular state.

A Notary's authority comes through a written authorization called a *commission* or *appointment*. Most states set a four-year term of office and empower Notaries to act anywhere within the state.

As public officials, Notaries must serve all persons who make lawful and reasonable requests for notarization. But since they owe allegiance to the laws of their states, Notaries must occasionally turn down employers, customers, friends or family members who request an improper act.

Notaries are ministerial officials and follow simple written rules, exercising discretion only within narrow limits. By acting beyond these limits, the Notary risks entering into the *unauthorized practice of law*. A Notary has no authority to advise others unless the Notary is also an attorney or expert in the particular field.

If a Notary acts improperly, he or she may be liable for financial damages. As a guarantee that the public will be protected, most states require Notaries to obtain surety bonds — from $500 to $15,000.

To best protect the public and themselves, Notaries must always remember that their commissions belong to them alone, and they should at all times use reasonable care in the performance of their duties. No one can share the Notary's responsibility for an improper act. ■

IMPORTANT TERMS

Appointment: Written authorization to perform notarial acts that is issued by a state's Governor, Secretary of State or other empowering official. Called a commission in some states and jurisdictions.

Bond: Written guaranty purchased from a surety (usually an insurance company) to guarantee payment to a victim of financial loss due to the improper action of a Notary.

Commission: To authorize to perform notarial acts; written authorization to perform notarial acts that is issued by a state's Governor, Secretary of State or other empowering official. Called an appointment in some states and jurisdictions.

Discretion: Freedom to act or judge on one's own, aware and mindful of the consequences.

Ethics: Principles of good conduct and professional responsibility; moral values.

Impartial Witness: Observer without bias; one who has no financial or beneficial interest in the transaction at hand.

Judicial Official: Public officer who uses considerable judgment or discretion in the performance of official duties.

Jurisdiction: Geographic area — a state or county — in which a Notary Public is authorized to perform notarial acts.

Ministerial Official: Public officer who follows written rules without having to use significant judgment or discretion. A Notary is a ministerial official.

Notarial Acts, Notarizations: Witnessing duties of a Notary that are specified by law. Most often, the Notary's duties involve signed documents and require the Notary to ensure a signer's identity and willingness to sign. Another common notarial act involves administration of an oath or affirmation.

Notary Public: Person of proven integrity appointed by a state government to serve the public as an impartial witness with duties specified by law. The Notary has the power to witness the signing of documents and to administer oaths.

Reasonable Care: Degree of concern and attentiveness that a person of normal intelligence and responsibility would exhibit.

Unauthorized Practice of Law: Practice of law by a person who is not a legal professional.

CHAPTER 1 TEST

In each blank, write the response — a, b, c or d — that best completes each of the following statements:

1. Notaries are commissioned by _____.

    a. Each state and given nationwide jurisdiction.

    b. The federal government and given statewide jurisdiction.

    c. Each state and given state or countywide jurisdiction.

    d. Each county and given countywide jurisdiction.

2. In their jurisdictions, Notaries must serve _____.

    a. County residents only.

    b. State residents only.

    c. U.S. citizens only.

    d. All persons.

3. Above all, a Notary should be guided by requirements of _____.

    a. The employer who paid for the Notary's commission.

    b. Customers and business clients.

    c. State law and regulation.

    d. Personal convenience.

4. At times, Notaries must use independent judgment, because _____.

    a. This is expected of all judicial officials.

    b. This is expected of all state-commissioned officers.

    c. Guiding laws may be too complicated to understand.

    d. Guiding laws may be vague or incomplete.

5. A truly impartial Notary should perform a notarial act _____.

    a. Whether or not a transaction is proper.

    b. Whether or not personally involved.

    c. Only when personally involved to ensure compliance with law.

    d. Never when personally involved.

6. A notarial commission _____.

    a. Is transferable from one state to another.

    b. Expires after four years in every state.

    c. Is issued to persons of proven integrity.

    d. Is for use in serving clients and customers only.

7. Notaries are authorized to _____.

    a. Fill out documents for others.

    b. Explain documents to persons who cannot read.

    c. Identify document signers.

    d. Determine the type of notarial act needed.

Explain in your own words:

8. Why is impartiality an essential quality for Notaries?

_____

_____

_____

See page 381 for correct responses.

CHAPTER 2

Notarization Defined

It will come as a surprise to many people that all notarizations are not alike and that there are actually different types of notarial acts. It is common, but incorrect, to believe that all notarizations involve the same procedures and achieve the same purpose. In fact, what we generally refer to as notarizations comprise a group of different official acts that can be performed by a Notary Public. Each of these notarial acts has a distinct and very specific purpose, and each accomplishes a unique result.

Broadly speaking, notarization is the authentication of a document as genuine or the verification that a statement was made under oath. The person who makes this authentication or verification is a public official, the Notary Public. Notarization provides assurance that the particular document is authentic and intended to be in force. For documents to be recorded in the public record (by a county recorder, for example), notarization is usually a requirement.

There are certain results that *no* notarial act ever accomplishes:

• Notarization does not guarantee the truth or accuracy of statements in a document. The Notary Public has no obligation to verify a document's contents.

- Notarization does not legalize or validate a document. A will or other legal paper that contains invalidating flaws before notarization will contain the same flaws afterward.

COMMON NOTARIAL ACTS

Of the various notarial acts, the three most common are acknowledgments, jurats and copy certifications. Brief descriptions of each follow, and Part III of this course covers these notarial acts in depth, detailing the procedures for performing each.

Acknowledgments

The purpose of an acknowledgment is to positively identify the signer.

The *acknowledgment* is the most widely performed notarial act. Its main purpose is positive identification of the document signer — to verify that the person named in the document is, in fact, the person who signed it. An acknowledgment provides assurance that a signer is not an impostor trying to benefit from a phony document.

In executing an acknowledgment, the Notary carefully identifies a document signer, who acknowledges having freely signed.

Acknowledgment of a signature before a Notary is an important step leading to a document's acceptance by a county recorder. Real estate deeds, for example, and many other papers relating to ownership of property must have the signatures acknowledged before the documents can be placed in the public record as authentic.

Jurats

A jurat is used to compel truthfulness from the signer.

Compelling a document signer to be truthful is the main purpose of the notarial act called a *jurat*. The Notary's function in executing a jurat is to appeal to the signer's conscience and to initiate a process that could result in a criminal conviction for perjury if the signer is found to be lying under oath.

In executing a jurat, the Notary must watch the person sign the document, then have the signer make either a solemn, oral promise of truthfulness to a Supreme Being (called an *oath*) or a promise on one's own personal honor (called an *affirmation*). The oath and affirmation have the same legal effect.

Jurats are common with documents that may be used as evidence in court proceedings, such as depositions and affidavits.

Oaths and affirmations also may be executed without reference to a document. An example would be the oath of office given to a public official. In this case, the oath or affirmation is a notarial act in its own right. Most often, though, Notaries administer oaths and affirmations for jurats in connection with documents.

Copy Certification

Certifying that a photocopy of a document is a complete and true reproduction of the original is the purpose of the notarial act called *copy certification*. In certifying a copy, the Notary carefully compares the copy to the original to ensure that they are identical.

> Copy certification ensures that a copy of a document is identical to the original.

Many states either do not allow Notaries to perform copy certifications or put restrictions on this type of notarization. In these states, a custodian-certified copy may be an acceptable alternative. This procedure requires the custodian of the original document — the person who is the document's permanent keeper — to sign a declaration that the copy is identical to the original. The Notary then notarizes this declaration with a jurat, witnessing the custodian's signature and administering an oath or affirmation.

Some documents should never be copy-certified by a Notary, including certain U.S. Citizenship and Immigration Services (USCIS) documents; vital records such as birth, death and marriage certificates; and recordable documents such as deeds.

Other Notarial Acts

In addition to acknowledgments, jurats and copy certifications, there are less common notarial acts that Notaries in certain jurisdictions may perform. These include accepting proofs of execution from a subscribing witness, protesting nonpayment of negotiable instruments on behalf of a payee, taking depositions, witnessing events and — in Maine, South Carolina, Florida, and one parish is Louisiana only — performing marriages.

DETERMINING THE NOTARIAL ACT

Often the request for notarization comes without sufficient instructions. The Notary may be handed a document and simply told, "I need this notarized." But without additional instructions from the signer or some indication on the document as to the type of notarization required, the Notary does not have enough information to proceed with the request.

As ministerial officials who follow but cannot issue instructions, nonattorney Notaries do not have the authority to determine the type of notarial act that is needed in a given instance. This is a legal decision, beyond the Notary's scope of expertise, and would be considered the unauthorized practice of law, a criminal offense.

Even though the Notary may have years of experience and may be certain of the appropriate notarial act to execute, the Notary may *never* make this decision. Instead, Notaries must be instructed by the signer as to what type of notarial act to perform before they can know how to proceed with a notarization.

In many cases, the decision already will have been made, and the document will indicate the type of notarization through the notarial wording that is provided on the document. If a document lacks notarial wording, it is the signer's responsibility to find out what notarization is appropriate by checking with the person or agency that prepared the document or will receive it. It is *never* the role of the Notary to decide what type of notarial act is needed for a given document, unless, of course, the Notary is also an attorney.

From the signer's perspective, it might seem reasonable for the Notary to refer to some "master list" to determine the type of notarization needed. Unfortunately, there is no definitive list to indicate the form of notarization required for every document type. The infinite variety of documents in use makes such a list virtually impossible to compile and update.

FUNDAMENTALS OF NOTARIZATION

In general, every notarization comprises five actions: 1) the signer's

The Notary does not decide what type of notarial act to perform. This decision is the responsibility of the document's issuing or receiving agency.

personal appearance before the Notary, 2) *identification* of the signer, 3) screening for *willingness* and *awareness*, 4) recording the act in a Notary *journal*, and 5) completing the notarial *certificate*. Brief descriptions of these steps follow here and are the subject of Part II.

Personal Appearance

The mandatory first step to every notarization is the signer's *personal appearance* before the Notary Public. The signer must appear in person, face to face, in the same room with the Notary at the time of the notarization — not before and not after. A telephone call does not constitute personal appearance, nor does mere recognition by the Notary of a familiar signature.

Personal appearance is the only way the Notary can assure positive identification of the signer and verify that he or she is signing the document willingly.

To have a document notarized, the signer must appear in person before the Notary.

Identification

Identification of the document signer assures that the person appearing before the Notary is who he or she claims to be. Positive identification means having no doubts about a person's identity.

A Notary can identify a document signer either through his or her own personal knowledge of the signer, identification documents (ID cards) or the sworn word of a credible identifying witness.

With acknowledgments, identification of the signer by the Notary is most critical — and almost always a requirement of law — but it is also a prudent practice with the other notarial acts, even if not mandated by law.

Positive identification of the document signer is a crucial step in notarization.

Willingness and Awareness

Screening for *willingness* makes sure the document signer is not being forced into signing a document against his or her will. The Notary should be confident that no one is trying to coerce or intimidate a signer into signing a document.

By screening for *awareness*, the Notary makes a commonsense judgment that the signer appears to understand what is being signed and

The Notary must determine that the document has been signed willingly and that the person appears aware of its significance.

▼

appears to be able to act responsibly. If a signer can coherently respond to questions and make a request for notarization, that person may generally be considered sufficiently aware for the purposes of notarization.

Journal Record

The journal entry — a detailed description of the notarial act preserved in a bound book — is a valuable public record and provides evidence that a notarization occurred. This record can be vital in the event that a notarized document is lost, stolen or challenged.

Entering a description of each notarial act in a bound journal provides a valuable public record.

In addition, the journal record helps to prove the Notary followed sound and proper procedures in executing the notarial act. This can be valuable if the Notary's credibility is ever called into question.

Notarial Certificate

The notarial certificate indicates what the notarization accomplished. The certificate contains wording that describes what procedures the Notary followed and is completed, signed and sealed by the Notary.

The notarial certificate states the procedures the Notary followed.

Notarial certificates may be in one of two forms: wording preprinted or typed on the document itself, or wording on a separate page attached to the document, known as a "loose certificate."

Not all states have specific laws that define identification standards, prescribe certificate wording or require a Notary to keep a journal. Such statutory omissions are not unusual. In many cases, state notarial laws do not adequately define the Notary's duties. When law and official directive do not detail how to perform a notarial act, Notaries must be guided by custom, ethical business principles and common sense.

DETERRING FRAUD

The purpose of all the steps in notarization — requiring document signers to personally appear, identifying each signer, screening for willingness and awareness, keeping a journal record and declaring facts on a certificate — is to deter *fraud*. Deterring fraud is the Notary's most important role.

The most important role of the Notary is to deter fraud.

Fraud is a deception aimed at causing a person to unknowingly surrender money, property, rights or advantages without compensation. The most common fraud involves theft of money or property through *forgery*; a signature is falsified on a document, which then is used to gain unauthorized or unlawful control of another's money or property.

Through careful identification of document signers, Notaries can detect *impostors* attempting to execute fraudulent documents that could result in devastating financial losses for innocent persons. The Notary's detailed and accurate notarial journal record can prove that certain fraudulent alterations were later made to a notarized document. Precautions in completing and attaching notarial certificates actually can prevent such later alterations.

In detecting and deterring fraud, Notaries perform their most valuable function as impartial witnesses in serving the public.

SUMMARY

Notarization is the authentication of a document as genuine or the verification that a statement was made under oath. It does not guarantee the accuracy of statements in a document and does not, on its own, legalize or validate a document.

The three most common notarial acts are acknowledgments, jurats and copy certifications. An acknowledgment verifies that the document signer is who he or she claims to be. The jurat is used to compel truthfulness through the taking of an oath or affirmation. Copy certification assures that a copy of a document is identical to the original.

Notaries may not determine the type of notarial act that is needed in a given instance. This decision is beyond the Notary's scope of expertise and might be considered the unauthorized practice of law, a criminal offense. Instead, Notaries must be instructed on what type of notarial act to perform in each instance.

Every notarization comprises five actions: the signer's personal appearance before the Notary, positive identification of the signer, screening for willingness and awareness, making a record of the act in a journal and completing the certificate that describes what procedures the Notary followed.

The purpose of the steps in notarization is to deter fraud. In detecting and deterring fraud, Notaries perform their most valuable function as impartial witnesses. ■

IMPORTANT TERMS

Acknowledgment: Notarial act in which a Notary certifies having positively identified a document signer who personally appeared before the Notary and admitted having signed the document freely.

Affirmation: Spoken, solemn promise on one's personal honor, with no reference to a Supreme Being, that is made before a Notary in relation to a jurat or other notarial act, or as a notarial act in its own right.

Awareness: Being able to understand a document's significance.

Certificate, Notarial: Wording completed, signed and sealed by a Notary that states the particulars of a notarization and appears at the end of a signed document or on a paper attached to it.

Copy Certification: Notarial act in which a Notary certifies that a copy of a document is a true and accurate reproduction of the original.

Copy Certification by Document Custodian: Alternative to a Notary-certified copy. The custodian of a document signs a declaration that a copy of the document is identical to the original; the Notary, using a jurat, then notarizes the custodian's signature on this declaration.

Document Custodian: Permanent keeper of an original document.

Forgery: False signature, writing, document or other creation made to imitate a genuine thing; the act of making such a false creation.

Fraud: Deception aimed at causing a person to unknowingly surrender money, property, rights or advantages without compensation.

Identification: Knowing who a person is without reasonable doubt or suspicion; positive identification.

Impostor: Person with false identity.

Journal, Notarial: Official record book of notarizations performed by a Notary Public.

Jurat: Notarial act in which a Notary certifies having watched the signing of a document and administered an oath or affirmation.

Oath: Spoken, solemn promise to a Supreme Being that is made before a Notary in relation to a jurat or other Notarial act, or as a notarial act in its own right.

Personal Appearance: Appearing in person, face to face, in the same room with the Notary at the time of the notarization — not before and not after.

Positive Identification: Knowing who a person is without reasonable doubt or suspicion.

Willingness: State of acting without duress or undue influence; state of acting voluntarily; volition.

CHAPTER 2 TEST

In each blank, write the response — a, b, c or d — that best completes each of the following statements:

1. The act of notarization _____.

    a. Guarantees the truth of statements in a document.

    b. Assures that a document's signature is authentic.

    c. Guarantees the legality of a document.

    d. Provides positive proof that a signer is honest.

2. A notarial certificate _____.

    a. Always comes with the document presented for notarization.

    b. Is completed by the signer before signing by the Notary.

    c. Is completed by the Notary before the document is signed.

    d. Indicates what the notarization accomplished.

3. The main purpose of acknowledgment before a Notary is to _____.

    a. Positively identify a document signer.

    b. Appeal to the conscience of a document signer.

    c. Subject a document signer to criminal penalties for falsehood.

    d. Point out and record flaws in a legal document.

4. An affirmation _____.

    a. Is a spoken promise of truthfulness to God.

    b. Is always made in relation to a jurat.

    c. Is the Notary's certification of positive identification.

    d. Is a pledge on one's personal honor.

5. It is proper for a Notary to _____.

    a. Decide what type of notarial act to perform.

    b. Legalize a document by affixing a notarial seal.

    c. Publicly record a document by keeping a copy in the journal.

    d. Rely on ID cards to identify a document signer.

6. Only Maine, South Carolina and Florida authorize Notaries to _____.

    a. Perform marriages.

    b. Execute protests.

    c. Certify copies.

    d. Administer oaths of office.

▼

7. Positive identification means _____.

    a. Relying only on personal knowledge of identity.

    b. Having no reasonable doubts about a signer's identity.

    c. A document signer has declared an identity under oath.

    d. A Notary has acknowledged the signer's identity under oath.

8. If a notarized document is lost _____.

    a. The Notary journal gives evidence the transaction occurred.

    b. The Notary certificate gives evidence the transaction occurred.

    c. A copy will always be on file with the local public recorder.

    d. A protest of loss can be filed by Notaries in many states.

Explain in your own words:

9. Why shouldn't a Notary select the type of notarization?

_____

_____

_____

See page 381 for correct responses.

PART II:
THE ESSENTIAL
STEPS

CHAPTER 3

Personal Appearance

THE FIRST STEP

Personal appearance is a requirement for all notarial acts.

Before any signature may lawfully be notarized, one all-important event must occur: the signer *must* appear in person before the Notary Public. This is the only way the Notary can properly identify the signer and verify that he or she is signing, or has signed, the document willingly, with understanding of its purpose and effect.

This *personal appearance* must be made at the time of the notarization — not before and not after — in the state and county indicated on the Notary's certificate.

Personal appearance means being face to face in the same room. A telephone call from the signer does not constitute personal appearance, nor does recognizing a familiar signature.

NOTARY CERTIFICATE WORDING

Every notarial certificate states that the signer was in the Notary's presence. This statement may be clear and direct, as in:

> On _____(date), **before me, a Notary Public, personally appeared** _____ (name of signer)....

▼

Or it may be less direct, as in:

> Subscribed and sworn to **before me** by _____ (name of signer)....

Thus, any Notary who does not require the physical presence of a document signer is blatantly neglecting a clear-cut responsibility of the Notary office and, in some states, may be prosecuted for issuing a false notarial certificate. This would be in addition to other criminal charges that could arise out of the Notary's willing participation in a fraud, as well as civil lawsuits filed against the Notary to recover losses from a forgery and the administrative penalty of commission revocation.

FAILURE AIDS FRAUD

There is no more serious violation by a Notary than failing to require the physical presence of a document signer at the time of notarization. Criminal prosecution, civil lawsuits and administrative penalties against the Notary are only part of the fallout from such an act.

By completing a notarial certificate without the presence of the signer, even the best-intentioned Notary facilitates a potential multitude of frauds that can inflict financial disaster on unsuspecting victims, especially when the fraud involves real estate.

While it is common for Notaries to have friends or employers ask that a signature be notarized without personal appearance, the Notary must, without exception, refuse such requests.

Sooner or later, almost every Notary will be approached by a trusted friend, relative, client, coworker, supervisor or business associate and asked as a favor to notarize the signature of a third party who is absent. "My wife is ill and can't come in," the excuse might be. Or, "It would be inconvenient for my husband to come all the way over here just to get this notarized." But when the Notary relinquishes to a third party the triple duty of verifying a signer's identity, willingness and awareness, the Notary surrenders control of the notarization.

In a surprisingly high percentage of the cases in which a spouse or business partner has asked a Notary to trust that the signature of an absent spouse or partner is genuine, the signature has proven to be a forgery.

It is an unfortunate reality that the individuals who most often take advantage of Notaries are not strangers with phony IDs, but trusted acquaintances. A vengeful spouse in a crumbling marriage or a disgruntled partner in a dissolving business may have other priorities than keeping faith with a Notary acquaintance — namely, wresting control of valuable property from the spouse or partner using a phony document with a forged signature and then pocketing the assets.

Courts Strict on Personal Appearance Requirement

Courts are generally uncompromising in interpreting statutes that require a signer's physical presence before a Notary. A case in point was the 1984 Nebraska Supreme Court ruling in *Christensen v. Arant.*

In that case, a real estate agent/Notary took the acknowledgment of a married couple who had received a $50,000 offer for sale of their home. The husband was in the same room with the Notary when his signature on the sales contract was notarized, but he asked that his ill wife be permitted to remain out of the Notary's sight in another room because she was "very contagious." The Notary cooperated, speaking to the unseen woman while performing the notarization. When the couple later accepted a $64,000 offer for the same house, they were able to have the first contract nullified because one of the signers had never actually appeared before the Notary.

So personal appearance means more than being under the same roof and within earshot. It also means being where the Notary can see each signer and communicate face to face.

Important

A telephone call is *not* considered personal appearance. "I just mailed you a deed," a caller might inform the Notary. "When you get it, please notarize my signature and mail it right back." But a Notary may not legally comply with such a request, even with a supposedly reliable third party present ("Here, call up my wife at this number — she'll verify her signature").

'EXCEPTIONS'

The law provides for two *very narrow* and *strictly controlled* "exceptions" to the rule prohibiting notarization of the signature of an absent person: 1) notarization through an attorney in fact and 2) notarization through a subscribing witness.

With these so-called "exceptions," it is technically the attorney in fact or the subscribing witness' signature being notarized and *not* the signature of the person named in the document (the absent *principal*). While the principal does not personally appear before the Notary, the attorney in fact and subscribing witness must.

Attorneys in fact and subscribing witnesses must personally appear before the Notary Public.

Attorney in Fact

A person who is appointed as *attorney in fact* for another individual (the principal) has authority to sign the principal's name and have this signature notarized without the principal being present before the Notary. Typically, the signature format might be as follows:

John R. Burns, by Mary S. Anderson , attorney in fact

Or an alternate such as:

Mary S. Anderson , attorney in fact for *John R. Burns*, principal

In these two examples, Mary S. Anderson is the attorney in fact signing on behalf of John R. Burns, the principal named in the document. The conscientious Notary would ask to see the *power of attorney* document that designates Mary S. Anderson as attorney in fact and verify that it authorizes the signer to act on behalf of the principal.

With notarization through an attorney in fact, the Notary actually is notarizing the signature of the attorney in fact — who acts on behalf of the principal — and *not* that of the principal. The personal-appearance rule applies to the attorney in fact, and it is the attorney in fact who must personally appear before the Notary.

Subscribing Witness

Most states allow a second very narrow exception to the rule banning notarization of the signature of an absent person: a *proof of execution by a subscribing witness.* The subscribing witness *proves* the document's signing by swearing under oath or affirmation before a Notary that he or she either watched another person (the principal) sign a document or took that person's acknowledgment of an already affixed signature.

With a proof of execution, the Notary actually is notarizing the subscribing witness' signature — appearing on the document in addition to the principal's — and *not* the signature of the principal. Most, but not all, states accept such a proof as equivalent to direct notarization of the principal's signature. As with attorneys in fact, the personal appearance requirement still stands but applies to the subscribing witness, who must personally appear before the Notary.

Proofs of execution by subscribing witnesses will be described in detail in Chapter 11.

Other than the two preceding "exceptions," there is no surer way for a Notary to avoid a civil or criminal lawsuit than to obey one simple rule: *Never notarize the signature of a person who is not in your presence at the time of the notarization.*

SUMMARY

For every notarization, the signer must appear in person before the Notary Public at the time of the notarization. Personal appearance means being face to face in the same room. A telephone call or recognition of a familiar signature does not count.

Because all notarial certificates state that the signer was in the Notary's presence, a Notary who fails to require the physical presence of a signer may be prosecuted for issuing a false notarial certificate, which is a criminal act. Other charges, as well as civil lawsuits, also could arise.

It is common for Notaries to be asked as a favor to notarize the signature of an absent third party. It is also common for these signatures to be proven forgeries later. Unfortunately, the individuals who most often take advantage of Notaries in such situations are not strangers, but trusted acquaintances.

Two narrow and controlled "exceptions" to the rule prohibiting

▼

notarization of the signature of an absent person occur with notarization through an attorney in fact and, in most states, notarization through a subscribing witness. But in both cases, it is the appearing attorney in fact or subscribing witness whose signature is being notarized, and not the principal's. So, while the principal does not appear before the Notary, the attorney in fact and subscribing witness must. ■

IMPORTANT TERMS

Attorney in Fact: Person who has authority to sign for another.

Personal Appearance: Appearing in person, face to face, in the same room with the Notary at the time of the notarization — not before and not after.

Power of Attorney: Document granting authority for a person to act as attorney in fact for another.

Principal: Person who is a signer of and party to a document.

Proof of Execution by Subscribing Witness: Notarial act where a person (called the *subscribing witness*) states under oath or affirmation before a Notary that he or she either watched another individual (called the *principal*) sign a document or took that person's acknowledgment of an already signed document. The witness must affix a signature to the document, in addition to the principal's.

CHAPTER 3 TEST

In each blank, write the response — a, b, c or d — that best completes each of the following statements:

1. Personal appearance before the Notary is required _____.

    a. Whenever it is practical for the signer to comply.

    b. For notarial acts involving only married signers.

    c. For every notarial act.

    d. Except when the signer's attorney dictates otherwise.

2. A phone call can establish personal appearance _____.

    a. Only when the Notary is personally familiar with the signature.

    b. If a business relationship with the signer has been established.

    c. At the time of notarization, but not before and not after.

    d. Under no circumstances.

3. Notarial certificate wording _____.

    a. Always states that the signer was in the Notary's presence.

    b. Most often states that the signer was in the Notary's presence.

    c. Sometimes states that the signer was in the Notary's presence.

    d. Never states that the signer was in the Notary's presence.

4. In interpreting laws requiring personal appearance, courts are _____.

    a. Generally uncompromising.

    b. Accommodating to Notaries who are helping out an employer.

    c. Strict in upholding a signer's right not to appear before a Notary.

    d. Strict in outlawing all subscribing witness notarizations.

5. Fraud is facilitated when _____.

    a. A Notary positively identifies a document signer.

    b. A Notary signs a certificate without requiring personal appearance.

    c. A Notary refuses to take an acknowledgment over the telephone.

    d. A Notary refuses to notarize a familiar signature of an absent signer.

6. In most states, a subscribing witness may _____.

    a. Not be required to appear before the Notary.

    b. Notarize documents in place of a Notary.

    c. Prove before a Notary the principal's signing of a document.

    d. Sign as attorney in fact on behalf of an absent principal.

7. The principal _____.

    a. May have his or her signature notarized by an attorney in fact.

    b. Must personally sign all documents in which he or she is named.

    c. May take an oath from a subscribing witness.

    d. May acknowledge a document before a subscribing witness.

8. A person who is appointed as attorney in fact _____.

    a. May sign documents for the principal.

    b. May notarize the principal's signature by recognizing it.

    c. May instruct a Notary to sign for the principal.

    d. May never sign the principal's name on a document.

9. The employer of a Notary does not have to personally appear _____.

    a. When the Notary recognizes the employer's signature.

    b. When a client will be lost if the notarization is delayed.

    c. If a subscribing witness can prove the signing of the document.

    d. If the employer serves as a subscribing witness.

Explain in your own words:

10. What does personal appearance mean?

_____

_____

_____

See page 381 for correct responses.

CHAPTER 4

Identifying the Signer

After the document signer appears before the Notary, the next step in performing a notarial act is to *positively identify* the signer. Here, the Notary must be certain that the signer actually is who he or she claims to be and that the signer has the authority to sign the document.

This crucial step provides credibility to signed documents and is often the primary reason notarization is required.

 NNA Recommendation

Although state laws usually require identification of a signer only for acknowledgments, careful Notaries also will identify signers for jurats, certified copies and every other notarial act. The National Notary Association strongly recommends that Notaries carefully identify all document signers.

Since not all states provide official guidelines on what constitutes positive identification, identifying a signer often can be a difficult step for the Notary. If there are no state guidelines, the Notary should rely on the procedures outlined in this chapter and, above all, exercise caution, prudence and reasonable care in performing this most important of all notarial duties.

METHODS OF IDENTIFICATION

The identity of a document signer is established either through the Notary's own *personal knowledge* of the signer, or through what is widely known as *satisfactory evidence* — satisfactory evidence being either an *identification document* (an ID card) or a *credible identifying witness*.

Notaries may use any of the three methods to determine a signer's identity.

The three typical methods used to identify a signer are personal knowledge, ID cards or credible identifying witnesses.

PERSONAL KNOWLEDGE OF IDENTITY

The safest and most reliable basis on which to identify a document signer is the Notary's reliance on his or her own personal knowledge of the signer's identity. A personal familiarity with another individual over a period of time almost always assures true identity.

But what are the criteria for determining whether a Notary has personal knowledge of a signer's identity? State laws seldom usefully define personal knowledge, but the courts have proven somewhat helpful in defining this term so that Notaries can know their responsibility in complying with state law.

For example, the Tennessee Supreme Court found that the acknowledgment certificate wording "with whom I am personally acquainted" means:

> Knowledge independent and complete in itself, and existing without other information, and...(that) imports more than a slight or superficial knowledge. (Figuers v. Fly, 137 Tenn. 358, 193 S.W. 117, 1916).

A California court held that personal knowledge:

> Involves...an acquaintance, derived from association with the individual in relation to other people.... Such an acquaintance cannot in its very nature be based upon the mere word of one or two or three individuals, but must be based upon a chain of circumstances surrounding the person in question, all of which

tend to show that they are what they purport to be. (Anderson
v. Aronsohn, supra, 181 Cal. 294, 1919).

So, a working definition of "personally known" might be this:

> A strong familiarity with an individual resulting from numerous
> interactions over a period of time sufficient to eliminate every
> reasonable doubt that the individual has the identity claimed.

To establish personal knowledge of identity, the Notary must know the signer over a long enough period of time to remove any reasonable doubt.

The familiarity should come from association with the individual in relation to other people and should be based on a series of circumstances surrounding the individual. The longer the Notary has known someone, the safer it is to rely on personal knowledge as a method to identify this individual. In general, however, Notaries must rely on their own good sense in deciding whether document signers are personally known.

For instance, the Notary might safely regard a longtime family friend and neighbor as personally known, but it would be foolish to consider a person met for the first time the previous day as such. A good friend from school known for several years might also be considered personally known, while an informal introduction of a stranger by a coworker or employer simply does not constitute personal knowledge.

Here is a safe rule to follow: if there is any doubt about whether the individual is personally known, consider the person *unknown* for the purposes of notarization and rely on another form of identification.

IDENTIFICATION DOCUMENTS

Today, business transactions between strangers are the norm, and identification documents, or ID cards, have become the predominant method used by Notaries to identify document signers. In most states, identification documents are regarded as satisfactory evidence of identity and equivalent to personal knowledge.

While many countries require their citizens to carry a national ID card, the United States has no such standard identification document. So, U.S. Notaries must rely on certain other identification documents issued by government and private agencies. These agencies include the U.S. Department of State (passports), the U.S. Department of Defense (military IDs) and state motor vehicle departments (driver's licenses and nondriver's IDs).

Notaries sometimes may rely on identification documents issued by colleges and universities (student IDs), large companies (employee IDs) and foreign governments (foreign passports and driver's licenses).

 State Laws Vary

The types of IDs legally acceptable for the purposes of notarization vary from state to state. A few states specify by name what identification documents are "legal." In these states, the Notary must follow this statutory list without exception and may not accept other IDs. Other states may suggest guidelines or give examples of acceptable IDs, allowing Notaries to use their own judgment. Most states offer no guidance at all. In those jurisdictions, the Notary should check with the Notary-regulating office for specific requirements. If none exist, the guidelines in the following section should be followed.

Acceptable Identification Documents

For a notarial act, the most reliable identification documents are government issued and contain a photograph, a physical description of the bearer and the bearer's signature. These elements provide a basis for comparison with the actual physical appearance and signature of the signer appearing before the Notary.

Identification documents should be government issued and have a photo, a physical description and a signature of the bearer.

Since state laws rarely indicate what type of document may serve as suitable identification of a signer, it is left to the Notary to make this determination. The National Notary Association urges Notaries to rely only on government-issued IDs bearing all three elements.

Examples of the most commonly used identification documents are:

Driver's licenses issued by each of the 50 states. Some states also allow driver's licenses from Canada or Mexico as identification.

Nondriver's IDs issued by most states as an option to nondriving residents for identification purposes.

Passports issued to U.S. citizens by the State Department to permit travel abroad. Also, foreign citizens visiting the U.S. may present their foreign passports as identification, provided that the passport bears a visa stamp of the U.S. Citizenship and Immigration Services. In addition, foreign students and temporary workers in the United States will have USCIS Form I-94 attached to their passports.

Federal IDs issued to employees of U.S. government agencies, including military personnel of the Army, Navy, Air Force, Marine Corps and Coast Guard.

State, county and local government IDs issued to employees or licensees. Barbers and taxi drivers, for example, may possess licensing papers with a photo.

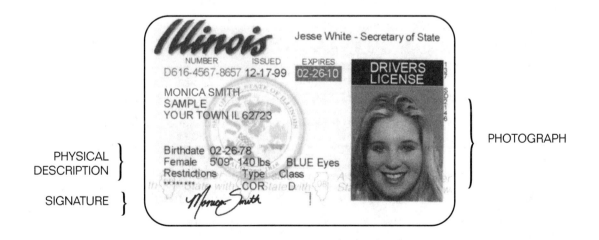

Above is an example of a reliable identification document for the purposes of notarization. It has been issued by a government agency and contains a photograph, physical description and signature of the bearer.

Lawful Permanent Resident Cards, also called *green cards*, issued to permanent-residents by the U.S. Citizenship and Immigration Services. These include Form I-151 and its replacement, Form I-551.

Border-crossing cards issued by the USCIS. Forms I-185 and I-186 permit citizens of Canada and Mexico, respectively, to enter the country. Crews aboard foreign aircraft and ships carry Form I-184.

Current identification documents are the most useful. But an expired ID, if not prohibited by state law, also may be acceptable if there are no suspicious circumstances, such as a lack of any other identification documents. Since physical appearance and even a personal signature can change over time, the photo, description and signature on an expired ID may not match its bearer's changed appearance and signature. In such cases, it is best for the Notary to request other identification.

A single acceptable identification document is enough to establish identity. However, Notaries are wise to ask any signer to present several IDs. The more IDs a Notary sees, the greater the likelihood of positively identifying a signer.

Signature and ID Discrepancies

Inevitably, there will be occasions when the name on the identification document will differ slightly from the signature or name on the document. In such instances, the Notary should follow a *less-but-not-more* policy, to determine if the ID is sufficient. That is, the signature name may be less but not more than the name on the ID.

For example, if the document signature and name read "Mark R. Simmons" and the ID shows "Mark Robert Simmons," then the ID is acceptable. But if the signature is "Jane K. Douglas" (the signer's maiden name) or "Jane K. Douglas-Smith" (a hyphenated name) and the ID says only "Jane K. Smith" (the signer's married name), then the ID does not sufficiently identify the signer. (For additional procedures, see Chapter 16.)

Supplemental Identification Documents

Supplemental IDs may be used in addition to primary IDs, but never alone.

Supplemental IDs, as the name implies, may be used to support a *primary ID* and can supply valuable additional information. (A primary ID would be one that is acceptable on its own for the purposes of notarization as discussed in the previous section.) Supplemental IDs alone, however, *never* should be the basis for identifying a stranger.

A supplemental ID may or may not contain a photograph, but it usually has at least a signature of the bearer.

Careful Notaries ask for supplemental IDs in addition to a primary ID, especially when there is some doubt about the genuineness of the primary ID. A signer's supplemental IDs — or failure to have any such IDs — can provide further evidence of fraud. But remember, supplemental IDs may not be the sole basis for identifying a signer.

Examples of supplemental identification documents include:

Social Security cards issued to workers in the United States to identify them as contributors to the national retirement pension system. These cards contain no photograph or physical description and are very easy to forge.

Credit cards issued to individuals by banks and retail stores. Even though some credit cards now include a photograph of the account holder, these plastic cards are of minimal value as identifiers, because there is virtually no screening for identification during the application and issuing process.

Other IDs, such as those described in the previous section as "commonly used identification documents," but which may not qualify in a particular state as acceptable identification. For example, a green card could serve as a supplemental ID if it were excluded as an acceptable ID for notarization in a particular state.

Birth certificates bear neither a photo, signature nor recent description and are relatively easy for anyone to obtain from a bureau of vital statistics. Thus, they are virtually worthless as identifying documents.

Fraudulent Identification

All identification documents should be carefully inspected for evidence of *imposture*, *alteration* and *counterfeiting*, because any document signer may be a criminal impostor presenting false IDs. When an individual poses as another in order to obtain an ID, this is called imposture. Alteration occurs when an ID is changed to conform to an unauthorized person. A false ID made from scratch is a counterfeit.

There is no absolute and foolproof method to detect every false ID, but many can be spotted through attention to detail, common sense and knowing common telltale signs.

Notaries should be familiar with the type of identification document they rely on to identify a signer in order to screen out IDs that clearly are false. A Georgia Notary, for example, might confidently accept a Georgia driver's license as proof of identity because of familiarity with the license's format. However, it would be risky to rely on an Oregon license if it were unfamiliar to the Notary. Books such as the *U.S. Identification Manual* and the *I.D. Checking Guide*, which contain sample IDs from all states, are helpful to all Notaries.

Chapter 18 describes how a Notary can detect false identification documents.

CREDIBLE IDENTIFYING WITNESS

When a document signer is not personally known to the Notary and is not able to present reliable identification documents, that signer can be identified on the oath or affirmation of a *credible identifying witness*. In most states, the word of a credible identifying witness is satisfactory evidence of identity and equivalent to personal knowledge.

A credible identifying witness, also often called a *credible witness*, is like a human ID card who identifies the document signer. The credible identifying witness must personally know the document signer and also should be personally known by the Notary. This establishes a

A credible identifying witness personally knows the document signer and establishes identity through an oath or affirmation.

chain of personal knowledge connecting the Notary with the signer.

For example, if a stranger without satisfactory IDs requests a notarization, the Notary need not turn this person away if the Notary has a friend present who personally knows the individual. The friend could serve as a credible identifying witness.

By definition, a credible identifying witness is a believable person. Credible identifying witnesses should be honest, competent and impartial to the matter at hand. This means that the credible identifying witness should neither have a beneficial interest in a notarized document nor be named in it.

Oath for a Credible Identifying Witness

To compel truthfulness, the Notary must administer an oath or affirmation to the credible identifying witness. The identifying witness must swear or affirm that the signer has the identity claimed. If not otherwise prescribed by law, the following oath (affirmation) may be used:

> Do you solemnly swear (or affirm) that you know the signer truly holds the identity he (or she) claims?

The oath or affirmation must be spoken aloud, and the credible identifying witness must answer affirmatively with, "I do," "Yes," or a similar response that indicates agreement.

Two Credible Witnesses

To identify a document signer, some states have the option of relying on *two* credible identifying witnesses who are *not* personally known by the Notary, as long as both have acceptable IDs. In others, such as Arizona, a Notary may identify a single credible witness who has acceptable identification.

IDENTIFYING THE REPRESENTATIVE SIGNER

In addition to determining that a document signer has the identity claimed, a Notary also may be required to determine that the person has a claimed *authority* to sign the document as a representative of another

The representative signer has the authority to sign for another person, organization or legal entity.

person, organization or legal entity. Such *representative capacities* include attorney in fact, corporate officer, partner, trustee and others.

Whether or not the Notary is required to do this will depend on the wording of the notarial certificate.

Certificate wording such as the following does *not* obligate a Notary to learn whether an individual has authority to sign:

> ...personally appeared _____, **known to me to be the person** who is described in and whose name is subscribed to the within instrument as the...

The Notary in this case is stating that the individual was described and signed as attorney in fact, corporate officer or partner, *not* that the Notary knew the person actually held the title.

In contrast, the Notary is obligated to establish that a signer is authorized to sign with such certificate wording as:

> ...personally appeared _____, **known to me to be the person and officer** whose name is subscribed to the within instrument as the...

Determining a Signer's Authority

A Notary establishes a signer's authority to sign in the same manner as establishing identity: by personal knowledge, by documentary proof or by sworn statement.

Personal knowledge. The Notary may depend on his or her own personal knowledge of the signer to determine authority to sign. The criteria for establishing personal knowledge of authority are essentially the same as for identity: a strong familiarity with an individual's status, resulting from numerous interactions over a period of time sufficient to eliminate every reasonable doubt that the individual has the authority claimed.

Documentary proof. Notaries who do not personally know a signer's representative status might depend on documentary evidence. A power of attorney document, for example, shows authority as an attorney in fact; a partnership agreement shows authority as a partner. Status as a corporate officer is sometimes difficult to obtain or recognize through documents. Relying solely on a business card as proof of status as a corporate officer is risky, since anyone can have a business card printed. With corporate officers, it is best to rely on a combination of different documents as evidence of authority. Notaries who cannot understand the documents presented as evidence of status as a corporate officer, partner, attorney in fact or other representative should refuse to notarize.

Proof on oath or affirmation. In some states, the Notary may be provided with a certificate requiring the signer to swear or affirm that he or she has authority to sign as a representative. This removes the responsibility of having to personally determine the signer's authority from the Notary. Following is an example of such a certificate:

> State of _____)
>   ) SS.
> County of _____)
>
> On this _____ day of _____ (month), _____ (year), before me appeared _____ (name of signer), to me personally known **who, being by me duly sworn (or affirmed), did say that he (or she) is the president (vice president, secretary, treasurer) of _____ (name of corporation)**, and that the seal affixed to the foregoing instrument is the corporate seal of said corporation, and that said instrument was signed and sealed on behalf of said corporation by authority of its board of directors, and the said _____ (name of signer) acknowledged the said instrument to be the free act and deed of said corporation.
>
> _____ (signature and seal of Notary)

Notaries in states not requiring proof of a signer's status as an attorney in fact, corporate officer or other empowered signer sometimes encounter certificates that do require such proof. Unless state law prohibits it, completing these certificates legally obligates the Notary to

The sworn word of a representative signer may be used to establish that person's authority to sign on behalf of another person or entity.

▼

51

know that a signer indeed holds a certain representative capacity and is empowered to act as described in the certificate.

SUMMARY

The first step in a notarization is for the Notary to ascertain the signer's identity and, if applicable, authority to sign the document. State laws usually require identification only for acknowledgments, but careful Notaries will identify signers for all notarial acts. Identity may be established through the Notary's personal knowledge of the signer, identification documents or the oath of a credible identifying witness.

The Notary's personal knowledge of a signer is the safest and most reliable method of identification. Personal knowledge of identity can be defined as a strong familiarity with an individual resulting from numerous interactions over a period of time sufficient to eliminate every reasonable doubt that the individual has the identity claimed.

Identification documents, or ID cards, are the predominant method used by Notaries to identify signers. The most reliable identification documents are government-issued and contain a photograph, physical description and signature of the bearer.

Every identification document should be examined for evidence of fraud — imposture, counterfeiting or alteration. When an individual poses as another in order to obtain an ID, this is called imposture. Alteration occurs when an ID is changed to conform to an unauthorized person. A false ID made from scratch is a counterfeit.

If a signer is not known to the Notary and has no acceptable identification documents, that signer can be identified on the oath or affirmation of a credible identifying witness, also known as a credible witness. A credible identifying witness must personally know the document signer and also should be personally known by the Notary. This establishes a *chain of personal knowledge* connecting the Notary with the signer. The credible identifying witness must swear or affirm that the signer has the identity claimed.

A Notary also may be required to determine that the signer has authority to sign the document as a representative. Representative

capacities include attorney in fact, corporate officer, partner and trustee;
and may be proven based on the Notary's personal knowledge,
documentation or the signer's sworn word. ∎

IMPORTANT TERMS

Alteration: Method of creating a false identification document by changing, or altering, its content.

Authority: Legal empowerment to sign for another person, organization or legal entity, as in the case of an attorney in fact, trustee, corporate officer, partner and others.

Capacity: Specific role of a representative signer — attorney in fact, trustee, corporate officer, partner or other — when signing for another person, organization or legal entity.

Chain of Personal Knowledge: Knowledge of identity linking the Notary with the signer through a credible identifying witness to establish the signer's identity. The Notary personally knows and can identify the credible witness, and the credible witness personally knows and can identify the document signer.

Counterfeit: False document made from scratch to imitate an authentic one.

Credible Identifying Witness: Believable person who identifies a document signer to the Notary after taking an oath or affirmation. The credible identifying witness must personally know the document signer and also should be personally known by the Notary.

Credible Witness: Credible identifying witness.

Green Card: Resident identification document (not actually green) issued by the U.S. Citizenship and Immigration Services, in the form of either the I-551 or the older I-151 card.

Identification Document (ID Card): Document or card which establishes the bearer's identity. Examples include passports, driver's licenses and nondriver IDs, among others.

Imposture: Pretending to have another identity.

Nondrivers' ID: Identification document similar to a driver's license issued by most states upon request to nondrivers, such as juveniles and the elderly.

Personal Knowledge: Familiarity with an individual resulting from random interactions over a period of time sufficient to eliminate every reasonable doubt that the individual has the identity claimed.

Positive Identification: Certainty that a person has the identity claimed.

Primary ID: Government-issued identification document with at least a photograph of the bearer that may be the sole basis for identification by a Notary.

Representative Signer: Person with the legal authority to sign for another individual, organization or legal entity. Representative signing capacities include attorney in fact, trustee, corporate officer and partner.

Satisfactory Evidence: Reliable identification documents, or the sworn or affirmed statement of a credible identifying witness, that satisfactorily proves that an individual has the identity claimed.

Supplemental ID: Identification document that, alone, does not provide positive identification of a signer due to its lack of a photograph, the ease with which it may be counterfeited and the low level of security in its issuance.

CHAPTER 4 TEST

In each blank, write the response — a, b, c or d — that best completes each of the following statements:

1. The most reliable basis for identifying a signer is _____.

   a. Primary identification documents.

   b. Supplemental identification documents.

   c. The Notary's personal knowledge.

   d. A personally known credible identifying witness.

2. Identification of a signer should not be based on a _____.

   a. U.S. passport.

   b. State nondriver's ID.

   c. Social Security card.

   d. Military ID.

3. Satisfactory evidence of identity means identification based on _____.

   a. Either personal knowledge or identification documents.

   b. Both personal knowledge and identification documents.

   c. Either identification documents or a credible identifying witness.

   d. Both identification documents and a credible identifying witness.

4. An acceptable identification document _____.

   a. Contains a signature, but no photo.

   b. Can safely be relied on by a Notary unfamiliar with its format.

   c. Is government-issued and has a photo, description and signature.

   d. Is the only permitted method to identify a document signer.

5. A Notary must verify a signer's status as corporate officer _____.

   a. When the notarial certificate wording so requires.

   b. For every signing by a corporate officer.

   c. Only when the Notary is not an employee of the corporation.

   d. At no time, since this is not a notarial duty.

6. Personal knowledge of identity would most safely be based on _____.

   a. A signer's introduction by a Notary's unsworn, trusted friend.

   b. The fact that a signer is a good business client with excellent credit.

   c. A signer and Notary having two casual acquaintances in common.

   d. A signer's repeated interaction with the Notary over many years.

7. To identify a signer, a credible identifying witness must _____.

    a. Also be named in the document.

    b. Swear or affirm that the signer has the identity claimed.

    c. Not have served as a witness for another signer.

    d. Be a blood relative of the signer.

Explain in your own words:

8. Why is a birth certificate all but worthless as an ID document?

_____

_____

_____

See page 381 for correct responses.

▼

CHAPTER 5

Determining Willingness and Awareness

Since the purpose of notarization is to detect and deter document fraud, the Notary must screen signers to assure that the execution of any document is honest and without deception.

Before performing a notarization, the conscientious Notary will be certain not only of the document signer's identity, but also of the person's *willingness* to sign the document and the person's *awareness* — the signer's basic ability to understand the document.

WILLINGNESS

Determining willingness is a relatively easy procedure. The Notary simply asks the signer if he or she has signed or is about to sign the document willingly, and then carefully watches for any indications to the contrary. Willingness means that the signing is a voluntary act and deed, freely made, without duress or undue influence.

Screening for willingness assures that the signer is not being forced to sign against his or her will.

If the Notary suspects that someone is being forced or coerced into signing against his or her own will, the Notary should refuse to perform the notarization.

In some situations, asking a potentially influential third party —

▼

someone who appears to be pressuring the signer — to leave the room during the notarization may assist the Notary in determining the signer's actual intent.

For many notarizations — usually acknowledgments — the wording of the notarial certificate will indicate to the Notary that determining the signer's willingness is critical. The certificate, for example, may state that the signer acknowledged acting "freely" or "of his/her own free will." Again, the Notary carefully must watch for signs to the contrary and refuse to proceed if there is reasonable doubt about the signer's intent.

The requirement to determine the signer's willingness is implied for *all* types of notarization — not just acknowledgments — and the Notary always should verify that any signer or witness is acting of his or her own free will.

AWARENESS

While state laws give Notaries clear authority to screen for identity and willingness, rarely does statute specifically require the Notary to determine awareness. This is understandable because even experienced physicians and attorneys can disagree over whether a given individual can understand the implications of signing a document.

The Notary makes a layperson's commonsense determination about the signer's awareness.

Since most Notaries are not medical or legal experts, they are only expected to make a *layperson's commonsense judgment* about whether a signer knows what he or she is doing.

It is decidedly in the public interest for Notaries to refuse to notarize for signers who clearly do not understand the consequences of their actions. Many lawsuits result from accusations that signers were "incompetent" to handle their legal affairs. And Notaries often are dragged into these suits either as defendants or witnesses. The safest policy for the Notary to follow is to refuse to perform the notarization if there is any doubt at all about the signer's awareness.

How to Determine Awareness

In the overwhelming majority of notarizations, ascertaining awareness presents no difficulty. There will be little doubt about the awareness of an individual who can approach the Notary, communicate a request for a notarial act and then respond to the Notary's inquiries about identification.

Extreme cases of unawareness are just as easy for the Notary to discern. For example, a hospitalized and unconscious man whose hand is moved by his wife in "signing" a document obviously does not know what he is doing at the time. An aware person must be conscious. Likewise, a woman so drugged that she cannot stand up or talk is certainly not fully aware at the moment. She may be conscious, but she is oblivious and unable to communicate. However, being merely tipsy or under the influence does not necessarily mean unawareness.

Medical experts attest that awareness and comprehension of one's surroundings can be transient. In other words, awareness may come and go. This is especially the case with elderly persons who may be labeled as "senile," but who may be lucid and significantly aware to handle their affairs at least part of the time.

In most situations, the best way to ascertain awareness is to talk to the signer. If the signer can communicate effectively during the conversation, then the Notary may consider the signer aware. Whenever a signer is unable to respond coherently to a Notary's basic questions about a notarial act, the Notary should refuse to notarize because awareness and comprehension are in doubt.

Notaries may consult any available expert, such as the person's physician or attorney, to determine awareness. If such an expert indicates a signer is comprehending, it is usually safe to notarize, noting the expert's remarks in the notarial journal.

However, the Notary's common sense should prevail in all cases and, if the signer cannot communicate intelligibly with the Notary, the person's awareness is in doubt and the notarization should not be performed.

Awareness and the Disabled

Determining awareness can be difficult and critical with signers who have certain disabilities. Simply because an individual has a physical or intellectual *disability* does not mean that this person is incapable of handling his or her own personal affairs. Special procedures may have to be used by the Notary in such cases. These are outlined in Chapter 14, "Meeting the Needs of Disabled Signers."

'Legal Competence' and Minors

Generally, *minors* are not considered "legally competent" to handle their own affairs. *Legal competence* in this context is related solely to the chronological age of the individual and not to the person's ability to understand a given document, which often may belie a youthful age.

Up to the age of majority (18 years in most U.S. localities), a parent or appointed guardian must sign for a child. But there are some exceptions, and these are covered in Chapter 15, "Notarizing for Minors."

SUMMARY

The Notary should screen document signers for willingness to sign and for awareness of the significance of a document.

Willingness means acting voluntarily and without undue influence. It can be determined by asking signers if they have signed willingly, then carefully watching for indications to the contrary.

Awareness is a signer's ability to understand the document. Notaries are not expected to render an expert legal or medical opinion about a signer's ability to comprehend, only a layperson's commonsense judgment. The best way to determine awareness is to draw the signer into a conversation. If available, medical or legal experts may be consulted.

A physical or intellectual disability does not necessarily make a signer unable to comprehend. Minors, under law, are generally not considered "legally competent" to handle their own affairs. ■

IMPORTANT TERMS

Awareness: Being able to understand a document's significance.

Disability: Physical or intellectual incapacity.

Layperson's Commonsense Judgment: Decision that would be reached by a person of reasonable intelligence, but without extensive legal or medical training.

Minor: Person who has not reached the age of majority (usually 18) and therefore is not considered "legally competent" to handle his or her own affairs.

Willingness: Acting freely without duress or undue influence.

CHAPTER 5 TEST

In each blank, write the response — a, b, c or d — that best completes each of the following statements:

1. Notaries must screen signers for willingness _____.

    a. Only in certain, very specific situations.

    b. Only when a document affects the signer's personal affairs.

    c. To assure the signing is without duress or undue influence.

    d. To be certain the signer is willing to pay the notarial fee.

2. Determining a signer's awareness _____.

    a. Is a notarial duty clearly spelled out in state law.

    b. Is not difficult for the Notary in most cases.

    c. Is a difficult task for the Notary in most cases.

    d. Should not be tried unless a physician or attorney is present.

3. A signer's physical or intellectual disability _____.

    a. Prevents notarization in all cases.

    b. May require special procedures to complete the notarization.

    c. Is of no concern to the Notary.

    d. Means that the individual is unaware in all cases.

4. There would be little doubt about the awareness of a signer _____.

    a. Who cannot speak understandably.

    b. Who is hospitalized and drifting in and out of consciousness.

    c. Who is unable to speak clearly and cannot stand without assistance.

    d. Who can read and write understandably.

5. The most important factor in determining awareness is _____.

    a. The signer's ability to communicate with the Notary.

    b. The signer's ability to write out a signature.

    c. The signer's ability to see the Notary.

    d. The signer's ability to hear the Notary.

6. A Notary's strong doubt about a person's awareness should _____.

    a. Always give way to the contrary opinion of a doctor.

    b. Always give way to the contrary opinion of an attorney.

    c. Not be relevant if the person is able to sign.

    d. Take precedence over the opinion of any other individual.

7. Generally, minors _____.

    a. Must have a parent or guardian sign for them.

    b. Are persons under the age of 16.

    c. Are considered "legally competent" to handle their affairs.

    d. Must never enter into contractual arrangements.

Explain in your own words:

8. What is the best way for the Notary to determine a signer's awareness?

    _____

    _____

    _____

See page 382 for correct responses.

▼

CHAPTER 6

The Journal of Notarial Acts

A *journal of notarial acts* is a detailed, chronological record of the Notary Public's official acts. The Notary's journal can provide valuable evidence in the event a notarized document is lost or altered, or if certain facts about the transaction are challenged later. The journal can protect the rights of individuals and help Notaries defend themselves against false accusations of wrongdoing.

A journal is a valuable public record of a Notary's official acts.

NNA Recommendation

While many states require Notaries to keep a journal, some do not. Nevertheless, every Notary should keep a record book of notarial acts, whether required by law or not. It is simply the prudent, commonsense thing to do and is a sound business practice.

To be most effective, the Notary journal should have *bound pages*, not loose-leaf, and the pages should be numbered to deter unauthorized removal. In addition, it is important that notarial acts are recorded *chronologically*, since this can point out later tampering with the dates of notarization.

	Month/Day/Year/Time of Notarization	Kind or Type of Notarization	Document Date (Month/Day/Year)	Document Kind or Type	Name and Address of Signer	
1	August 9, 2001 3:30 p.m.	Corporate Acknowledgment	August 9, 2001	Contract Amendment	Richard Mason 1423 S. Olive St. Anytown, US 00000, phone 222-555-2324	☐ Pers ☐ ID C ☒ Cre
2	August 12, 2001 10:00 a.m.	Jurat	August 12, 2001	Affidavit of Residence	Diana Martinez 245 Vista Place Anytown, US 00000, phone 222-555-7184	☒ Pe ☐ ID ☐ C
3	August 12, 2001 1:20 p.m.	Attorney in Fact Acknowledgment	August 12, 2001	Grant Deed	Brian L. Carver 1200 Valley Spring Lane, #8 Anytown, US 00000, phone 222-555-7687	☐ Pe ☐ ID C ☐ Cred
						☐ Per

❶ ❷ ❸ ❹ ❺

Above is an example of a journal page and entries for typical notarial acts: 1) the date and time of the notarial act; 2) the type of notarial act; 3) the date of the document; 4) the title or type of the document; 5) the printed name,

JOURNAL ENTRIES

Some states specify in law what information a Notary must record in the journal. However, by recording the following data, as applicable, a Notary will fulfill the requirements of any state:

- The date and time of the notarial act.
- The type of notarial act.
- The date of the document.
- The title or type of the document or transaction.
- The printed name and address of each signer and witness.
- How each signer was identified.
- Any other pertinent information.
- The notarial fee charged, if any.
- The signature of each signer and witness.
- The right thumbprint of the signer.

Each notarization requires its own journal entry. If a signer presents several documents for notarization, the Notary should record each document as a separate notarization with separate journal entries.

If signatures from multiple individuals are being notarized on a single document at one time, then each signer's information — identification, name, address, signature, etc. — should be recorded on a separate line

Identification of Signer	Additional Information	Notary Fee	Signature of Signer	Right Thumbprint of Signer	
☐ Personally Known by the Notary ☐ ID Cards — Describe each card below ☒ Credible Witness(es) — Include signature of each witness John Tyson John Tyson, 221 Main St, Carson City, NV	signed as president of United Software, Inc.	$5.00	x Richard Mesa	[thumbprint]	1
☒ Personally Known by the Notary ☒ ID Cards — Describe each card below ☐ Credible Witness(es) — Include signature of each witness NV Driver's License #370202800154 Exp. 5/24/10		$5.00	x Diana Martinez	[thumbprint]	2
☐ Personally Known by the Notary ☒ ID Cards — Describe each card below ☐ Credible Witness(es) — Include signature of each witness NV Driver's License #283266066733 Exp. 8/30/11	signed as attorney in fact for Vivian Grayson, his grandmother	$5.00	x Brian L Carrea	[thumbprint]	3
☐ Personally Known by the Notary					

❻   **❼**   **❽**   **❾**   **❿**

address and phone number of the document signer; 6) how each signer was identified; 7) additional pertinent information; 8) the notarial fee charged; 9) the signature of each signer; and 10) the signer's right thumbprint.

in the journal. In some states, ditto marks or signing along a diagonal line are acceptable techniques to avoid rewriting the same information.

Date and Time of Notarization

This is the month, day, year and time of day (e.g., 1:45 p.m.) the signer appeared before the Notary. Recording this information provides helpful evidence if there is a dispute later about whether the signer actually appeared before the Notary.

All parts of a notarization — identifying the signer, making the journal entry and completing the certificate — must be performed on the same day at the same time and place.

Type of Notarial Act

Here the Notary indicates the official act performed, whether an acknowledgment, jurat, copy certification or other type of notarization. In addition, the type of acknowledgment — attorney in fact, corporate, partnership or other — should be noted.

Date of Document

In most cases, the document date is the date of the document's signing. If there is more than one signer, it is the date of the final signing. If others will sign the document after the notarization at hand, the

▼

document date would be the date of the most recent signing.

The document's date of signing may *precede* or *coincide* with the date of notarization, but never *follow* it. A document dated to follow the date on its notarial certificate risks rejection by a recorder, who may question how the document could have been notarized before it was signed. An exception may occur when a document must be circulated to collect different signatures and notarial certificates. In this case, the document date — indicating the date of the final signing — may follow the dates on all but the last notarial certificate.

Predating and *postdating* documents and notarial certificates are deceptive and often illegal acts. They misrepresent the actual date of signing or notarizing and often are done to take advantage of certain deadlines. Falsifying a notarial certificate is a criminal act. As a trusted public official, a Notary must never be a knowing party to a deception, whether involving dates or any other matter.

Title or Type of Document

The entry should include a description of the document notarized — that is, either its exact title, as in "Affidavit of Support," or its general type, as in "Grant Deed" or "Power of Attorney."

If there is no document involved, as might be the case with the administration of an oath, a description of the procedure or event should be recorded. For example, the Notary might write "oath of office for deputy commissioner."

Printed Name and Address of Each Signer

Recording the printed names of signers is important because signatures can be very difficult to read.

The home or business address — and even the phone number — where the signer may be contacted is extremely helpful if there are any later questions about the notarization.

The address also should be entered for any subscribing witness, credible identifying witness or witness to a signing by mark. A subscribing witness's address goes in the address column. A credible identifying witness's address may be placed in the journal's identification column and a signature-by-mark witness's address in the additional information column, if space allows. Otherwise, additional journal-entry lines may be used to accommodate such witnesses' information.

Identification

The journal entry should indicate in detail which of the three methods the Notary used to identify each signer. The Notary would enter either "personal knowledge"; "credible identifying witness," plus the witness' signature, printed name and address; or the identification document's title or type, issuing agency, serial number (Texas and Oregon Notaries are prohibited from recording the serial number in the journal) and date of issuance or expiration.

Other Pertinent Data

Any other information that the state may require or that the Notary may feel is important also may be recorded. Such entries include, but are certainly not limited to, observations about the signer's behavior; the address where the notarization is performed, if not at the Notary's office; any further description of the document, including number of pages, attachment of a loose certificate, names of other signers and any fraud-deterrent measures taken by the Notary, such as use of an embosser.

Also in this category, the Notary should record the reason for refusing or failing to complete a notarization.

Notarial Fee

Here the Notary would indicate the fee charged, if any, for performing the notarization.

Some states require a record of notarial fees to be maintained by the Notary in a "fee book." A fee entry in the Notary journal is an acceptable alternative and simplifies the Notary's recordkeeping.

Signature of Each Signer

The signature of each document signer and oath-taker comprises one of the most important entries in the Notary's journal. A journal signature provides strong evidence that the signer indeed appeared before the Notary. This serves as a deterrent to signers with second thoughts about a document who might otherwise falsely claim not to have appeared before the Notary. Also, the journal signature can be a great obstacle to a forger who may have difficulty duplicating the document signature without taking an undue amount of time and arousing the Notary's suspicion.

In addition to the signature of the document signer, the signature and printed name should be entered for each credible identifying witness, subscribing witness and witness to a signing by mark. Since the credible identifying witness identifies the signer, this individual's signature may be recorded in the identification area if space permits. Otherwise, an additional journal-entry line may be used. The subscribing witness would sign in the signature column, and the witness to a signing by mark would write the marker's name next to the mark in the signature column and sign his or her own name in the additional information column.

All journal signatures must be made at the time of notarization, not before and not later. There can be no exceptions.

The Notary should compare the journal signature to the signature on the document and on any identification documents presented. These must match to a certain degree ("Pat R. Jones" instead of "Patrick Ronald Jones," for example).

A shortcut to relieve the signer from making multiple signatures in the journal when several documents are notarized at the same time may be allowed in some states. In such cases, the Notary makes a separate entry for each notarization, but the signer signs along a diagonal line drawn across the signature spaces of all the entries on one page. However, this shortcut is not allowed with documents notarized on separate appearances before the Notary. If the signer leaves and then returns a few minutes later with another document, this is a separate appearance requiring a separate signature and separate journal entry.

Thumbprint

Notaries increasingly are asking signers to affix a thumbprint in the journal. This practice deters impostors who will not want to leave behind such absolute evidence of an attempted fraud and provides proof that the signer actually appeared before the Notary, should this fact later be challenged.

A simple inking device is all that is required. The signer touches the device with the right thumb and then touches the journal page to leave a print. The print is taken of the right thumb because law enforcement and other government agencies use this digit for fingerprint identification. If the signer is missing the right thumb, a left thumb or other digit may be used, and the Notary should note which digit made the print.

The type of Notary journal best suited for recording thumbprints is one with designated spaces for prints. If the journal does not have thumbprint spaces, the print may be affixed in the "additional information" column or on a second entry line, providing the print is not obscured by preprinted information or intersecting lines.

In California, a Notary journal thumbprint is mandated by law for signers of deeds affecting real property and powers of attorney.

 NNA Recommendation

To prevent a document signer from leaving before vital data has been recorded, the careful Notary always will complete the journal entry before filling out the notarial certificate and affixing his or her signature and official seal.

OTHER NOTARIAL RECORDS

In addition to the journal, it may be necessary or prudent for the Notary to keep certain other notarial records. These might include duplicates of certified copies and written remarks from a physician about a signer's ability to understand.

DISPOSITION OF NOTARIAL RECORDS

The journal of notarial acts and related records should be kept in a secure place, preferably in a locked and fireproof drawer, file or safe.

If the journal is stolen, lost, destroyed or damaged, it may be prudent — if not required by law — to inform the state's Notary-regulating authority in writing, as well as the agency to which the journal would eventually have been surrendered. If a criminal act is suspected, local law enforcement authorities should be contacted.

If a Notary changes jobs, the journal — and the seal — go with the Notary. Even if an employer paid for the journal and seal, these are official tools of the notarial office, and their possession or use by anyone but the Notary may be a criminal act.

When a notarial commission is resigned or revoked, or when a commission expires without renewal for any reason, the Notary may be required to turn in all notarial records to a designated agency. Depending on state law, the records may have to be deposited with a county clerk, county recorder, probate judge, secretary of state or other official.

States often set criminal penalties for concealing, defacing or destroying the journal or failing to turn it in at an appropriate time. The penalties may apply either to Notaries or, if they are deceased, to the administrators of their estates.

SUMMARY

A journal of notarial acts is a detailed record of the official acts of a Notary. The journal can provide valuable evidence if a notarized document is lost, altered or challenged. It also can protect the Notary from baseless accusations that notarial duties were improperly performed.

To prevent tampering, the journal should be a bound book with consecutively printed page numbers.

For each notarial act, the journal entry should include: the date and time of day the notarization was performed, descriptions of the notarization and document, the signature, name and address of each signer and witness, how each signer and witness was identified and the fee charged. Other entries might include the thumbprint of the signer, observations about the signer's behavior and demeanor, and an additional description of the document. Also important is noting why a notarization was refused.

It is wise to record the journal entry before completing the notarial certificate to prevent the signer from leaving without signing the journal or providing other important information.

In addition to the journal, other records may be kept by the Notary, such as duplicates of certified copies or a physician's statement about a signer's ability to understand.

The journal should be kept in a safe place. If it is lost or stolen, the Notary should inform the Notary-regulating authority. If the Notary changes jobs, the journal (as well as the Notary seal) goes with the Notary. When a notarial commission is terminated for any reason, the Notary must forward the journal to the designated agency, if required. ■

IMPORTANT TERMS

Bound Pages: Pages that are securely fastened together to deter their unauthorized removal or replacement.

Chronological: In the sequence of occurrence.

Date of Document: Date of signing, or, in the case of multiple signers, of the most recent or final signing.

Journal Entry: Information recorded in a journal describing a particular notarization.

Journal of Notarial Acts: Detailed, chronological record of the official acts of a Notary Public.

Postdate: Deceptive and sometimes illegal act of dating a document with a time after the actual signing or execution.

Predate: Deceptive and sometimes illegal act of dating a document with a time before the actual signing or execution.

CHAPTER 6 TEST

In each blank, write the response — a, b, c or d — that best completes each of the following statements:

1. A journal of notarial acts _____.

    a. Should contain permanently bound pages.

    b. Must be surrendered to an employer when quitting a job.

    c. May be filled in at the end of each week.

    d. Can be in the form of papers distributed in office files.

2. Requiring a person to sign the journal of notarial acts is _____.

    a. Unnecessary if the signer is the Notary's employer.

    b. Unnecessary if the signer is personally known to the Notary.

    c. An invasion of privacy, if not required by law.

    d. Strongly recommended, even when not required by law.

3. When a Notary resigns his or her commission, the journal _____.

    a. Must be destroyed as soon as possible.

    b. Must be surrendered to a designated public agency, if required.

    c. Must be safeguarded by the Notary's employer in a fireproof file.

    d. Must be surrendered to any available Notary.

4. The proper sequence for performing a notarial act is _____.

    a. Journal entry, identification, certificate completion.

    b. Identification, certificate completion, journal entry.

    c. Identification, journal entry, certificate completion.

    d. Certificate completion, journal entry, identification.

5. Notaries are not recommended to keep _____.

    a. Copies of every document notarized.

    b. Proof of their commissioning and bonding.

    c. Duplicates of copies certified.

    d. Written remarks from a physician about a signer's awareness.

6. The document signer's journal signature _____.

    a. Should be obtained only when there is doubt about identity.

    b. Need not be obtained if a credible identifying witness signs.

    c. Eliminates the need for a credible identifying witness or ID.

    d. Should be obtained even with personal knowledge of identity.

▼

7. Notaries need not record in their journals _____.

    a. The time of day of notarization.

    b. The fees charged for notarial services.

    c. The document signer's address.

    d. The time of day of the document's signing.

8. When a journal entry is made, a certificate is completed _____.

    a. At the same time, with the document signer there.

    b. Any time later, if the signer is there.

    c. Any time the same day, with or without the signer there.

    d. At the same time, with or without the document signer there.

9. The following document signing date and notarization date recorded in the journal are unacceptable: _____.

    a. Document date: May 10. Notarization date: May 10.

    b. Document date: May 10. Notarization date: May 11.

    c. Document date: May 11. Notarization date: May 10.

    d. Document date: April 10. Notarization date: May 10.

10. A person who presents five documents for notarization at different times _____.

    a. May sign the journal once if ditto marks are used four times.

    b. Need not sign if he or she signed before for a notarization.

    c. Need not sign if he or she left a sample signature in the front.

    d. Must sign the journal at each of the five appearances.

Explain in your own words:

11. Why should the journal entry be made before a certificate is completed?

_____

_____

_____

12. Make a journal entry for the following notarial act:

    Today at 3:15 p.m., Harold P. Garvey, a close friend, appears before you to acknowledge his signature on a grant deed signed yesterday.

He lives at 4321 Elm Street in your town and zip code. You do not
charge for the notarization.

	Month/Day/Year/Time of Notarization	Kind or Type of Notarization	Document Date (Month/Day/Year)	Document Kind or Type	Name and Address of Signer	
1						☐ Perso ☐ ID / ☐ C
						☐ Pe

Identification of Signer	Additional Information	Notary Fee	Signature of Signer	Right Thumbprint of Signer	
☐ Personally Known by the Notary ☐ ID Cards — Describe each card below ☐ Credible Witness(es) — Include signature of each witness			x	Top of thumb here	1
☐ Personally Known by the Notary					

See page 382 for correct responses.

CHAPTER 7

The Notarial Certificate and Seal

THE NOTARIAL CERTIFICATE

In notarizing any document, the Notary must complete, sign and seal wording to indicate exactly what the notarization has certified. This wording is called the notarial certificate and indicates the procedures that the Notary followed in performing the notarization. Filling out the notarial certificate is the final step of a notarial act.

The notarial certificate is wording that describes what the Notary certified in performing the notarial act.

Because the Notary certifies a different set of facts in each type of notarial act, each requires different wording in the notarial certificate. Acknowledgments, jurats, copy certifications and other notarial acts have distinctly different notarial certificates.

 State Laws Vary

Many states require specific certificate wording as set forth in law for each type of notarial act. Other states prescribe no wording at all and allow for a range of certificates. The Notary must be familiar with his or her state's certificate requirements and follow them exactly.

The notarial certificate may be in one of two forms: wording preprinted or typed on the document itself (typically following the document's signature space) or wording that appears on a separate sheet of paper attached to the document, known as a *loose certificate*, which is usually stapled to the document's signature page.

CONTENTS OF NOTARIAL CERTIFICATES

While each type of notarization requires a unique notarial certificate, certificates for notarial acts have five components: 1) a *venue*, 2) a *statement of particulars*, 3) a *testimonium clause* (optional), 4) the *signature of the Notary*, and 5) an imprint of the *official seal of the Notary* (if state law requires).

Venue

The *venue* indicates where the notarization is being performed. "State of _____, County of _____," is the standard venue wording, with the state and county names inserted in the blanks.

Sometimes, the letters "SS." or "SCT." appear after or to the right of the venue. These letters abbreviate the traditional Latin word *scilicet*, meaning "in particular" or "namely."

Statement of Particulars

The portion of a certificate that describes what the Notary has certified and what the notarization has accomplished is called the *statement of particulars*. In other words, the statement of particulars specifies what the Notary actually did in performing the notarial act.

The statement of particulars is the wording that tells what the Notary has certified.

Since a Notary certifies different facts in the various types of notarial acts, it is the statement of particulars that is unique for each type of notarization. For example, a typical acknowledgment certificate would include such wording as:

> On this _____ day of _____ (month), _____ (year), before me, _____ (name of Notary), the undersigned Notary Public, personally appeared _____ (name of signer[s]), personally known to me (or proved to me on the basis of satisfactory evidence) to be the person(s) whose name(s) is/are subscribed to the within instrument and acknowledged that he/she/they freely executed it.

▼

Acknowledgment

State of _____)
) SS.   } VENUE
County of _____)

On this _____ day of _____ (month), _____ (year), before me, _____ (name of Notary), the undersigned Notary Public, personally appeared _____ (name of signer[s]), personally known to me (or proved to me on the basis of satisfactory evidence) to be the person(s) whose name(s) is/are subscribed to the within instrument and acknowledged that he/she/they freely executed it.   } STATEMENT OF PARTICULARS

Witness my hand and official seal.   } TESTIMONIUM CLAUSE

_____ (signature and seal of Notary)   } SIGNATURE AND SEAL OF NOTARY

Jurat

State of _____)
) SCT.   } VENUE
County of _____)

Subscribed and sworn to (or affirmed) before me this _____ day of _____ (month), _____ (year), by _____ (name of signer[s]).   } STATEMENT OF PARTICULARS

_____ (signature and seal of Notary)   } SIGNATURE AND SEAL OF NOTARY

Above are examples of an acknowledgment certificate and a jurat certificate. Completing any notarial certificate requires the Notary to carefully read the wording and then fill in the appropriate information. In this jurat certificate, the testimonium clause is implied, and the fact that the certificate is signed and sealed by the Notary is adequate without the ceremonial wording "Witness my hand and official seal."

A jurat certificate typically would include such wording as:

Subscribed and sworn to (or affirmed) before me this _____ day of _____ (month), _____ (year), by _____ (name of signer[s]).

Testimonium Clause

The testimonium clause immediately follows the statement of particulars and typically appears as, "Witness my hand and official seal," or similar wording. ("Hand" means signature.) In this short sentence, the

Notary formally attests to the truthfulness of the preceding facts in the certificate. Note that it is the truthfulness of the facts in the certificate that the Notary verifies, not the facts in the document.

In some cases, the somewhat ceremonial testimonium clause will be omitted, and the simple fact that the Notary signed and sealed the certificate will serve as sufficient confirmation of the facts in the certificate. However, in some certificates, the testimonium clause will contain the date of notarization, as in "Witness my hand and official seal this _____ day of _____ (month), _____ (year)"; in such cases, the clause must not be omitted.

Signature of the Notary

The signature of the Notary certifies that Notary performed the actions stated in the certificate for the particular notarial act and that the venue, date and other information are correct.

The Official Seal of the Notary

The imprint of the official seal of the Notary authenticates the Notary's signature and makes the act official. The seal signifies that the Notary is a public officer commissioned in a particular state. It also provides information such as the county where the Notary's commission, bond and oath of office are on file, as well as the commission number and expiration date.

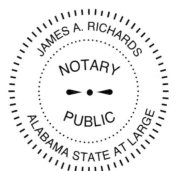

Above are examples of typical notarial seals. The two on the left are common formats for inking seals; on the right is an example of an embosser seal format. (Embosser seals make images in relief on a sheet of paper.)

There are two types of official Notary seals: the modern inking stamp and the traditional embosser. The most common inking seal is a rubber stamp, and it imprints a photographically reproducible image on the document. The embosser is a press-like device that imprints an image in relief on a paper surface.

Increasingly, the inking seal is being used by Notaries because its image may be readily photocopied and microfilmed. However, some states allow only traditional embosser seals to be used.

State Laws Vary

Some states require Notaries to use inking seals, some require an embossing seal, and some allow either. (See Appendix 2, "State Notary Officials and Key Law Provisions," page 363.) In many states, the inking seal is replacing the traditional embossing seal because it affixes an image that is readable on microfilm.

COMPLETING THE NOTARIAL CERTIFICATE

Because of the wide variety of different forms, completing the notarial certificate can be a confusing step in the notarization process. However, the Notary should keep in mind that most notarial certificates require the same basic information. Completing a certificate, then, is simply a matter of carefully reading the wording and filling in the appropriate information.

In completing a notarial certificate, the Notary should type or print legibly in ink. Dark ink, preferably black, always should be used to facilitate microfilming by a recorder.

Indicating the Venue

The venue must be completed so that it indicates the state and county where the notarization takes place.

The venue must be filled in with the state and county (and sometimes city) where the notarization is being performed. This is not necessarily where the Notary's commission is filed, where the Notary's business is located or where the Notary or signer resides.

If the venue is preprinted or already filled in with a state or county other than where the notarization is being performed, the Notary must correct it by lining through (a single line only) the incorrect state and/or county, writing in the correct location and then initialing and dating the change. Dating the correction is not necessary if it is made at the time of notarization.

▼

Filling in the Statement of Particulars

With the statement of particulars, the Notary fills in the blanks with the appropriate date, his or her own name (if required) and the name of the signer or signers.

Many certificates indicate what information goes in each blank with descriptions either below the blank or in parentheses following the blank. However, some do not, requiring the Notary to carefully read the certificate to determine what information is required.

The opening phrase in most certificates indicates the actual day, month and year that the signer or signers appeared before the Notary. This phrase may have been completed prior to the notarization and may require correction by the Notary to reflect the actual date of notarization.

On many certificates, the Notary must choose between alternate wording. The certificate may provide options allowing the Notary to indicate, for example, how the signer was identified or whether the signer took an oath or an affirmation. These choices may be in the form of check-off boxes or phrases beginning with "or" that appear in parentheses. The Notary selects the proper phrase by checking the appropriate box or by lining through the inapplicable phrase. For example, with a certificate bearing the wording "...personally known to me (or proved to me on the basis of satisfactory evidence)...," the Notary would either line through the words "personally known to me" or the words "(or proved to me on the basis of satisfactory evidence)," to indicate how the signer was identified.

Any plurals are to be crossed out for a solo signer or left intact for two or more signers — the "(s)" in "person(s)," for instance, would be crossed out or left as is for one or multiple signers, respectively. The correct verbs are similarly chosen — either "is" or "are" in "is/are" being crossed out to reflect one or multiple signers.

In addition, the Notary must indicate the correct pronouns — he, she or they — as required. These are usually printed in the form "he/she/they" or "___he___." With "he/she/they" the Notary crosses out the pronouns not applicable, leaving the correct one unmarked — for one male signer, for example, "she" and "they" would be crossed out

The core of the notarial certificate is the statement of particulars. The Notary fills in the blanks, crosses out inapplicable wording and selects plurals, verbs and pronouns to comply with the number and gender of the signer or signers.

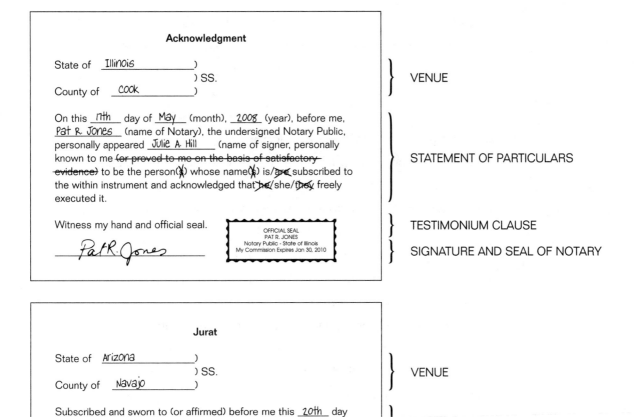

Acknowledgment

State of _Illinois_)
) SS.
County of _Cook_)

On this _17th_ day of _May_ (month), _2008_ (year), before me, _Pat R. Jones_ (name of Notary), the undersigned Notary Public, personally appeared _Julie A. Hill_ (name of signer, personally known to me (or proved to me on the basis of satisfactory evidence) to be the person(s) whose name(s) is/are subscribed to the within instrument and acknowledged that he/she/they freely executed it.

Witness my hand and official seal.

Pat R. Jones

OFFICIAL SEAL
PAT R. JONES
Notary Public - State of Illinois
My Commission Expires Jan 30, 2010

} VENUE

} STATEMENT OF PARTICULARS

} TESTIMONIUM CLAUSE

} SIGNATURE AND SEAL OF NOTARY

Jurat

State of _Arizona_)
) SS.
County of _Navajo_)

Subscribed and sworn to (or affirmed) before me this _20th_ day of _March_ (month), _2008_ (year), (by _John F. Oh_).

Paul C. Fontana

PAUL C. FONTANA
Notary Public - Arizona
Navajo County
My Comm. Expires Dec 15, 2010

} VENUE

} STATEMENT OF PARTICULARS

} SIGNATURE AND SEAL OF NOTARY

Above are examples of completed certificates for an acknowledgment and a jurat.

leaving "he." With "___he___" the blanks are left empty for one male signer or are filled with letters to construct the words "she" or "they" as appropriate. Sometimes the pronouns "his/her/their" are included as well. These are to be handled similarly.

In crossing out inapplicable wording on a notarial certificate to indicate a choice, it is not necessary for the Notary to initial and date the cross-out; initialing and dating are required only when making corrections.

Because of its sometimes legalistic language, the statement of particulars can be difficult to understand. The Notary must read it carefully to assure that he or she actually has done what the certificate

▼

says. Also, the Notary must make sure the certificate substantially complies with any certificate wording that may be mandated by law.

A Notary who is unable to understand a given notarial certificate must decline to use it.

Signing and Sealing the Certificate

A notarization is not complete without the Notary's signature and, as required in most states, an imprint of the Notary's official seal. These often follow a testimonium clause, "Witness my hand and official seal."

The Notary must sign the certificate exactly as the name appears on the Notary's commissioning paper. The signature must be an original. A signature stamp is not allowed.

Some certificate wording includes the phrase, "Signature and quality of officer," or, "Signature and title of official" where the Notary signs. "Quality of officer" and "title" mean the same. When one of these phrases appears, the Notary should write "Notary Public" — the Notary's official title — following his or her signature.

The seal imprint should be placed as close to the Notary's signature as possible without overprinting it. To assure legibility, the seal imprint should not be placed over any wording in the document. If there is no room for the seal, the Notary may have to use some ingenuity in finding space for it — perhaps affixing its impression in a margin or using an attached loose certificate instead of the preprinted certificate. Only with the permission of the document's recipient may the seal be placed over wording if there is no room at all for it elsewhere. In no case should a Notary attach an additional sheet of paper with only the seal imprint.

On many certificates, the letters "L.S." appear, indicating where the seal is to be located. These letters abbreviate the Latin term *locus sigilli*, meaning "location of the seal." The inking seal should be placed near but not over any of the letters, so that wording imprinted by the seal will not be obscured. An embossing seal may be placed directly over the letters.

Many Notaries in states that require an inking seal recommend using an embossment in addition to (but not over) the inked seal impression as a deterrent to fraud, especially with multipage documents or attached loose certificates. Embossing a document and certificate together makes their fraudulent replacement more difficult, since a tamperer would have to duplicate the Notary's embossment. An embosser may be used in addition to a legally required inking seal. In some states, the embosser is the required seal.

Some states do not require Notaries to use seals, or they allow seals without commission expiration dates. In such jurisdictions, Notaries may be required to write, type or stamp a commission expiration date or other information on the certificate. A large percentage of Notaries in states not requiring seals still opt to use them instead of adding this mandatory information.

No matter where a notarized document is destined, Notaries must comply with the seal requirements in their own states. Remember, a Notary's first allegiance is to the laws of his or her state.

Notaries never should merely stamp and sign a document without filling out certificate wording. Without such wording, a Notary's seal and signature are meaningless.

Do Not Pre-Sign or Pre-Seal Certificates

A Notary never should sign and/or seal certificates ahead of time or permit other persons to attach pre-signed or pre-sealed loose notarial certificates to documents. In particular, a Notary should not send an unattached, signed and sealed, loose certificate through the mail, even if adamantly requested to do so by a signer who previously appeared before the Notary. These actions may facilitate fraud or forgery and could subject the Notary to lawsuits to recover damages resulting from the Notary's neglect or misconduct.

False Certificate

If a Notary knowingly completes a notarial certificate with false information, he or she may be subject to criminal penalties, including fines and imprisonment. The Notary also may have his or her commission suspended or revoked. In addition, the Notary may be held liable for damages resulting from the improper act. A Notary would be completing a false certificate, for example, if he or she signed and sealed a certificate indicating a signer personally appeared when the signer actually did not.

LOOSE CERTIFICATES

When certificate wording is not preprinted on the document, or when the preprinted certificate wording does not comply with state requirements (as is often the case when documents are prepared in a state other than where they are to be notarized), a loose certificate may be attached. Loose certificates also may be used when there is no room for a required notarial seal imprint or when additional signatures are notarized at a later date.

A loose certificate is a separate sheet of paper with notarial wording that the Notary attaches to a document.

The loose certificate often is a smaller size than the document page and is stapled to the left margin on top of the document's signature page. Only one side of the certificate should be stapled, so it can be lifted to allow viewing of the document beneath. If the certificate is a full-page sheet, it may be attached preceding or following the signature page and in the same manner — stapled at the top, side or corner — as other pages of the document.

If a loose certificate is used because the certificate wording printed on the document does not comply with the requirements of the Notary's state, then the Notary should line through or cross out the preprinted wording and write or type, "See attached certificate."

Loose certificates must never be completed and attached in addition to completing the provided wording on a document. This facilitates fraud by inviting removal of the loose certificate and using it on another document.

To prevent a loose certificate from being removed and fraudulently placed on another document, there are precautions a Notary can take. The Notary can emboss the certificate and document together and write: "Attached document bears embossment" on the certificate. Or the Notary can write a brief description of the document on the certificate: e.g.,

A loose certificate may be used when the document has no notarial wording or when the wording provided does not comply with state law.

"This certificate is attached to a _____ (title or type of document), dated _____, of _____ (number) pages, also signed by _____ (name[s] of other signer[s])."

To avoid rejection by a recorder, Notaries never should affix an inking seal imprint half on a document and half on a loose certificate in an attempt to prevent the certificate from being lifted from the document. However, this may be done with a seal embossment that is affixed on a certificate in addition to a full seal impression.

While fraud-deterrent steps such as these can make it much more difficult for a loose certificate to be removed and misused, there is no absolute protection against its removal and misuse. Notaries must absolutely ensure that while a certificate remains in their control, it is attached only to its intended document. A Notary must never give or mail a signed and sealed notarial certificate to another person and trust that person to attach it to a particular document. This would be an all-but-indefensible action in a civil court of law.

SELECTING THE NOTARIAL CERTIFICATE WORDING

As discussed in Chapter 2, nonattorney Notaries do not have the authority to determine the type of notarial act required for a particular document. So, if a document is presented for notarization without certificate wording, the Notary may not independently select a certificate, since this is essentially the same as determining the type of notarial act. Such a decision by a Notary may well be considered the unauthorized practice of law.

The document signer must instruct the Notary as to what type of notarization to perform and, therefore, what certificate is needed.

Instead, the Notary must ask the signer what type of notarization to perform, and this will tell the Notary what certificate wording is required. The Notary then may type the appropriate wording on the document or attach a preprinted loose certificate.

If the signer does not know the type of notarization needed, it is his or her responsibility to find out. The signer may do so by checking with the person or agency that prepared the document or will receive it, or the signer may consult an attorney.

SUMMARY

The final step of a notarization is completing, signing and sealing the notarial certificate. This form describes the procedures that the Notary followed and specifies exactly what the Notary is guaranteeing. Since each type of notarial act has different procedures and guarantees, each act requires distinct certificate wording. Many, but not all, states mandate the wording to be used for each type of notarization.

The venue of the certificate indicates the state and county where the notarization is being performed. The statement of particulars describes what the Notary has certified and usually includes the date, the signer's name and the Notary's name. Here the Notary also selects between alternate wording and crosses out any inapplicable plural terms. In the testimonium clause, the Notary formally attests to the facts in the certificate. To certify the notarization and make the act official, the Notary signs his or her name and affixes an imprint of his or her official seal of office. The signature name must be exactly as on the Notary's commissioning paper. Some states require an inking seal, some an embosser, some allow either, and some states do not require a seal at all.

Notaries never must sign or seal a document without certificate wording. And notarial certificates never should be signed or sealed in advance.

Notaries who knowingly complete notarial certificates with false information may be subject to criminal penalties and liable for any resulting financial loss.

If certificate wording is not preprinted on the document, or if the preprinted wording does not comply with the requirements of the Notary's state, the Notary may attach a separate sheet of paper to the document with appropriate notarial wording. Such an attachment is called a loose certificate. The Notary may not select the certificate wording needed for a particular document. The signer must tell the Notary what type of notarization to perform. If the signer does not know, it is his or her responsibility to find out what type of notarization is required by checking with the document's issuing agency or receiving agency, or with an attorney. Only then may the Notary add the appropriate wording to the document or attach a loose certificate. Loose certificates never may be provided to a signer or other person unless attached to a document. ■

IMPORTANT TERMS

Embosser Seal: Plier- or press-like device that imprints a raised image into a paper surface to form a notarial seal.

False Certificate: Notarial wording that contains incorrect information.

Hand: Signature.

Inking Seal: Device that imprints ink on paper to form a photocopiable notarial seal.

Instrument: Document.

Loose Certificate: Notarial certificate wording on a separate sheet of paper that is attached to a document. Used when no wording is provided, when the provided certificate wording does not comply with state requirements, when there is no room for the seal on the document or when a preprinted certificate has already been used by another Notary.

L.S.: Abbreviation of the Latin term *locus sigilli*, meaning "place of the seal." Traditional element indicating where the seal imprint is to be placed.

Photographically Reproducible: Image that can be readily photocopied or microfilmed.

Quality of Officer: Term sometimes appearing on notarial certificates and meaning "title of official," such as "Notary Public."

Seal of Notary: Inking or embossing device that imprints the Notary's name, title (Notary Public) and jurisdiction on a notarized document. Also may include such information as the county where the commission and bond are on file, commission number and date of commission expiration.

Signature of Notary: Handwritten name of and by the Notary, matching exactly with the name on the Notary's commissioning paper.

SS. or SCT.: Abbreviations of the Latin word *scilicet*, meaning "in particular" or "namely." Traditional element appearing after or to the right of the venue in a notarial certificate.

Statement of Particulars: Wording in a notarial certificate that describes what the Notary has certified.

Testimonium Clause: Wording in a notarial certificate where the Notary formally attests to the facts. Typically phrased as, "Witness my hand and official seal."

Venue: Wording in a notarial certificate that indicates the state and county where the notarization takes place.

CHAPTER 7 TEST

In each blank, write the response — a, b, c or d — that best completes each of the following statements:

1. The venue in a notarial certificate is the _____.

   a. State and county where the Notary's commission is filed.

   b. State and county where the notarization takes place.

   c. Jurisdiction of the Notary.

   d. State and county where the document will be recorded.

2. An embosser seal imprint _____.

   a. Is an image that is readily captured by a microfilm camera.

   b. Should not be affixed over the letters "L.S."

   c. Should be affixed over the Notary's signature.

   d. May be affixed to deter replacement of attached loose certificates.

3. An inking seal imprint _____.

   a. Should be affixed over the letters "L.S."

   b. Should be affixed half on the document, half on an attached loose certificate to deter removal of the certificate.

   c. Should be affixed as close to the Notary's signature as possible.

   d. Is required of Notaries in every state.

4. If a document has no certificate wording, the Notary may _____.

   a. Attach an appropriate loose certificate only when the signer has instructed the Notary as to the type of notarial act needed.

   b. Attach an appropriate loose certificate only when the signer does not know the type of notarial act needed.

   c. Attach an appropriate loose certificate only when the signer has instructed the Notary to decide the type of notarial act needed.

   d. Simply sign and seal the document without notarial wording.

5. If there is no room for the Notary seal imprint, it _____.

   a. May be omitted.

   b. May be affixed over the Notary's signature.

   c. May be affixed on the back of the document.

   d. May be affixed on a loose certificate that is attached to the document and contains the notarial wording.

6. A loose certificate _____.

   a. May be completed and mailed to the signer or receiving agency separate from the document when necessary.

   b. May be completed and attached to a document when the notarial wording on the document clearly does not comply with state law.

   c. May be completed and attached to a document in addition to completing the notarial wording on the document.

   d. Must be completed and attached to every document notarized, because notarial wording included on documents is usually wrong.

7. The Notary's signature on the certificate _____.

   a. Must represent exactly the same name appearing on the Notary's commissioning paper.

   b. May be affixed with a signature stamp to assure legibility.

   c. May be abbreviated with initials when space is limited.

   d. Should be made on certificates in advance to expedite the lengthy process of notarization.

In each blank, write the response — a, b, c or d — that best completes each of the following statements:

8. For a notarization completed on May 4, 2008, for a document dated May 2, 2008, the notarial certificate date should read, "On this the _____ day of _____ , _____...."

   a. 2nd.

   b. 4th.

   c. 2005.

   d. May.

9. When notarizing for two signers, the Notary should _____ the certificate wording "...he/she/they..." and _____ "...person(s)...."

   a. Cross out.

   b. Cross out the "he/she" in.

   c. Leave as is.

   d. Cross out the "(s)" in.

▼

10. When notarizing for one signer, a woman, the Notary should _____ the certificate wording "...he/she/they..." and _____ "...person(s)...."

    a. Cross out "he" and "they" in.

    b. Cross out the "he/she" in.

    c. Leave as is.

    d. Cross out the "(s)" in.

Complete the notarial certificates for the following notarizations.

11. Today, a woman named Grace C. Winslow appears before you in your county to have her signature notarized on a grant deed. The document was signed and dated two days earlier and concerns property located in Gotham County in your state. You identify her through a driver's license, indicating a residence at 1234 Main Street in Metropolis County. Complete the following certificate:

State of _____)

) SS.

County of _____)

On this _____ day of _____, _____, before me, _____, the undersigned Notary, personally appeared _____, personally known to me (or proved to me on the basis of satisfactory evidence) to be the person(s) whose name(s) is/are subscribed to the within instrument and acknowledged that he/she/they freely executed it.

Witness my hand and official seal.

_____   L.S.

(Signature and Quality of Officer)

12. Today, in your state and county, a man named Robert T. Simons appears before you to have an affidavit notarized. You watch him sign

the document, and he opts to take an affirmation rather than an oath. Complete the following jurat:

State of _____)

) SS.

County of _____)

Subscribed and sworn (or affirmed) to before me on this _____ day of _____, _____, by _____.

_____   L.S.

(Signature and Title of Official)

See pages 382–383 for correct responses.

PART III: NOTARIAL ACTS

CHAPTER 8

Acknowledgments

In this and the four chapters that follow, we will tie together the concepts outlined in the first seven chapters and present them as complete notarial acts. The common types of notarization — acknowledgment, jurat, copy certification and proof of execution — will be discussed in depth, and the essentials for performing each will be explained step by step from beginning to end.

THE MOST COMMON NOTARIAL ACT

Of all the types of notarial acts, the acknowledgment is the most prevalent. The average Notary Public likely will perform far more acknowledgments than all other notarial acts combined.

The acknowledgment helps assure that a signature was not forged or made while the signer was coerced or incompetent.

Since an acknowledgment provides strong evidence that a signature on a particular document is genuine, this notarization is required by law for a variety of important documents, from deeds to powers of attorney to loan agreements. For documents to be accepted by county recorders, the acknowledgment of the signatures before a Notary is extremely crucial. Deeds, loan agreements and other papers relating to ownership of real estate, for example, must have their signatures acknowledged so that they may be regarded as authentic before they are placed in the public record.

THREE FACTS CERTIFIED

The primary function of an acknowledgment is positive identification of the document's signer — verifying that the person who signed the document is, in fact, the person named in it. To do this, the Notary certifies three things:

An acknowledgment guarantees that the signer appeared before the Notary, was identified by the Notary and stated that he or she signed the document willingly.

1. Personal Appearance. The document signer must appear in person before the Notary at the time of the notarial act.

2. Positive Identification. The Notary must positively identify the signer.

3. Acknowledgment of Signature. The signer must acknowledge to the Notary that he or she willingly signed the document.

Additionally, many acknowledgment certificates require the certification of other facts by the Notary. For example, determining the authority of the signer to act in a claimed representative capacity is often a requirement in many states, and some states require signers to take an oath or affirmation in conjunction with an acknowledgment.

Important

The Notary is obligated by law to verify any claims made in the notarial certificate. For example, if the certificate states that the signer is "known to be the president of …(a particular corporation)," the Notary must indeed know this to be true. Careful reading of the certificate will reveal any facts the Notary must verify.

Personal Appearance

As explained in Chapter 3, the document signer's personal appearance before a Notary Public is the first step in any notarization.

The signer must appear in person before the Notary on the date and at the location (state and county) stated on the notarial certificate.

Personal appearance means that the signer is in the Notary's physical presence — face to face in the same room. A phone call cannot constitute personal appearance, nor can a voice heard from an adjacent room, recognition of a familiar signature, a written note from an absent signer, nor the casual, unsworn word of a third party about an absent signer's intent.

Identifying the Document Signer

Chapter 4 described how to positively identify the document signer. In performing an acknowledgment, the Notary must positively identify the document signer through either the Notary's own personal knowledge of the signer's identity, the oath or affirmation of a credible identifying witness who personally knows the signer, or a reliable identification document.

Acknowledgment of Signature

Acknowledge means to recognize as one's own. In the notarial act called an acknowledgment, the document signer recognizes before a Notary Public that a signature on a document is his or her own and that the signer made it voluntarily.

The signer makes or gives the acknowledgment, and the Notary takes, executes or performs it.

The signer must acknowledge that the signature is his or her own. It is not required that the Notary watch the signature being made.

Since a signer usually will not know what to say to the Notary in making an acknowledgment, the Notary may help by asking, "Do you acknowledge that this is your signature and that you signed willingly?" or words to this effect. A "yes" constitutes the signer's acknowledgment.

If a signer happens to sign the document in front of the Notary, that action may be taken as tacit acknowledgment of the signature. However, the Notary still may ask the signer if the signing was done voluntarily.

With an acknowledgment, the Notary is not required to watch the signature being placed on the document. The document signer need only acknowledge having made the signature to the Notary. While the signature does not have to be made in the presence of the Notary, the signer always must personally appear before the Notary to acknowledge the signature at the time of notarization. The signature could have been made minutes, hours, days, weeks, months or even years before the signer brings the document to the Notary.

Representative Capacities

It is sometimes necessary for one individual to sign as representative of another (usually as attorney in fact or guardian) or of a legal entity, such as a corporation, partnership or trust (as officer, partner, trustee, attorney in fact, etc.). Documents signed in a representative capacity generally require special acknowledgment certificates that specify who or what is being represented.

Depending on state law or the wording of the particular acknowledgment certificate, the Notary may or may not be required to verify the signer's representative status.

Determining a signer's authority to sign in a particular representative capacity may be done in several ways: through the Notary's personal knowledge, by documentary proof or by vouching under oath or affirmation by the signer. (Refer to Chapter 4 for more on how this is done.)

Some states do not require Notaries to require proof of a signer's representative capacity. Nonetheless, Notaries in these states sometimes encounter certificates that require such proof. Completing these certificates legally obligates the Notary to verify that a signer is empowered to act as described in the certificate.

ACKNOWLEDGMENT CERTIFICATES

In taking an acknowledgment, the Notary must complete a notarial certificate that describes what has been guaranteed, as with other notarial acts. Generally, acknowledgment certificate wording indicates the three facts certified by the Notary: 1) the signer's personal appearance before the Notary, 2) identification of the signer by the Notary, and 3) the signer's acknowledgment to the Notary.

Note how the three guarantees are embodied in a typical acknowledgment certificate:

Documents may be signed in representative capacities. That is, one person may sign as a representative of another person or of a legal entity, provided this individual has been given the authority to do so.

State of _____)
) SS.
County of _____)

On this _____ day of _____ (month), _____ (year), before me, _____ (name of Notary), the undersigned Notary Public, personally appeared _____ (name[s] of signer[s]), personally known to me (or proved to me on the basis of satisfactory evidence) to be the person(s) whose name(s) is/are subscribed to the within instrument and acknowledged that he/she/they freely executed it.

Witness my hand and official seal.

_____ (signature and seal of Notary)

The phrase, "*before me _____ (name of Notary), the undersigned Notary Public, personally appeared _____ (name[s] of signer[s])*," indicates the signer's personal appearance before the Notary — that the document signer was in the presence of the Notary on the date and at the location indicated in the venue. In the appropriate blanks, the Notary fills in his or her own name and the signer's name.

Next, "*personally known to me (or proved to me on the basis of satisfactory evidence) to be the person(s) whose name(s) is/are subscribed to the within instrument*" specifies that the signer was positively identified by the Notary — either by the Notary's personal knowledge of the signer or by "satisfactory evidence" (one or more credible witnesses or an acceptable identification document).

And "*acknowledged that he/she/they freely executed it*" indicates the signer's acknowledgment that the signature is his or her own and that it was made voluntarily.

A few terms occur repeatedly in acknowledgment certificates: *instrument*, which means document; *within*, which means attached; *foregoing*, which means preceding; *subscribed*, which means signed; and *party* and *principal*, which mean a signer participating in a transaction.

Acknowledgment Certificate Wording

The actual wording in acknowledgment certificates can vary considerably for several reasons. First, there are differences in state law.

Second, there are different representative capacities a document signer may have — attorney in fact, corporate officer, trustee, etc. Third, there are special circumstances, such as when a signer has been identified by a credible identifying witness or when a person unable to write his or her name instead signs by making a mark or "X."

The signature by mark will be covered in Chapter 14, "Meeting the Needs of Disabled Signers." The others are discussed in the following sections.

If Uncertain, Refuse

If a Notary is uncertain about which notarial certificate to use, about what a certificate means, or about how to complete any particular certificate, the Notary should refuse to perform the notarization.

Certificate Wording Prescribed by State Law

Most states prescribe specific wording for common acknowledgment certificates, and Notaries must use only certificate wording that substantially complies with these formats. Some states prescribe no certificate formats at all and allow a wide range of wordings to be used. Notaries must be keenly aware of their state's requirements.

An out-of-state acknowledgment certificate may be used if it substantially complies with the form prescribed by law in the Notary's state. Notaries should read any preprinted certificate wording carefully before signing it to make sure it is acceptable for use in their state.

Some states prescribe specific wording for acknowledgment certificates; others may allow more latitude. Notaries must make sure that the certificates they sign and seal comply with state law.

If certificate wording on a document does not comply with the requirements of the Notary's state, the Notary must either write or type the approved standard wording on the document or attach a loose certificate containing the approved wording.

Sometimes Notaries are told that only the acknowledgment wording preprinted on the document is acceptable or that attached loose certificates are not to be used. Even so, if the wording does not comply with the Notary's state law, the Notary must replace it with certificate wording that does comply. As state-appointed officials, Notaries must always follow the laws of their own state.

Just about all states will recognize and accept for public recording documents that have been notarized in another state with that other state's prescribed acknowledgment certificate wording.

Short-Form Acknowledgment Certificates

A state may prescribe or allow what is called a short-form acknowledgment certificate as an alternate to a long-form or standard certificate.`Although the wording on the short-form version is minimal and may not indicate that the signer was even identified by the Notary, use of a short form does not "shorten" the Notary's obligation to guarantee personal appearance, identity and acknowledgment.

Following is an example of a short-form acknowledgment certificate:

State of _____)
) SS.
County of _____)

The foregoing instrument was acknowledged before me by
_____ (name[s] of signer[s]) on this _____ day of
_____ (month), _____ (year).

Witness my hand and official seal.

_____ (signature and seal of Notary)

Individual Acknowledgment Certificates

An individual acknowledgment is executed for a person who has signed a document on his or her own behalf.

Following is wording for an individual acknowledgment certificate:

State of _____)
) SS.
County of _____)

On this _____ day of _____ (month), _____ (year), before
me, _____ (name of Notary), the undersigned Notary
Public, personally appeared _____ (name[s] of
signer[s]), personally known to me (or proved to me on the
basis of satisfactory evidence) to be the person(s) whose
name(s) is/are subscribed to the within instrument and
acknowledged that he/she/they freely executed it.

Short form certificates have abbreviated wording, but Notaries still must verify personal appearance, identity and acknowledgment of the signer.

When not serving in a representative capacity, a person signs as an individual.

Witness my hand and official seal.

_____ (signature and seal of Notary)

Attorney-In-Fact Acknowledgment Certificate

An attorney in fact is an individual who has been authorized to sign for another person through a document called a power of attorney.

An attorney-in-fact acknowledgment certificate is used when one person has authorized another to sign legal documents on his or her behalf, and the signature of the attorney in fact must be acknowledged.

The person granting the authority to sign, known as the principal, first executes an authorizing document called a power of attorney. The individual given power to sign is called an attorney in fact — though this person is not necessarily an attorney or lawyer.

An attorney in fact signs the document for the principal — for example, "David R. White, principal, by Jennifer A. Peterson, attorney in fact." (See "Attorney in Fact" in Chapter 3, page 34.)

When notarizing for an attorney in fact, the conscientious Notary would ask to see the power of attorney document to verify that the signer does have the authority to act on behalf of the principal. Even when the certificate wording does not require the Notary to examine the power of attorney, the prudent Notary will do so.

Following is an example of an attorney in fact acknowledgment certificate, with key wording that specifies the representative capacity as attorney in fact highlighted in boldface:

State of _____)
) SS.
County of _____)

On this the _____ day of _____ (month), _____ (year), before me, _____ (name of Notary), the undersigned Notary Public, personally appeared _____ (name of attorney in fact), personally known to me (or proved to me on the basis of satisfactory evidence) **to be the person whose name is subscribed to the within instrument as the attorney in fact of _____ (name of principal), and he/she acknowledged to me that he/she subscribed the principal's name thereto and his/her own name as attorney in fact.**

Witness my hand and official seal.

_____ (signature and seal of Notary)

Corporate Acknowledgment Certificate

When a corporate officer or other representative signs on behalf of a corporation, a corporate acknowledgment certificate is used.

A corporation is an entity under law with the legal rights of a person. Like a person, a corporation legally commits itself when a corporate officer or other designated representative signs on behalf of the corporation. Such designated officers may include the president, vice president, treasurer, secretary, attorney in fact and agent, among others.

Only officers and specially designated agents may sign on behalf of a corporation.

As with an attorney in fact acknowledgment, the Notary may be required to determine that the person is, in fact, an officer or representative of the corporation and has the claimed authority to sign the document. The certificate wording will indicate if this is required. (Chapter 4 explained how to determine when it is necessary to verify the signer's representative capacity.)

A typical corporate acknowledgment certificate follows. In boldface is the wording that names the representative capacity of the signer as corporate officer:

State of _____)
) SS.
County of _____)

On this the _____ day of _____ (month), _____ (year), before me, _____ (name of Notary), a Notary in and for said state, personally appeared _____ (name of officer), personally known to me (or proved to me on the basis of satisfactory evidence) **to be the person who executed the within instrument as _____ (title of officer) on behalf of the corporation herein named, and acknowledged to me that the corporation executed it.**

Witness my hand and official seal.

_____ (signature and seal of Notary)

Partnership Acknowledgment Certificates

A partnership acknowledgment certificate is used when a partner signs on behalf of a partnership.

Under law, a partnership is an association of two or more persons (called partners) who agree to share profits and losses in a business venture. Like a corporation, a partnership may commit itself by signing a

▼

Documents involving partnerships normally require the signatures of all partners.

document. However, unlike a corporate document, which often bears the signature of only one corporate officer, a partnership document usually bears the signatures of all partners.

A typical partnership acknowledgment certificate follows. The wording that states that the signer's representative capacity is that of a partner acting on behalf of a partnership is in boldface:

State of _____)
) SS.
County of _____)

On this the _____ day of _____ (month), _____ (year), before me, _____ (name of Notary), the undersigned Notary Public, personally appeared _____ (name[s] of partner[s]), personally known to me (or proved to me on the basis of satisfactory evidence) **to be the person(s) who executed the within instrument on behalf of the partnership herein named and acknowledged to me that the partnership executed it.**

Witness my hand and official seal.

_____ (signature and seal of Notary)

Other Representative Acknowledgment Certificates

A trustee may sign documents on behalf of a trust; an executor on behalf of an estate; and a public officer on behalf of a public agency.

Besides corporations and partnerships, there are other legal entities that may sign documents through a designated representative. For example, a trustee may sign for a trust, an executor for an estate, or a public officer for a public agency.

The following acknowledgment certificate is typical of those used by signers who are trustees, executors or public officers. Again, the wording describing the signer's particular representative capacity is shown in boldface:

State of _____)
) SS.
County of _____)

On this the _____ day of _____ (month), _____ (year), before me, _____ (name of Notary), the undersigned Notary Public, personally appeared _____ (name of trustee, executor or public official), personally known to me (or proved to me on the basis of satisfactory evidence) **to be the person who executed the within instrument as trustee/ executor/public official on behalf of said trust/estate/public entity herein named, and acknowledged to me that the trust/estate/public entity executed it.**

Witness my hand and official seal.

_____ (signature and seal of Notary)

Combined Certificates

Occasionally, attorney in fact, corporate and partnership acknowledgment certificates are combined in special certificates to accommodate persons who are signing in more than one representative capacity at the same time.

For example, there are certificates for attorneys in fact signing either for corporations or partnerships, certificates for corporations signing as attorney in fact for other corporations, and certificates for partnerships signing as partners in other partnerships.

The certificate below is an example of wording that might be used for a corporation signing as a partner in a partnership. In this example, the wording that lists the signer's representative capacity as corporate officer and the corporation's capacity as partner is shown in boldface:

State of _____)
) SS.
County of _____)

On this the _____ day of _____ (month), _____ (year), before me, _____ (name of Notary), the undersigned Notary Public, personally appeared _____ (name of signer), personally known to me (or proved to me on the basis of satisfactory evidence) **to be the person who executed the within instrument as the _____ (title of officer) of _____ (name of corporation), the corporation that executed the within instrument on behalf of _____ (name of partnership), the partnership that executed the within instrument, and acknowledged to me that such corporation executed the same as such partners and that such partnership executed the same.**

Witness my hand and official seal.

_____ (signature and seal of Notary)

A person may represent more than one other person or entity when signing a document.

▼

113

Credible-Identifying-Witness Acknowledgment Certificates

As outlined in Chapter 4, when a signer is not personally known to the Notary and does not have adequate ID, a credible identifying witness may be used to establish the identity of a stranger. In such cases, a special notarial certificate — a credible-identifying-witness acknowledgment certificate — that names the credible identifying witness is sometimes used.

It is not always necessary to use a credible-identifying-witness acknowledgment form. In many states, it suffices merely to indicate on the acknowledgment certificate that the signer's identity was "proven on the basis of satisfactory evidence," or words to that effect. Satisfactory evidence includes credible identifying witnesses and identification documents.

A typical credible-identifying-witness acknowledgment certificate follows, with the credible identifying witness wording in boldface:

State of _____)
) SS.
County of _____)

On this _____ day of _____ (month), _____ (year), before me, _____ (name of Notary), the undersigned Notary Public, personally appeared _____ (name[s] of signer[s]), **proved to me on the basis of satisfactory evidence, in the form of the oath/affirmation of _____ (name of credible identifying witness) to be the person(s) whose name(s) is/are subscribed to the within instrument** and acknowledged that he/she/they freely executed it.

Witness my hand and official seal.

_____ (signature and seal of Notary)

All-Purpose Acknowledgment Certificates

A few states prescribe what is termed an all-purpose acknowledgment certificate. This certificate may not require the Notary to indicate the signer's title (partner, attorney in fact, etc.) or the entity or person represented by the signer.

The following example is the all-purpose acknowledgment certificate

With credible identifying witnesses, Notaries have the option of using a special certificate that names the witness.

An all-purpose acknowledgment certificate may not specify the signer's representative capacity.

prescribed by Hawaii statutes. Note how the capacity of the signer is not specified in the highlighted wording:

State of _____)
) SS.
County of _____)

On _____(insert date)_____ (year), before me personally appeared _____ (name of signer[s]), to me personally known, who, being by me duly sworn (or affirmed), did say that such person(s) executed the foregoing instrument as the free act and deed of such person(s), **and if applicable, in the capacity shown, having been duly authorized to execute such instrument in such capacity.**

_____ (signature and seal of Notary)

My commission expires _____ (expiration date)

(The above certificate is also an example of an acknowledgment where an oath or affirmation is required. With this particular certificate, the Notary certifies that the signer has sworn, rather than just acknowledged, that he or she signed the document in a duly authorized capacity. When using this certificate, any Notary must give the oath or affirmation without exception, even if the document is being notarized in a state where an oath or affirmation are not generally required.)

 ### California

California is unique in authorizing its Notaries to use one, and only one, acknowledgment certificate, an all-purpose form, on documents that will be filed in the state. Neither the signer's representative capacity nor the person or entity represented are noted on the certificate.

PERFORMING A TYPICAL ACKNOWLEDGMENT

Now, we will put together all the steps for performing an acknowledgment using an imaginary situation to illustrate the act. First, the situation will be outlined, and then the procedures will be detailed. You'll note that the steps are organized similarly to Chapters 4 through 7, with some additional steps included from other chapters.

▼

The Situation

Judith M. Hill and her husband David R. Hill appear before Notary Olivia P. Simms in Arlington County, Virginia, on July 17, 2008, to acknowledge their signatures on a Grant Deed signed the previous day.

Mr. and Mrs. Hill are from Pennsylvania and are not personally known to the Notary. Mr. Hill offers as proof of identity a Pennsylvania driver's license; Mrs. Hill has no picture ID. The Hills are accompanied by a friend and local resident, James K. Hawkins, who is personally known to the Notary, Ms. Simms.

The deed contains preprinted acknowledgment certificate wording.

Step 1: Personal Appearance

Mr. and Mrs. Hill appear in person before the Notary, Ms. Simms, to request a notarial act, so personal appearance has been established.

Step 2: Determining the Type of Notarial Act

The deed has preprinted acknowledgment wording, and this serves as instructions to the Notary that an acknowledgment is required.

Step 3: Identifying the Signers

Since the Notary does not know either of the Hills, satisfactory evidence of identity — an identification document or a credible identifying witness — will be required.

Mr. Hill's current Pennsylvania driver's license establishes his identity. The Notary, Ms. Simms, is familiar with the Pennsylvania driver's license format, and Mr. Hill's shows no signs of alteration or counterfeiting.

Mrs. Hill, however, has no acceptable ID. So, the Hills' friend, James Hawkins, will serve as a credible identifying witness to identify her. The Notary personally knows Mr. Hawkins who personally knows Mrs. Hill, establishing the necessary chain of personal knowledge. Mr. Hawkins does not have a financial interest in the transaction and agrees to vouch for Mrs. Hill's identity. The Notary tells Mr. Hawkins to raise his right hand and asks, "Do you solemnly swear that you know Judith M. Hill truly holds the identity she claims?" Mr. Hawkins answers, "Yes, I do."

Step 4: Acknowledgment

Next, the Notary asks each of the Hills, "Do you acknowledge that this is your signature and that you signed willingly?" Both respond, "Yes." This is where the Hills make or give their acknowledgment.

Step 5: Willingness and Awareness

The "yes" answer and the Hills' demeanor also establishes their willingness to sign the document.

Awareness is established because the Notary has engaged the Hills in conversation about the notarization: She asks the Hills questions about the document, their identity and their acknowledgment. Since they appear to the Notary to communicate coherently during the conversation, she may consider the Hills to be able to comprehend.

Step 6: The Journal Entry

Next, the Notary begins to make the journal entry. Since there are two signers, two journal line entries are required.

She records the date and time of notarization, "July 17, 2008, 3:30 p.m."; the type of notarial act, "acknowledgment"; the document date, "July 16, 2008"; the document type, "Grant Deed"; the names, addresses and telephone numbers of the signers, David and Judith Hill.

Then the Notary records how she identified each of the Hills. For Mr. Hill, the Notary checks the box beside "ID Cards" and records the issuing state, serial number and expiration date of Mr. Hill's driver's license. For Mrs. Hill, our Notary checks the box beside "Credible

	Month/Day/Year/Time of Notarization	Kind or Type of Notarization	Document Date (Month/Day/Year)	Document Kind or Type	Name and Address of Signer	
1	July 17, 2008 3:30 p.m.	Acknowledgment	July 16, 2008	Grant Deed	David R. Hill 4546 Sycamore Street Anytown, US 00000 (717) 555-2386	☐ Per ☒ ID ☐ Cred
2	"	"	"	"	Judith M. Hill 4546 Sycamore Street Anytown, US 00000 (717) 555-2386	☐ Per ☐ ID ☒ Cr
						☐ Per

Illustrated above is the left side of the journal entries for Mr. and Mrs. Hill's acknowledgment of their grant deed.

Identification of Signer	Additional Information	Notary Fee	Signature of Signer	Right Thumbprint of Signer	
☐ Personally Known by the Notary ☒ ID Cards — Describe each card below ☐ Credible Witness(es) — Include signature of each witness Penn. DL #90 909 021 exp. 8/31/2012		$5.00	x _David R Hill_	Top of thumb here	1
☐ Personally Known by the Notary ☐ ID Cards — Describe each card below ☒ Credible Witness(es) — Include signature of each witness _James K. Hawkins_ James K. Hawkins 325 Polk St., Arlington VA		$5.00	x _Judith M. Hill_	Top of thumb here	2
☐ Personally Known by the Notary					

The right-side continuation of the journal entries for the Hills' acknowledgment.

Witness(es)," writes Mr. Hawkins' name and address, and has Mr. Hawkins sign his name.

Our Notary then records the fee she charged, $5.00 for each signer.

And finally, the Hills each sign the journal and leave a thumbprint.

Step 7: Completing the Certificate

The last step in performing the acknowledgment is completing, signing and sealing the notarial certificate. The acknowledgment certificate printed on the deed appears as follows:

State of _____)
) SS.
County of _____)

On this _____ day of _____ (month), _____ (year), before me, _____ (name of Notary), the undersigned Notary Public, personally appeared _____ (name[s] of signer[s]), personally known to me (or proved to me on the basis of satisfactory evidence) to be the person(s) whose name(s) is/are subscribed to the within instrument and acknowledged that he/she/they freely executed it.

Witness my hand and official seal.

_____   L.S.
(signature and seal of Notary)

My commission expires _____

The Notary reads the certificate carefully to ensure that it is appropriate for her state and the particular notarization. It is, so she begins.

First, she fills in the venue — the state in which the notarization is performed (and that commissioned the Notary) and the county where the notarization takes place (not necessarily the county in which the Notary's oath of office is filed).

State of ___Virginia___)
) SS.
County of ___Arlington___)

Then, the Notary writes in the day, month and year in which the Hills appeared before her to give their acknowledgment. This must be the same time that the Notary recorded the notarization in her journal and completed the certificate.

On this __17th__ day of ___July___ (month), __2008__ (year)...

Our Notary, Ms. Simms, then writes her own name in the appropriate space. The name must be exactly as it appears on her official commissioning papers and in her signature and official seal, later to be affixed to the certificate.

...before me, __Olivia P. Simms__ (name of Notary), the undersigned Notary Public...

Next, the names of both signers are written in.

Since both appear before the Notary at the same time and place, one acknowledgment certificate may be used. However, if Mrs. Hill had appeared before Ms. Simms to acknowledge her signature at 1:15 p.m., then left at 1:20, and Mr. Hill appeared before Simms at 2:15, two separate acknowledgment certificates would be required.

Even when signers appear before the same Notary at the same time and place, the Notary still has the option of using separate certificates. This may be necessary if the blank does not provide enough space for the names of both signers. If there is too much blank space, the Notary should line through the unused space to deter later unauthorized insertion of other names.

▼

...personally appeared _David R. Hill and Judith M. Hill_
(name[s] of signer[s])...

Then the Notary indicates how she identified the Hills.

She crosses out "personally known to me (or," because the alternate language provided — "proved to me on the basis of satisfactory evidence" — applies to how she identified both the Hills — Mr. Hill through an identification document (his driver's license) and Mrs. Hill through a credible identifying witness (Mr. Hawkins).

Because there are two signers included on one certificate, the plural "s" is left after "person(s)" and "name(s)." The plural verb "are" also is indicated by crossing out the singular "is."

If one of the Hills were identified through personal knowledge and the other by an identification document, then two certificates would be necessary. One certificate would indicate "personally known to me" as the identification method, the other, "proved to me on the basis of satisfactory evidence." If the Notary's state required the use of a credible-witness certificate, two certificates again would be needed — one for Mr. Hill indicating personal knowledge as the identification method and one for Mrs. Hill with the wording, "proved to me on the oath of _____ ," to indicate that she was identified by a credible identifying witness (Mr. Hawkins' name would go in the blank.)

..~personally known to me (or proved to me on the basis of satisfactory evidence) to be the person(s) whose name(s) ~is~/are subscribed to the within instrument...

Also, the plural "they" is indicated by crossing out the singular terms "he" and "she."

...and acknowledged that ~he/she/~they freely executed it.

If only Mr. Hill were named, the "s" would be crossed out in person(s)" and "name(s)," and "he" would be left with "she" and "they" crossed out.

Finally, the Notary signs where indicated, makes an imprint of her seal and completes any additional wording. This particular certificate also asks the Notary to write her commission expiration date, a common requirement, since this information will not always be contained within the notarial seal. (Some states do not require their Notaries to use seals, though many Notaries still opt to use them.) As discussed previously, "L.S." indicates the location of the seal, though these letters are not always printed on certificates.

Witness my hand and official seal.

Olivia P. Simms

L.S.

OLIVIA P. SIMMS
Notary Public
Commonwealth of Virginia
My Commission Expires June 21, 2012

(signature and seal of Notary)

My commission expires *June 21, 2012*

SUMMARY

The acknowledgment is the most common type of notarial act. Many categories of documents, in particular documents relating to the transfer of real estate, often require an acknowledgment in order to be publicly recorded.

The primary function of an acknowledgment is to positively identify the signer. An acknowledgment certifies that the signer appeared before the Notary, was positively identified by the Notary, and acknowledged to the Notary having made the signature willingly on the document. In addition, many acknowledgments require the Notary to determine that the signer has authority to act in a particular representative capacity, such as attorney in fact or corporate officer.

Like all notarial acts, an acknowledgment requires a notarial certificate. The acknowledgment certificate wording can vary because of differences in state law and in the representative capacities of different signers. Most states prescribe specific wording for common acknowledgments, while others prescribe no wording at all and allow a wide variety of certificates.

The first step in performing an acknowledgment is to require the signer to personally appear before the Notary. The signer either requests an acknowledgment, or the Notary is directed by the certificate wording on the document to perform an acknowledgment. The Notary then

▼

identifies the signer. Next, the signer must acknowledge that the signature is his or her own and that it was made willingly. If the signer can communicate coherently as the Notary asks questions, then the signer may be considered competent.

The Notary then makes the journal entry, recording the date and time of notarization, the type of notarization, the document date, the kind of document, the signer's name and address, how the signer was identified, the fee charged, and any other pertinent information. The signer signs the journal and leaves a thumbprint (which is optional except in California for deeds, quitclaim deeds and deeds of trust).

Lastly, the Notary completes the certificate, indicating the venue, the date, his or her own name (if required), the signer's name and how the signer was identified. The Notary crosses out inappropriate terms to indicate the number and gender of signers. The Notary then completes the certificate by signing the exact name that appears on the commission and by making an imprint of the official Notary seal. ■

IMPORTANT TERMS

Acknowledge: To recognize as one's own. In the notarial act called an acknowledgment, the document signer recognizes before a Notary that a signature on a document is his or her own and indicates it was made voluntarily.

All-Purpose Acknowledgment Certificate: Acknowledgment certificate wording that is adaptable to any signer's representative capacity.

Annexed: Attached or accompanying.

Combined Acknowledgment Certificate: Acknowledgment certificate wording indicating a person signed as having two or more representative capacities.

Corporation: Legal entity with many of the rights of an individual that may own property and sign contracts through its officers and agents.

Foregoing: Preceding.

Long-Form Certificate: Standard or unabridged notarial certificate wording.

Partnership: Legal association of two or more persons — called partners — who agree to share profits and losses in a business venture.

Party: Signer participating in a transaction; principal.

Publicly Recorded: Placed in the public record or filed with a county recorder as authentic.

Representative Capacity: Status of signing or acting on behalf of another person or on behalf of a legal entity, such as a corporation, partnership or trust.

Short-Form Certificate: Notarial certificate with abridged or condensed wording.

Substantially Complies: In agreement, but not necessarily verbatim.

Trust: Arrangement under law in which one person — called the trustee — manages property for the benefit of another person or legal entity.

Within: Attached or accompanying.

CHAPTER 8 TEST

In each blank, write the response — a, b, c or d — that best completes each of the following statements:

1. An acknowledgment does not guarantee that the signer _____.

    a. Personally appeared before the Notary.

    b. Signed the document before the Notary.

    c. Was identified by the Notary.

    d. Admitted to the Notary having freely signed the document.

2. The acknowledgment is the most common notarial act because _____.

    a. It is an all-purpose notarization.

    b. It provides strong evidence that a document's signature is genuine.

    c. It requires signers to take an oath or affirmation.

    d. It is the easiest to perform of all notarial acts.

3. Acknowledge means a person recognizes before a Notary that _____.

    a. A document's signature is his or her own and made willingly.

    b. A signature of another is, in fact, the signature of that person.

    c. A signature is that of his or her employer, partner or spouse.

    d. A signature on the document is made on penalty of perjury.

4. The date of acknowledgment on the Notary certificate _____.

    a. Always coincides with the document's date of signing.

    b. May coincide with or follow the document's date of signing.

    c. May precede or coincide with the document's date of signing.

    d. May precede or follow the document's date of signing.

5. With a short-form acknowledgment certificate _____.

    a. The Notary is not required to identify the signer.

    b. The signer is not required to appear before the Notary.

    c. The notarial certificate is filled in by the signer.

    d. The Notary has the same duties as with a longer certificate.

6. A corporate acknowledgment certificate is required when _____.

    a. A person signs for a corporation as an officer or agent.

    b. A person signs a document that will be sent to a corporation.

    c. Articles of incorporation are signed and notarized.

    d. A person signs a document while in a corporate environment.

7. Documents signed by a person in a representative capacity require an acknowledgment certificate that _____.

    a. Adapts to any person or entity represented.

    b. Always specifies that the signer is under oath.

    c. Specifies who or what the signer is representing.

    d. Describes documentary proof of the signer's status.

8. The wording in acknowledgment certificates must substantially comply with the prescribed statutory wording of _____.

    a. The state where the document is created.

    b. The state where the document is recorded.

    c. The state where the document is signed.

    d. The state where the document is notarized.

Explain in your own words:

9. When may a Notary use a notarial certificate from out of state?

    _____

    _____

    _____

10. What are the three facts an acknowledgment certifies?

    _____

    _____

    _____

Complete the journal entry and notarial certificate for the following notarization.

11. Today, at this hour, a woman named Michelle C. Wong appears before you to acknowledge her signature on a power of attorney. The document was signed and dated yesterday and names Ms. Wong's daughter, Marjorie A. Jackson as attorney in fact. You and Ms. Wong are longtime neighbors and friends. Ms. Wong lives at 4525 State Street in your city and zip code. You charge $2.00 for the notarization. Complete the following journal entry:

Month/Day/Year/Time of Notarization	Kind or Type of Notarization	Document Date (Month/Day/Year)	Document Kind or Type	Name and Address of Signer	
1					☐ Pers ☐ ID ☐ Cr
					☐ Per

Identification of Signer	Additional Information	Notary Fee	Signature of Signer	Right Thumbprint of Signer	
☐ Personally Known by the Notary ☐ ID Cards — Describe each card below ☐ Credible Witness(es) — Include signature of each witness			x _____	Top of thumb here	1
☐ Personally Known by the Notary					

12. Complete the following certificate for the same notarization:

State of _____)

) SS.

County of _____)

On this _____ day of _____, _____, before me,

_____, the undersigned Notary, personally

appeared _____, personally known to me (or

proved to me on the basis of satisfactory evidence) to be the

person(s) whose name(s) is/are subscribed to the within instrument

and acknowledged that he/she/they freely executed it.

Witness my hand and official seal.

_____ L.S.

(Signature and Quality of Officer)

See pages 383–384 for correct responses.

CHAPTER 9

Oaths, Affirmations and Jurats

Oaths, affirmations and jurats are notarial acts that have the same effect: inducing a person to be truthful. Jurat certificates are used for written statements, where oaths and affirmations are spoken.

For Notaries, the jurat is seen more frequently than oaths or affirmations on their own. Oaths and affirmations usually are administered by Notaries in conjunction with jurats or other notarial acts.

Because understanding oaths and affirmations is crucial to understanding jurats, this chapter will begin there and then go on to discuss the more common jurat.

OATHS AND AFFIRMATIONS

Simply put, oaths and affirmations are spoken promises of truthfulness or loyalty, and both achieve the same legal result. An oath is a solemn, spoken pledge to a Supreme Being. An affirmation is a solemn, spoken pledge on one's own personal honor, with no reference to a Supreme Being. A person who objects to taking an oath may instead be given an affirmation.

Historically, an oath was a spoken promise of truthfulness that asked divine punishment for falsehood. It often involved a religious object in a solemn ceremony. In the past, Christians showed the seriousness of their oaths by kissing the Bible. Today, oaths and affirmations are less elaborate pledges but still have important legal purposes. A person who takes an oath or affirmation in connection with certain official proceedings may be prosecuted for perjury should he or she fail to be truthful.

Oaths and affirmations may be administered as part of a notarial act (such as with a jurat, explained later in this chapter). They may be administered in conjunction with performing a notarization (such as when swearing in a credible identifying witness); or they may stand on their own as a notarial act. An oath of office, for example, is a full-fledged notarial act in its own right when administered by a Notary, even when there is no document or certificate. Most often, Notaries will administer oaths or affirmations as part of the execution of a jurat or when swearing in a credible identifying witness.

Terminology

It is important to use the proper terminology relating to oaths and affirmations. A Notary administers or gives an oath or affirmation to a person who takes the oath or affirmation. Or the person may swear or affirm, respectively, to an oath or affirmation. In this context, swear means to promise under oath; affirm means to promise under affirmation.

The person who takes an oath is called the oath-taker, and the person taking an affirmation is called either the affirmation-taker or affirmant.

A Notary can be said to swear in an oath- or affirmation-taker, and an oral or written declaration taken under oath or affirmation can be described as sworn or sworn to.

TWO REQUIREMENTS

The main function of oaths and affirmations is to compel an individual to be truthful. This is done by appealing to the oath-taker's or affirmant's conscience and fear of criminal penalties for perjury, or untruthfulness. When an oath or affirmation is taken, a legal process is begun that could result in criminal punishment if the oath-taker or affirmant is later found to have lied.

When administering an oath or affirmation, the Notary must require two actions:

With oaths and affirmations, the Notary certifies that a person appeared and took a pledge.

1. Personal Appearance. The individual must personally appear before the Notary.

2. Oath or Affirmation Taken. The individual must speak aloud before the Notary a solemn promise of truthfulness.

NNA Recommendation

Cautious Notaries will take the additional step to positively identify each oath- or affirmation-taker just as they would with the signer in an acknowledgment. While this might not be a legal requirement, the National Notary Association recommends that Notaries make an effort to identify all persons for whom they perform notarial acts.

Personal Appearance

To take an oath or affirmation, one must appear in person before the oath-giving officer, the Notary Public. This personal appearance must be at the time the oath or affirmation is spoken aloud. The oath-taker or affirmant must be face to face in the same room with the Notary. Oaths and affirmations cannot be given over the phone, from another room, through the mail or through a third person.

Oath or Affirmation

The oath-taker or affirmant must formally state out loud his or her promise of truthfulness. It is not acceptable for the oath or affirmation to be silently taken or administered unless a written statement is signed in lieu of making an oral declaration.

Identifying the Oath-Taker or Affirmant

Even though the Notary is not generally required to positively identify

While not always required, it is wise to identify the taker of an oath or affirmation.

the oath-taker or affirmant, the prudent Notary will take this additional step. Doing so indicates a high standard of reasonable care and helps ensure that an impostor is not taking an oath or affirmation for another.

Oath-takers and affirmants can be identified through either the Notary's personal knowledge, a credible identifying witness, or a state-approved identification document. Chapter 4 outlined how to establish positive identification.

 ### No Representative Oaths or Affirmations

A person may not take an oath or affirmation in a representative capacity for another person or entity such as a corporation. An oath or affirmation is a personal commitment of conscience that individuals can only make for themselves. So, while attorneys in fact, trustees, corporate officers and other representatives may take an oath or affirmation to confirm their representative status, they may not take an oath or affirmation for another individual.

ADMINISTERING OATHS AND AFFIRMATIONS

To administer an oath or affirmation, the Notary usually first makes an oral statement, and the oath-taker or affirmant then indicates his or her agreement by repeating the statement or by saying the words "I do" or "I will." (A person incapable of speaking could indicate compliance in other ways, including a nod or a written note.)

There are occasions when the oath or affirmation might appropriately be said aloud in its entirety by the oath-taker or affirmant. This might be the case with an oath of office. In these situations, the Notary may read the oath or affirmation one phrase at a time, with the oath-taker or affirmant repeating each phrase, or the oath-taker or affirmant may read the oath or affirmation.

Oaths and affirmations must be spoken or agreed to formally. Compliance with an oath or affirmation may not be silently implied.

Wording for Oaths and Affirmations

State laws, regulations or customs do not always prescribe exact wording for a particular oath or affirmation. And the oath- or affirmation-taker may or may not furnish the Notary with the necessary wording. If there is no wording provided in a given instance, the following examples may be acceptable:

Document signer (jurat) oath or affirmation:

OATH: Do you solemnly swear that the statements in this document are true, so help you God?

AFFIRMATION: Do you solemnly affirm that the statements in this document are true?

Credible identifying witness oath or affirmation:

OATH: Do you solemnly swear that you know the signer truly holds the identity he (or she) claims, so help you God?

AFFIRMATION: Do you solemnly affirm that you know the signer truly holds the identity he (or she) claims?

Witness statement or testimony oath or affirmation:

OATH: Do you solemnly swear that the information you are about to give (or have given) is the truth, the whole truth and nothing but the truth, so help you God?

AFFIRMATION: Do you solemnly affirm that the information you are about to give (or have given) is the truth, the whole truth and nothing but the truth?

Oath of office or affirmation for taking office:

OATH: I do solemnly swear that I will support the Constitution of the United States, the Constitution of the State of _____, and that I will faithfully discharge the duties of the office of _____ during the term for which I have been elected (or appointed), so help me God.

AFFIRMATION: I do solemnly affirm that I will support the Constitution of the United States, the Constitution of the State of _____, and that I will faithfully discharge the duties of the office of _____ during the term for which I have been elected (or appointed).

Note that the three preceding oaths refer to a Supreme Being, both

▼

directly with the phrase "...so help you God?" and indirectly by use of the term "swear." The affirmations do not refer to a Supreme Being, since there is no mention of the term, "God."

Ceremony and Gestures

> Notaries are urged to convey the seriousness of the oath or affirmation by incorporating some ceremony and formality into the procedure.

To impress upon the oath-taker or affirmant the importance of truthfulness, the Notary is encouraged to lend a sense of ceremony and formality to the oath or affirmation. During the administration of an oath or affirmation, the Notary and oath-taker or affirmant traditionally raise their right hands, palms forward, though this is not a legal requirement in most states. Notaries generally have discretion to use the ceremony and gestures they feel will most compellingly appeal to the conscience of the oath-taker or affirmant.

In administering oaths, the Notary may ask the oath-taker to place one hand on the Bible or other appropriate religious text with the other hand raised in a pledging gesture.

Although the religious element is not included, an affirmation may still involve some ceremony. Raising one's right hand or placing it over the heart are traditional gestures adaptable to either the oath or affirmation.

To further underline the seriousness of taking an oath or affirmation, the Notary also may wish to tell the oath-taker or affirmant that perjury is a serious criminal offense.

	Month/Day/Year/Time of Notarization	Kind or Type of Notarization	Document Date (Month/Day/Year)	Document Kind or Type	Name and Address of Signer	
1	August 9, 2008 1:30 p.m.	Oath of Office for Town Council Representative	n/a	n/a	Donna E. Williams 768 Orange Street Anytown, US 00000 (908) 555-7184	☐ Pers ☒ ID/ ☐ C ☐ Pe

Identification of Signer	Additional Information	Notary Fee	Signature of Signer	Right Thumbprint of Signer	
☐ Personally Known by the Notary ☒ ID Cards — Describe each card below ☐ Credible Witness(es) — Include signature of each witness NJ DL #55524 39770 02126 exp. 10/16/2011 ☐ Personally Known by the Notary	Oath provided by Ms. Williams	$2.50	x *Donna E. Williams*		1

Above is a typical journal entry for an oath of office.

Certificate

When the oath or affirmation is not associated with another notarial act (such as with a jurat or swearing in a credible identifying witness), there is generally no document or notarial certificate involved. Oaths or affirmations as notarial acts in their own right do not require notarial certificates because they are simply oral statements.

Journal Entry

There should always be an entry in the Notary's journal to record an oath or affirmation given as a notarial act by itself. The entry should include the date and time the oath or affirmation was administered, the type of oath or affirmation (e.g., "mayor's oath of office"), the name and address of the oath-taker or affirmant, how the individual was identified, the fee charged and the signature of the oath-taker or affirmant. The illustration on page 134 shows a typical journal entry for an oath of office.

Who May Give Oaths and Affirmations?

Besides Notaries, certain other officials — including some federal, state, county and city employees, electees and appointees — also may administer oaths and affirmations due to powers of their offices.

JURATS

Closely associated with oaths and affirmations is the jurat. Jurat is Latin for "he/she swears" and certifies that a written statement has been sworn to or affirmed. In simplistic terms, a jurat is used when a promise of truth or loyalty appears as a written statement.

Like the acknowledgment, the jurat is a very common notarial act. (Acknowledgments and jurats are the two most common.) But a jurat has a very different purpose than an acknowledgment. As the previous chapter outlined, an acknowledgment serves to certify the signer's identity and willingness to sign a particular document. A jurat, on the other hand, certifies that the signer has sworn or affirmed to the truthfulness of the statements in the signed document.

A jurat certifies that a written statement has been sworn to or affirmed.

Notaries usually execute jurats on documents such as affidavits and depositions that may be submitted as evidence in trials and other official proceedings, as well as on other forms of written verification requiring an oath or affirmation. (A deposition is a signed transcript of an individual's oral statements taken down for use in a judicial proceeding. An affidavit is a signed statement made under oath or affirmation and is used for a variety of purposes both in and out of court. Verification is a declaration that a statement or pleading is true.)

CERTIFIES THREE FACTS

As with oaths and affirmations, a jurat's primary function is to compel the document signer to be truthful by appealing to the signer's conscience, as well as the individual's fear of criminal penalties for perjury. Like oaths and affirmations, the jurat initiates a legal process that could eventually result in criminal arrest, conviction and punishment if the signer is later found to have lied.

In executing a jurat, the Notary certifies three things:

1. Personal Appearance. The document signer appeared in person before the Notary.

> To execute a jurat, the Notary must require the signer to appear, sign the document in the Notary's presence and take an oath or affirmation.

2. Witnessing of Signature. The Notary watched the document signer sign his or her name on the document.

3. Administration of Oath or Affirmation. The signer took an oath or affirmation from the Notary, in which the signer declared the statements in the document to be truthful and accurate.

State Laws Vary

Some states also require Notaries to positively identify each signer when executing a jurat, just as they would with an acknowledgment. While this is not a requirement in all states, the National Notary Association strongly recommends that Notaries identify all document signers for jurats as well as acknowledgments.

Personal Appearance

With jurats, the document signer must appear in person before the Notary Public on the date and at the location stated in the notarial certificate, as with all notarizations.

To achieve personal appearance, the signer must be face to face in the same room with the Notary. A telephone call, a voice from another room, recognizing a familiar signature, a written note from an absent signer, or the word of a third person about an absent signer's intent will not suffice.

Witnessing the Signature

In executing a jurat, the Notary witnesses the signing of the document. This means the Notary must actually see the signer write his or her signature on the document. If it has already been signed, the signer must sign again in front of the Notary.

For a jurat, the document must be signed in front of the Notary.

This requirement represents a significant difference from the acknowledgment, which allows the document to be previously signed out of the presence of the Notary. It also reinforces the requirement for personal appearance, because witnessing the signature would be impossible without the signer appearing before the Notary.

Oath or Affirmation

To accomplish the primary purpose of a jurat, compelling truthfulness, the Notary must administer an oath or affirmation to the document signer.

Identifying the Signer

In some states, the Notary must take the additional step of identifying the document signer when executing a jurat. As with acknowledgments, signers for jurats can be identified through either the Notary's personal knowledge of the signer, a credible identifying witness who personally knows the signer, or a state-approved identification document.

Though not always required, identifying the signer when executing a jurat is a prudent step for the Notary.

Most states do not have an identification requirement for jurats. In these states, cautious Notaries still will take the extra step of identifying each signer when performing jurats because it helps assure the signer is not an impostor.

Chapter 4 outlined how to establish positive identification of a document signer.

No Representative Jurats

Because one person may not take an oath or affirmation for another person or entity, it is not possible to execute certain jurats for signers who are acting in a representative capacity. An oath or affirmation is a personal commitment of conscience that individuals only can make for themselves. While attorneys in fact, trustees, corporate officers and other representatives may swear to or affirm facts and sign documents requiring jurats in their own individual names, they may not sign affidavits, depositions and other sworn documents in the name of another.

THE JURAT CERTIFICATE

Jurat certificate wording is generally simpler than acknowledgment certificate wording.

In executing a jurat, the Notary must complete a notarial certificate that is either contained within or attached to the signed document. The jurat wording is far simpler than the wording for an acknowledgment discussed in the previous chapter.

The jurat certificate describes the three facts the notarial act certifies: 1) the signer's personal appearance before the Notary, 2) the signature being witnessed by the Notary and 3) the signer's taking of an oath or affirmation. Following is a example of typical jurat wording:

State of _____)
) SS.
County of _____)

Subscribed and sworn to (or affirmed) before me this _____ day of _____ (month), _____ (year), by _____ (name of signer).

_____ (signature and seal of Notary)

The words "before me" indicate that the document signer appeared before the Notary. "Subscribed" denotes that the document was signed before the Notary. And "sworn to (affirmed)" specifies that the signer took an oath or affirmation administered by the Notary.

> **⚠ Important**
>
> The term jurat is frequently misused. Many persons mistakenly refer to all notarial certificates — even to acknowledgment certificates — as jurats. When a signer asks that a Notary "attach a jurat" to a document, the Notary should question the person to determine what is really meant.

The actual wording of jurat certificates can vary considerably from one document to the next and from one state to another. For affidavits, the jurat certificate often will be divided into two parts, with the venue appearing at the beginning of the document, the jurat wording (the statement of particulars plus the signature and seal of the Notary) at the end, and the document's text and affiant's signature in between. (The signer of an affidavit is called the affiant.)

The following example of an affidavit shows how the jurat certificate sandwiches the affiant's statement.

State of _____)
) SS.
County of _____)

_____ (name of signer), having been duly sworn (affirmed) before me, makes this his/her affidavit and states that, to the best of his/her knowledge and belief...

(affiant's statement continues).

_____ (signature of affiant)

Subscribed and sworn to (or affirmed) before me by _____ (name of signer) this _____ day of _____ (month), _____ (year).

_____ (signature and seal of Notary)

As in the above example, the affiant's statement is often preceded by an introductory statement by the Notary. The Notary completes this introductory statement by filling in the name of the document signer and by selecting the correct pronouns ("he" or "she") and terms ("sworn" or "affirmed").

PERFORMING A TYPICAL JURAT

Using an imaginary situation as an example, we will now put all the steps together for executing a jurat.

The Situation

Katherine P. Dutton appears before Notary Dorothy L. Maguire in Suffolk County, New York, on September 15, 2008, at 11 a.m. to swear to and have her signature notarized on an affidavit of loss that will be submitted to her insurance company.

Ms. Dutton, a longtime close friend of Ms. Maguire, signed the affidavit the previous day.

The affidavit contains preprinted jurat wording.

Step 1: Personal Appearance

Ms. Dutton appears in person before the Notary, Ms. Maguire, to request the notarial act, so personal appearance has been established.

Step 2: Determining the Type of Notarial Act

The preprinted jurat wording on the affidavit indicates to the Notary that a jurat is the notarial act required.

Step 3: Identifying the Signer

Although identification is not expressly required by law for a jurat in New York, Ms. Maguire is a careful Notary and chooses to identify all document signers.

Since Ms. Dutton is personally known to the Notary, the process of identification is simplified.

If the Notary did not personally know Ms. Dutton, identification documents or credible identifying witnesses could serve the purpose of identifying her.

Step 4: Witnessing of Signature

Next, the Notary asks Ms. Dutton to re-sign the document. Even though the document is already signed and the Notary easily recognizes the signature as that of her close friend, it must be signed again in her presence so the making of the signature can be officially witnessed, as required for a jurat.

Step 5: Oath or Affirmation

The next step is for the Notary to administer an oath or affirmation to Ms. Dutton. Ms. Dutton prefers to take an oath.

The Notary first informs Ms. Dutton that perjury is a serious criminal offense. Then, the Notary asks Ms. Dutton to raise her right hand in a pledging manner and asks her, "Do you solemnly swear that the statements in this document are true, so help you God?" Ms. Dutton replies, "I do."

Step 6: Willingness and Awareness

Since the document was signed in the presence of the Notary and Ms. Dutton took an oath, both without any apparent hesitation, willingness to sign has been reasonably established.

Throughout the notarization, the Notary has engaged Ms. Dutton in conversation, and since Ms. Dutton appears to communicate effectively, the Notary considers her to be aware of the document's significance.

Step 7: The Journal Entry

Next, the Notary makes the journal entry. She records the date and time of notarization, "September 15, 2008, 11:00 a.m."; the type of notarial act, "jurat"; the document date, "September 15, 2008"; the document type, "Affidavit of Loss"; and the name and address of the signer, Ms. Dutton. Then she records how she identified Ms. Dutton by checking "personal knowledge" in the identification section. The Notary then records the fee she charges, $2.00 for the notarization of one signature. Finally, Ms. Dutton signs the journal and leaves her thumbprint.

Month/Day/Year/Time of Notarization	Kind or Type of Notarization	Document Date (Month/Day/Year)	Document Kind or Type	Name and Address of Signer	
1	sept. 15, 2008 11:00 am.	Jurat	sept. 15, 2008	Affidavit of Loss	Katherine P. Dutton 191 Empire Avenue Anytown, US 00000 (516) 555-6975	

Identification of Signer	Additional Information	Notary Fee	Signature of Signer	Right Thumbprint of Signer	
☒ Personally Known by the Notary ☐ ID Cards — Describe each card below ☐ Credible Witness(es) — Include signature of each witness ☐ Personally Known by the Notary	Document was re-signed in my presence.	$2.00	✗ Katherine P. Dutton		1

Above is the journal entry for the jurat performed on Ms. Dutton's affidavit.

Step 8: Completing the Certificate

The last step in performing the jurat is completing, signing and sealing the notarial certificate. The jurat certificate printed on the affidavit appears as follows:

State of _____)
) SS.
County of _____)

_____ (name of signer), having been duly sworn (affirmed) before me, makes this his/her affidavit and states that, to the best of his/her knowledge and belief…

(affiant's statement continues).

_____ (signature of affiant).

Subscribed and sworn to (or affirmed) before me this _____ day of _____ (month), _____ (year), by _____ (name of signer).

_____
(signature and seal of Notary)

First, the Notary fills in the venue — the state and the county where the notarization takes place.

State of __New York__)
) SS.
County of __Suffolk__)

Then, the Notary completes the introductory statement by writing in the signer's name and by crossing out the inapplicable pronouns and terms.

> _Katherine P. Dutton_ (name of signer), having been duly sworn ~~(affirmed)~~ before me, makes this ~~his~~/her affidavit and states that, to the best of ~~his~~/her knowledge and belief...

Next, the Notary moves to the jurat at the end of the document and selects between "sworn" (for an oath) and "affirmed" (for an affirmation) by crossing out the inapplicable term.

> Subscribed and sworn to ~~(or affirmed)~~ before me...

The Notary then completes the day, month and year in which Ms. Dutton appeared before her to sign the document and take her oath, then writes in Ms. Dutton's name.

> ...this _15th_ day of _September_ (month), _2008_ (year), by _Katherine P. Dutton_ (name of signer).

And lastly, the Notary signs where indicated and makes an imprint of her official seal.

> _Dorothy L. McGuire_
> (signature and seal of Notary)
>
> **DOROTHY L. MCGUIRE**
> **Notary Public - State of New York**
> **No. 12-3456789**
> **Qualified in Nassau County**
> **My Commission Expires Oct 1, 2012**

Note how the venue is separated from the jurat by the affiant's statement and signature. This is typical with affidavits. Also typical is the absence of wording indicating that the affiant was identified by the Notary. However, a prudent Notary always will identify any signer.

SUMMARY

Oaths, affirmations and jurats are notarial acts that are used to compel truthfulness.

Oaths and affirmations are spoken promises of truth or loyalty. An oath is a pledge to a Supreme Being; an affirmation is a pledge on one's own personal honor. Both have the same legal effect and begin a process that could result in criminal penalties for failing to abide by the spoken promise.

Jurat certificates are used when an individual attests to the truth or accuracy of a written statement. In executing a jurat, the Notary must witness the individual sign the document, administer an oath or affirmation to the signer and complete a special notarial certificate. Notaries usually execute jurats on documents such as affidavits and depositions.

Notaries most often will administer oaths or affirmations as part of the execution of jurats or the swearing in of credible identifying witnesses. But oaths and affirmations can be complete notarial acts on their own, as with an oath of office.

In administering an oath or affirmation, the Notary must require the oath-taker or affirmant to personally appear and to speak aloud the appropriate words, which may be as brief as "I do" or "I will." The Notary and oath-taker or affirmant traditionally raise their right hands.

A jurat certifies that the signer appeared before the Notary, signed the document in front of the Notary and took an oath or affirmation administered by the Notary.

Even though identification of oath-takers, affirmants and jurat signers is not required in most states, prudent Notaries take this additional step. A Notary may not administer an oath or affirmation or execute a jurat for a person acting in a representative capacity, only for a person acting on his or her own behalf.

There always should be an entry in the Notary's journal to record the administration of an oath or affirmation or the execution of a jurat.

In executing a jurat, the Notary must complete a notarial certificate that typically is worded, "Subscribed and sworn to (or affirmed) before me on ...(date)... by ...(name of signer)." Often, the jurat certificate will be divided into two parts, with the venue at the beginning of the document, the jurat wording with the signature and seal of the Notary at the end, and the document's text in the middle. ■

IMPORTANT TERMS

Administer: To give formally, as in "giving" an oath or affirmation.

Affiant: Signer of an affidavit.

Affidavit: Written statement signed before a Notary or other authorized official by a person who swears or affirms to the Notary that the statement is true.

Affirm: To make an affirmation; to make a solemn promise on one's own personal honor with no reference to a Supreme Being.

Affirmant, Affirmation-Taker: One who makes an affirmation.

Deponent: Person who, under oath or affirmation, gives oral testimony that is transcribed for use in a legal proceeding.

Deposition: Written statement that is transcribed from words spoken by a person (deponent) under oath or affirmation that is usually signed by this person and used in a lawsuit.

Oath of Office: Oath promising to faithfully discharge the duties of a particular office.

Oath-Taker: One who takes an oath.

Perjury: Crime of making a false statement under oath or affirmation in an official proceeding.

Personal Honor: Individual conscience.

Subscribed: Signed.

Supreme Being: God or other entity considered to be the principal object of faith and worship.

Swear: To make an oath; to state under oath. To make a solemn promise to a Supreme Being.

Verification: Declaration that a statement or pleading is true.

Witness: One who has personally seen something; to observe.

CHAPTER 9 TEST

In each blank, write the response — a, b, c or d — that best completes each of the following statements:

1. The primary function of jurats, oaths and affirmations is to _____.

    a. Compel an individual to tell the truth.

    b. Compel an individual to identify a signer.

    c. Compel an individual to sign a document.

    d. Compel the Notary to be truthful.

2. An oath differs from an affirmation in that _____.

    a. An oath is a spoken vow; an affirmation is unspoken.

    b. An oath refers to God; an affirmation does not.

    c. Oath-takers are subject to perjury penalties; affirmants are not.

    d. An oath requires ceremony; an affirmation does not.

3. A jurat may not always guarantee that the document signer _____.

    a. Personally appeared before the Notary.

    b. Signed before the Notary.

    c. Was given an oath or affirmation by the Notary.

    d. Was positively identified by the Notary.

4. Jurat refers to _____.

    a. The phrase, "State of _____, County of _____."

    b. The phrase, "Witness my hand and official seal."

    c. The phrase, "Subscribed and sworn to before me...."

    d. All notarial certificates.

5. If an affidavit has not been signed in the Notary's presence, _____.

    a. It must be discarded, redrawn and signed again.

    b. It must be signed in the Notary's presence.

    c. It is acceptable, since signing before a Notary is not required.

    d. The signature must be acknowledged.

6. The parts of an affidavit most often occur in this sequence: _____.

    a. Venue — affiant statement — jurat — Notary signature and seal.

    b. Jurat — affiant statement — venue — Notary signature and seal.

    c. Notary signature and seal — affiant statement — venue — jurat.

    d. Affiant statement — venue — Notary signature and seal — jurat.

▼

7. In executing a jurat, the oath the Notary administers might be _____.

 a. "Do you swear that the statements in the document are true?"

 b. "Do you affirm that the statements in the document are true?"

 c. "Do you acknowledge before me that the statements in the document are true?"

 d. "Do you confirm before me that the statements in the document are true?"

8. Both a jurat and an acknowledgment require _____.

 a. Administration of an oath or affirmation.

 b. Face-to-face communication between signer and Notary.

 c. Signing the document in the Notary's presence.

 d. Presence of a credible identifying witness.

9. A Notary is responsible for the truth of _____.

 a. The affiant's written declaration in an affidavit.

 b. Written questions for a deposition.

 c. The written venue in an affidavit.

 d. All statements transcribed in a deposition.

Explain in your own words:

10. Why is there no such certificate as an attorney in fact jurat?

 _____

 _____

 _____

Complete the journal entry and notarial certificate for the following notarization.

11. Today, at this hour, William R. Cochrane appears before you to take an oath and have his signature notarized on an Affidavit of Residency. The affidavit contains preprinted jurat wording. Mr. Cochrane lives at 122 2nd Street in your city and zip code. He offers his driver's license as identification, number N39705503, for your state, expiring May 3, 2009. You charge $2.00 for the notarization. Complete the following journal entry:

Month/Day/Year/Time of Notarization	Kind or Type of Notarization	Document Date (Month/Day/Year)	Document Kind or Type	Name and Address of Signer	
1					☐ Pers ☐ ID ☐ C
					☐ Per

Identification of Signer	Additional Information	Notary Fee	Signature of Signer	Right Thumbprint of Signer	
☐ Personally Known by the Notary ☐ ID Cards — Describe each card below ☐ Credible Witness(es) — Include signature of each witness			x _____	Top of thumb here	1
☐ Personally Known by the Notary					

12. Complete the following certificate and affidavit introduction for the same notarization:

State of _____)

) SS.

County of _____)

_____ (name of affiant), having been duly sworn (affirmed) before me, makes this his/her affidavit and states that, to the best of his/her knowledge and belief...(affiant's statement continues)....

_____ (signature of affiant)

Subscribed and sworn to (or affirmed) before me by _____ this _____ day of _____, _____.

_____ L.S.

(Signature and Quality of Officer)

See pages 384–385 for correct responses.

CHAPTER 10

Copy Certification

Though not nearly as common as acknowledgments or jurats, copy certification is the third major type of notarization. Copy certification verifies that a reproduction or photocopy of an original document is true, complete and correct.

THE CERTIFIED COPY

A certified copy is a document that has been officially certified to be an accurate reproduction of another document, the original. An original is any document of which a reproduction has been made.

Actually, verification of a copy may be performed by any person or agency responsible for holding and preserving any original document. However, only Notaries and certain other public officials, including county recorders, are authorized to issue certified copies without retaining permanent custody of the original document. Anyone may verify the accuracy of a copy, but only a Notary or other officer may certify a copy.

Making a certified copy lets the document owner or custodian provide proof of its existence and contents without losing custody of it. The original may be kept safe while the copy is sent elsewhere.

A common request is to certify a copy of a college diploma, since only one such document exists and most people do not want to risk parting with the original when proof of their graduate status is required by a prospective employer or school.

 State Laws Vary

Copy certification is not an authorized notarial act in all states. A few states either prohibit Notaries from certifying copies or set certain restrictions. For instance, New York Notaries may not certify copies of any document, while California Notaries only may certify copies of powers of attorney and, when requested by the California Secretary of State, entries in their own notarial journals. Many state laws make no reference to copy certification. Before a Notary attempts to certify a copy, he or she should check to be certain copy certification is allowed and, if so, what limitations exist. In states where a Notary-certified copy is prohibited, a custodian-certified copy (see page 157) is an alternative that is often used.

FOUR REQUIREMENTS

Copy certification ensures that a copy is an accurate reproduction of the original document. To execute a certified copy, four requirements must be met:

1. Personal Appearance. It is strongly recommended that the individual requesting the certified copy appear before the Notary.

2. Original Presented. The original document must be provided to the Notary.

The original must be presented to the Notary. The Notary must determine that a copy of the particular document may be lawfully certified and then carefully compare the original and copy to determine that they are identical.

3. Certification Lawful. The Notary must verify that certifying a copy of the particular document is a legal act.

4. Accuracy Verified. The Notary must ensure that the copy is a true, exact and unaltered reproduction of the original.

Personal Appearance

The permanent custodian of the original document should appear in person to request a certified copy.

While it is possible that a certified copy request might come by mail or over the phone (such as when the Notary already has access to the original), Notaries should refrain from providing such certifications. Notarization always should involve a face-to-face interaction between two or more people.

In addition, the careful Notary will positively identify the document custodian when executing a copy certification. While most states do not require identification for copy certifications, it is a prudent practice for the Notary. Identification can be through the Notary's personal knowledge, a credible identifying witness, or an identification document. (Chapter 4 described how to establish positive identification.)

Original Presented to Notary

To certify a copy, the Notary must be provided with the original document at the time and place of the copy certification. Otherwise, it would be impossible for the Notary to compare the copy to the original to assure that they are identical.

Copy certification may not be based on the Notary's memory of a document previously seen. It may not be based on the word of another person, regardless of how reliable that person may be. Nor may it be based on the assumption the copy is accurate because the person or agency making the copy is reputable, official or authoritative.

May a Copy Be Certified Legally?

Some types of documents may not be certified by a Notary.

Notaries may not certify copies of certain vital or public records. A Notary's improper "certification" of such copies may lend credibility to what is actually a counterfeit or altered document.

In general, any one-and-only document in the rightful custody of a private individual may be copied and certified by a Notary whose state permits such certification, as long as it is not publicly recordable.

Ideally, a photocopy should not serve as the original for a certified copy. If it is unavoidable that a certified copy be made of a photocopy, the certified copy should be described on the Notary's certificate as "a photocopy of a photocopy...."

Documents of which Notaries may not certify copies include:

Vital Records. Copies of vital records may not be certified by a Notary. Vital records include birth or death certificates, marriage licenses and divorce decrees. Copies of these documents may only be certified by officials in the respective public record office.

Recordable Documents. Many states specifically prohibit Notaries from certifying copies of recordable documents. A recordable document is one that may be filed with an official agency. An example would be a property deed filed with the county recorder. A document does not have to be recorded but merely recordable for the Notary to be prohibited from making a certified copy. Certified copies of recordable documents, such as deeds, should be issued by a public recorder.

Immigration Documents. It may be a violation of federal law to copy certain documents issued by the U.S. Citizenship and Immigration Services. These documents include the Certificate of Naturalization, the Certificate of Citizenship and the Declaration of Intention to Become a Citizen. Imprisonment and fines may be imposed for unlawful copying of these USCIS documents. (See "Immigration Documents," in Chapter 16, page 233, for more information.)

Institutional or Corporate Documents. A Notary should not certify a copy of a document intended to be kept in an institutional or corporate office. For example, a copy of a college transcript only should be certified by an official of the college; and a copy of a corporate record only by a designated corporate officer. If the Notary is custodian of such records, he or she should certify copies using the institutional or corporate letterhead or seal, not the Notary's.

Verify Accuracy of Copy

To minimize the opportunity for fraud, Notaries only should certify photocopies that have been made under their control or in their presence. This makes it easy for the Notary to assure absolutely that the copy is identical to the original. If it is unavoidable that the photocopy be made without the Notary's control or presence, the Notary must carefully compare the original and the copy — line by line, word for word — to make certain that they match exactly.

A Notary may never certify a copy of an original document that is not in the Notary's hands at the time of the certification. The Notary must be permitted to examine the original when certifying a copy.

The Notary also should keep a duplicate of the certified copy as a notarial record. A duplicate can provide evidence that a certified copy has later been altered, and it may prove useful if the certified copy and its original are lost.

 NNA Recommendation

Though some states allow certification of a transcription or a hand-rendered or typed reproduction, the National Notary Association strongly recommends that Notaries certify only photocopies made by the Notary or, at least, made in the Notary's presence.

COPY CERTIFICATION CERTIFICATE

When certifying a copy, a notarial certificate must be completed to detail exactly what the certification means. The certificate wording may be typed, stamped or printed on the copy or on a paper attached to it like any other loose notarial certificate.

It is preferable to fasten the notarial certificate as a cover sheet, rather than as an attachment to the signature page, as is done with most other notarial certificates.

Depending on the circumstances of the certification, the notarial certificate wording will vary somewhat — for example, if the copy is of an original presented to the Notary, or if the copy is of an original in the Notary's custody such as a notarial record.

Certified Copy of Original Presented to Notary

For a certified copy of an original document presented to the Notary by the document's custodian — a college diploma or a contract, for example — typical notarial certificate wording would be as follows:

State of _____)
) SS.
County of _____)

On this _____ day of _____ (month), _____ (year), I certify that the attached or preceding document of _____ (number of pages) pages is a true, exact, complete and unaltered photocopy of _____ (name or description of original document), presented to me by _____ (name of original document's custodian), and that, to the best of my knowledge, the original document is neither a public record nor a publicly recordable instrument.

_____ (signature and seal of Notary)

With the wording, "I certify that the attached or preceding document of _____ (number of pages) pages is a true, exact, complete and unaltered photocopy of _____ (name or description of original document)," the Notary officially certifies that the copy is an identical reproduction of the original. In the appropriate blanks, the Notary fills in the number of pages and describes the document ("Last Will and Testament," "Collaboration Agreement" or other). If a particular certificate does not ask for the number of pages, the Notary should include this with the document description. Indicating the number of pages can later show whether a page of the copy has been improperly added or removed.

"Presented to me by _____ (name of original document's custodian)" indicates that the original document was provided by the custodian to the Notary on the date and at the location indicated in the venue of the certificate. The blank is to be completed with the document custodian's name. This wording is also an indirect reference to the appearance of the document custodian before the Notary.

The closing phrase, "to the best of my knowledge, the original document is neither a public record nor a publicly recordable instrument," is the Notary's verification that a certified copy of the original is a lawful notarial act.

Certified Copy of Notarial Record

Occasionally, a Notary will be requested to provide a certified copy of a particular notarial record or journal entry. In these situations, typical certificate wording would be:

State of _____)
) SS.
County of _____)

On this _____ day of _____ (month), _____ (year), I certify that the attached or preceding document of _____ (number of pages) pages is a true, exact, complete and unaltered photocopy of _____ (name or description of original document), an official notarial record in my possession.

_____ (signature and seal of Notary)

The significance of this wording is that it describes the original as "an official notarial record in my possession" rather than as a document presented to the Notary by another person.

COPY CERTIFICATION BY DOCUMENT CUSTODIAN

A custodian-certified copy is an alternative often used in states where a Notary-certified copy is prohibited. This procedure requires the custodian of the original document to sign a declaration that a copy is identical to the original and take an oath or affirmation before the Notary. The custodian's signature is then notarized on the declaration with a jurat.

Basically, a copy certification by document custodian is an affidavit signed and sworn to by the custodian, with a jurat as the notarization.

A typical custodian's declaration, with accompanying notarial certificate, follows:

State of _____)
) SS.
County of _____)

I, _____ (name of custodian of original document), hereby swear (or affirm) that the attached reproduction of _____ (description of original document) is a true, correct and complete photocopy of a document in my possession.

_____ (signature of document custodian)
_____ (address of document custodian)

Subscribed and sworn to (or affirmed) before me by _____ (name of signer) this _____ day of _____ (month), _____ (year).

_____ (signature and seal of Notary)

With copy certification by document custodian, the keeper of the original certifies the copy.

In this declaration and certificate, the custodian — not the Notary — guarantees that the original and copy are identical. The document custodian completes the declaration (beginning with "I..." and ending with the signature and address of the custodian); the notarial certificate ("State of..." through the signature and seal of the Notary) is completed by the Notary.

Important

A copy certification by document custodian may not always be an acceptable substitute for a Notary certified copy. The Notary should recommend that the person requesting the act check with the agency that will receive the copy to be sure a notarized custodian-certified copy will serve the required purposes.

THE CONFORMED COPY

Occasionally, a Notary will notarize a document with carbon or NCR (no carbon required) copies attached, and the notarial seal impression unfortunately will not carry through the carbon. Or sometimes a document will be photocopied and certain words will not reproduce on the photocopy. In either case, it may be necessary to conform the copies so that they contain all the information appearing on the original document.

A conformed copy is a reproduction of an original document whose unreproduced parts are filled in on the copy by hand. While conforming a copy is not a notarial act, Notaries occasionally are asked to execute conformed copies in conjunction with a notarization.

Unreproduced portions of a copy may be completed by hand if so noted on the copy. A copy altered in this manner is called a conformed copy.

There are two steps in conforming a copy. First, printing, typing or stamping all missing words in the same location as on the original document. Signatures should be printed or typed. A notarial seal may be affixed as on the original. Second, printing the words "conformed copy" in large letters across the top or in the margin or other available area of the copy, without obscuring any text. While any person may conform a copy, only a Notary should affix a notarial seal on a conformed copy.

The fact that conformed copies were made (and the number made) should be noted in the notarial journal as additional information related to notarization of the original document.

PERFORMING A TYPICAL COPY CERTIFICATION

With the following example, we will illustrate the steps in performing a typical copy certification, starting again by setting up the situation.

The Situation

On March 19, 2008, at 3:00 p.m., Linda R. Owens appears before Notary Paul C. Fontana in Bexar County, Texas, to have a copy of her college diploma certified.

Ms. Owens lives in San Antonio and offers her Texas driver's license as identification.

She hands the diploma to Mr. Fontana.

Step 1: Personal Appearance

Ms. Owens appears in person before the Notary, Mr. Fontana, to request a notarial act, so personal appearance has been established.

Step 2: Determining the Notarial Act

Ms. Owens specifically asks for a certified copy, thereby instructing the Notary as to the type of notarial act to perform.

Step 3: Identifying the Document Custodian

Though not required for a copy certification, the Notary asks Ms. Owens for identification because the Notary is careful and prudent. Ms. Owens obliges by providing her driver's license.

If no suspicious circumstances were present, the Notary still could proceed even if Ms. Owens could not be positively identified.

Step 4: Original Presented

When she requested the certified copy, Ms. Owens provided the original document to the Notary. A Notary may never certify a copy of a document that is not in the hands of the Notary.

Step 5: Copy Certification is Lawful

Since a college diploma is a one-of-a-kind document, it may be copied and certified by any Notary whose state permits such certification, provided the document is the rightful possession of a private individual.

It is easy to see that a diploma with Ms. Owens' name on it is rightfully in her custody, since she was positively identified by the Notary. In addition, copy certification is a lawful notarial act in Texas, as long as the original is not recordable in the public record. A college diploma is not a recordable document.

So the Notary has determined that he may lawfully certify a copy of Ms. Owens' diploma.

Step 6: Verify Accuracy of Copy

Because the Notary makes the photocopy himself, he is absolutely sure that the copy is identical to the original. In addition, he makes a copy for his notarial records.

If the copy to be certified was made outside the Notary's control or presence, he must carefully compare the original and the copy to make certain that they are identical.

Step 7: The Journal Entry

Next, the Notary records the notarial act in his journal. He records the

	Month/Day/Year/Time of Notarization	Kind or Type of Notarization	Document Date (Month/Day/Year)	Document Kind or Type	Name and Address of Signer	
1	March 19, 2008	copy	June 15, 1977	college Diploma	Linda R. Owens	☒ Pers ☐ ID/ ☐ ☐
	3:00 p.m.	certification			13031 Johnson Road	
					Anytown, US 00000 (210) 555-9978	☐ Per

Identification of Signer	Additional Information	Notary Fee	Signature of Signer	Right Thumbprint of Signer	
☐ Personally Known by the Notary ☒ ID Cards — Describe each card below ☐ Credible Witness(es) — Include signature of each witness	Uni. of Texas diploma	$6.00	x *Linda R. Owens*	[thumbprint]	1
Texas DL	Linda R. Owens, MS Psychology				
Expires 5/31/12	Made copy myself.				
☐ Personally Known by the Notary					

Illustrated above is the journal entry for the copy certification of Ms. Owen's college diploma.

date and time of notarization, "March 19, 2008, 3:00 p.m."; the type of notarial act, "copy certification"; the document date, "June 15, 1977"; the document type, "college diploma"; the name and address of the document custodian, Ms. Owens.

The Notary then records how he identified Ms. Owens by checking "ID Cards" in the identification section and recording the ID description, serial number and expiration date.

Next, in the additional information section, the Notary describes the document in detail ("University of Texas diploma, Linda R. Owens, M.S. Psychology") and indicates that he made the copy.

The Notary then records the fee he charged, $6.00.

Finally, Ms. Owens signs the journal and leaves her thumbprint.

Step 8: Completing the Notarial Certificate

The last step in the copy certification is completing, signing and sealing the notarial certificate.

Since Ms. Owens provided only the original document, the Notary will need to provide the notarial certificate. He uses a preprinted certificate with the following wording:

State of _____)
) SS.
County of _____)

On this _____ day of _____ (month), _____ (year), I certify

that the attached or preceding document of _____ (number of pages) pages is a true, exact, complete and unaltered photocopy of _____ (name or description of original document), presented to me by _____ (name of original document's custodian), and that, to the best of my knowledge, the original document is neither a public record nor a publicly recordable instrument.

_____
(signature and seal of Notary)

First, the Notary fills in the venue — the state and the county where the notarization takes place.

State of __Texas_____)
) SS.
County of __Bexar_____)

Next, the date of notarization is completed. This is the date that Ms. Owens appeared before the Notary to request the certified copy.

On this __19th__ day of __March_____ (month), __2008__ (year)...

Then, the Notary completes the portion of the wording that describes the copy the Notary certified — the number of pages (note how "pages" became the singular "page") and title of the document.

I certify that the attached or preceding document of __1____
(number of pages) page**x** is a true, exact, complete and
unaltered photocopy of __University of Texas MS diploma__
(name or description of original document)...

Next, the Notary places Ms. Owens' name in the blank indicating who the original document's custodian is.

...presented to me by __Linda R. Owens_____ (name of
original document's custodian)...

And finally, the Notary signs where indicated and makes an imprint of his official seal.

▼

Paul C. Fontana

(signature and seal of Notary)

SUMMARY

Copy certification verifies that a reproduction of an original document is true, complete and correct. Verification of a copy may be performed by the person or agency responsible for holding and preserving the original document. Notaries and certain other public officials, including county recorders, are the only officers empowered to issue official certified copies.

Some states either do not allow Notaries to certify copies or impose restrictions on that act. And Notaries in states that allow copy certification may not certify copies of certain documents, including vital records, recordable documents, certain USCIS documents and documents intended to be kept in a institutional or corporate office. Generally speaking, any one-of-a-kind original document in the rightful custody of a private person may be copied and certified by a Notary. Notaries also may honor requests for certified copies of their notarial records or journal entries.

Ideally, Notaries should certify only photocopies, not hand-rendered or typed reproductions. The photocopy should be made by the Notary to minimize the chance of fraud. If the photocopy is not made by the Notary, the original and the copy must be carefully compared to assure that they are identical. A Notary may never certify a copy of an original that is not in the Notary's hands. The Notary should make a duplicate of the certified copy to keep as a notarial record.

A completed notarial certificate must accompany the certified copy. The certificate wording may be typed, stamped or printed on the copy or on a loose certificate attached to it. With multipage documents, it is preferable to fasten the certificate as a cover sheet.

In states where a Notary-certified copy is prohibited, copy certification by document custodian is an alternative. This procedure involves a written declaration that a copy is identical to the original. This declaration is signed and sworn to by the custodian, with a jurat as the notarization.

▼

A conformed copy is a reproduction — either a carbon copy or photocopy — on which any unreproduced parts are filled in by hand. Conforming a copy is not a notarial act, but Notaries occasionally are asked to conform copies in conjunction with a notarization. The words "conformed copy" should be printed in large letters across top, in the margin or in another available area of the copy. ■

IMPORTANT TERMS

Carbon Copy: Reproduction of a document produced by carbon paper.

Certificate of Naturalization or Certificate of Citizenship: Documents that authenticate the granting of U.S. citizenship that are issued by the U.S. Citizenship and Immigration Services.

Certified Copy: Document certified by an official, such as a Notary, to be an accurate reproduction of an original.

Conformed Copy: Reproduction of an original document whose unreproduced parts are filled in on the copy by hand.

Custodian or Document Custodian: Keeper of a document.

Custodian-Certified Copy: Document verified to be an accurate reproduction of an original by the original document's permanent custodian.

Declaration of Intention to Become a Citizen: Document issued by the U.S. Citizenship and Immigration Services that is used in the process of becoming a U.S. citizen.

Immigration Document: Document used in the process of becoming a legal resident of the United States, such as the Affidavit of Support (I-134/I-864).

NCR or No Carbon Required: Special duplication paper that does not require an intervening sheet of carbon paper.

Original: Any document of which a reproduction has been made.

Photocopy: Reproduction of a document made through exact photographic duplication of the original's image, rather than through approximation of its image by hand-copying or other methods.

Recordable Document: Document that may be filed with an official agency such as a County Recorder.

Vital Record: Birth certificate, death certificate, marriage license or other public record of demographic data.

CHAPTER 10 TEST

In each blank, write the response — a, b, c or d — that best completes each of the following statements:

1. An original is _____.

    a. Any reproduction of a document.

    b. Any document of which a reproduction has been made.

    c. Any document photocopied by a Notary.

    d. Any photocopy of a document.

2. A custodian is the document's _____.

    a. Certifier.

    b. Photocopier.

    c. Signer.

    d. Keeper.

3. In all states _____.

    a. Notaries may certify copies.

    b. Notaries may not certify copies.

    c. Custodians may certify copies.

    d. Custodians may not certify copies.

4. Notaries generally are authorized to certify a copy of _____.

    a. A birth certificate.

    b. An entry in their notarial journal.

    c. A naturalization certificate.

    d. A college transcript.

5. A Notary employed by a corporation should certify copies of _____.

    a. Corporate records, using the notarial seal.

    b. Corporate records, using the corporate seal.

    c. Notary journal entries, using the corporate seal.

    d. Notary journal entries, using the corporate letterhead.

6. Notarial certificate wording for a certified copy _____.

    a. Is not required, since certifying a copy is not a notarial act.

    b. Should be attached to the last page of a multi-page copy.

    c. Should be duplicated and kept in the Notary journal.

    d. May be typed, stamped or printed on the copy or an attachment.

▼

7. A custodian-certified copy is _____.

    a. Sometimes acceptable in place of a Notary-certified copy.

    b. Always acceptable in place of a Notary-certified copy.

    c. Never acceptable in place of a Notary-certified copy.

    d. Exactly the same as a Notary-certified copy.

8. The following is not a step in conforming a copy: _____.

    a. Typing a missing number on the copy.

    b. Affixing a missing Notary seal on the copy.

    c. Having the signer re-sign the copy.

    d. Printing "conformed copy" across the copy.

Explain in your own words:

9. What should a Notary do when asked to certify copies of a deed?

    _____

    _____

    _____

10. Why should Notaries keep duplicates of certified copies as part of their notarial record?

    _____

    _____

    _____

Complete the journal entry and notarial certificate for the following notarization.

11. Today, at this hour, Anna Lisa Bradshaw appears before you and asks you to issue a certified copy of her Last Will and Testament, which she presents. The three-page document is dated September 29, 1996. Ms. Bradshaw has been a close friend of yours for 10 years, and she lives at 400 McArthur Boulevard, Apartment 303, in your city and zip code. You make the photocopy of the document yourself and use a preprinted, loose notarial certificate. You charge no fee for the certification. Complete the following journal entry:

Month/Day/Year/Time of Notarization	Kind or Type of Notarization	Document Date (Month/Day/Year)	Document Kind or Type	Name and Address of Signer	
					☐ Pers ☐ ID/ ☐ C
1					
					☐ Pe

Identification of Signer	Additional Information	Notary Fee	Signature of Signer	Right Thumbprint of Signer	
☐ Personally Known by the Notary ☐ ID Cards — Describe each card below ☐ Credible Witness(es) — Include signature of each witness			x _____		1
☐ Personally Known by the Notary					

12. Complete the following certificate for the same notarization:

State of _____)

) SS.

County of _____)

On this _____ day of _____, _____, I certify that the attached or preceding document of _____ (number of pages) pages is a true, exact and unaltered photocopy of the _____ (name or description of original document) presented to me by _____ (name of original document's custodian), and that, to the best of my knowledge, the original document is neither a public record nor a publicly recordable instrument.

_____   L.S.

(Signature and Title of Officer)

See pages 385–386 for correct responses.

CHAPTER 11

Proofs of Execution

Occasionally, situations arise when a signed document must be notarized, but the document signer is unable to personally appear before a Notary. The signer, for example, may have been suddenly called out of the country. In these instances, a notarization called a proof of execution by subscribing witness — allowing a third party who has witnessed the signing to appear before a Notary with the document in place of the signer — often may be performed.

SUBSCRIBING WITNESS

With proofs of execution, the principal's signature is notarized through this third party, called a subscribing witness. The subscribing witness "proves" the authenticity of the principal's signature to the Notary rather than the principal acknowledging it.

A subscribing witness is a person who watches a principal sign a document (or who personally takes the principal's acknowledgment) and then subscribes (signs) his or her own name on the document at the principal's request. This witness brings that document to a Notary on the principal's behalf and takes an oath or affirmation from the Notary to the

When a signer cannot appear before a Notary, the signature may often be proved by a third person, called a subscribing witness.

The subscribing witness must witness the signing or personally take the principal signer's acknowledgment. The witness then subscribes (signs) his or her name to the document.

effect that the principal willingly signed (or acknowledged signing) the document and also requested the witness sign the document.

 State Laws Vary

Not all states allow proofs of execution. Some prohibit them; others limit their use, such as California, where proofs are not permitted with Mortgages, security agreements, Deeds of Trust and Grant Deeds. In addition, some states allow proofs only if the subscribing witness watches the principal sign. But in other states, this is not necessary, provided that the principal acknowledges having signed the document to the witness.

The subscribing witness typically must be personally known by the Notary. In addition, the ideal subscribing witness personally knows the principal signer and has no beneficial or financial interest in the document or transaction. It would be foolish of the Notary, for example, to rely on the word of a subscribing witness presenting for notarization a power of attorney that names this very witness as the attorney in fact.

ALTERNATIVE TO AN ACKNOWLEDGMENT

Proofs are generally acceptable in lieu of acknowledgments. However, not all agencies allow proofs because of the potential for abuse.

In most states, a proof of execution is regarded as an acceptable substitute for an acknowledgment on recordable documents.

However, proofs, as they are sometimes called, may never be used for documents requiring a jurat. Jurats require oaths or affirmations, and no person may take an oath or affirmation for another.

While many states allow proofs of execution for deeds and other recordable documents, some persons, agencies and companies may not accept documents notarized in this way because proofs have a high potential for fraudulent abuse. Relying only on the word of a third party, without the signer present, a Notary cannot determine for certain that the signature of the principal was not forged, coerced or incompetently made. But a Notary can reduce the possibility of fraud by refusing to notarize in cases in which the honesty or impartiality of a witness is questionable.

> **Important**
>
> Due to their potential for fraud, proofs of execution should only be performed as a last resort. They should not be used merely to avoid inconveniencing a friend, client or employer.

FOUR REQUIREMENTS FOR PROOFS

To execute a proof of execution by subscribing witness, four requirements must be met:

1. Personal Appearance. The subscribing witness must personally appear before the Notary.

2. Identification of Witness. The Notary must personally know or positively identify the subscribing witness.

3. Witness Signs Document. The subscribing witness must sign the document.

4. Oath or Affirmation. The subscribing witness must swear or affirm that he or she either witnessed the principal sign, or the principal acknowledged having signed the document to the subscribing witness.

Personal Appearance

While the principal signer does not appear before the Notary for a proof of execution, the subscribing witness must. A proof is the only notarial act that may be performed in this manner — without the presence of the principal signer or an authorized representative (such as an attorney in fact, guardian or conservator) of the principal who signs for the principal. These circumstances would be unacceptable for an acknowledgment or a jurat, but the appearance of a subscribing witness before the Notary does meet the personal-appearance requirement for a proof of execution.

To establish personal appearance, the subscribing witness must be face to face in the same room as the Notary at the time the proof is executed. A proof cannot be taken over the phone, from an adjacent room or through the mail.

Identification of Subscribing Witness

The subscribing witness must be positively identified by the Notary. The more reliably a Notary can identify a subscribing witness, the more reliable the proof of execution will be.

Most state laws specifically require every subscribing witness to be personally known by the Notary. This is a good, prudent practice for all Notaries to follow for proofs, as it reduces the potential for fraud.

One state, North Carolina, expressly allows Notaries to rely on identification documents to identify subscribing witnesses. Other states may allow use of a personally-known credible identifying witness to identify a subscribing witness.

! Important

The terms credible identifying witness and subscribing witness can be confusing, but these are very different types of witnesses. A credible identifying witness vouches for the identity of a signer appearing before a Notary. A subscribing witness vouches for the genuineness of the signature of a person who does not appear before the Notary (See Chapter 4 to review credible identifying witnesses).

Witness Signs Document

The subscribing witness is so named because this person also must subscribe (sign) his or her name on the document as a witness, in addition to the principal's signature.

Witness Takes Oath or Affirmation

To compel truthfulness, the Notary administers an oath or affirmation to the subscribing witness. The subscribing witness swears or affirms that he or she watched the principal sign the document or personally took the principal's acknowledgment, depending on the circumstances and the allowed procedures. Additionally, the witness must swear or affirm that the principal requested the witness to sign the document as a witness and bring it to the Notary.

Following are examples of a typical oath and affirmation for a subscribing witness:

> OATH: Do you solemnly swear that you witnessed _____ (name of the document signer) sign his/her name to this document and/or acknowledge to you having executed it for the purposes therein stated, so help you God?

> AFFIRMATION: Do you solemnly affirm that you witnessed _____ (name of the document signer) sign his/her name to this document and/or acknowledge to you having executed it for the purposes therein stated?

CERTIFICATE FOR PROOFS OF EXECUTION

Proofs of execution are complex notarial acts. They involve an absent principal, a subscribing witness, identification, plus an oath or affirmation. Certificates for proofs are complex as well.

But the Notary should not shy away. Careful reading of the certificate wording will show the Notary's responsibilities.

A typical example of a proof-of-execution-by-subscribing-witness certificate follows:

> State of _____)
>) SS.
> County of _____)

> Before me, _____ (name of Notary), on this day personally appeared _____ (name of subscribing witness), personally known to me (or proved to me on the oath of _____ [name of person identifying the subscribing witness]) to be the person whose name is subscribed as a witness to the foregoing instrument, and who, after being duly sworn (or affirmed) by me, stated on oath (affirmation) that he/she saw _____ (name of principal signer), the person who executed the foregoing instrument, subscribe the same (or acknowledge in his/her presence having executed the same) for the purposes and considerations therein expressed, and that he/she had signed the same as a witness at the request of the person who executed the same.

Given under my hand and seal of office this _____ day of
_____ (month), _____ (year).

_____ (signature and seal of Notary)

While this wording is lengthy and intricate, looking at it phrase by phrase helps to "decode" the meaning.

"Before me, _____ (name of Notary), on this day personally appeared _____ (name of subscribing witness)" indicates that the subscribing witness appeared before the Notary at the time of notarization. In the first blank, the Notary writes his or her own name; in the second one, the subscribing witness's name.

The wording "personally known to me (or proved to me on the oath of _____ [name of credible identifying witness])" says that the subscribing witness was identified by the Notary and how — by personal knowledge or by a credible identifying witness. The inappropriate wording is to be be lined through, and if a credible identifying witness is used, his or her name is written in the blank.

With, "the person whose name is subscribed as a witness to the foregoing instrument," the certificate states that the subscribing witness signed the document as a witness.

The phrase "who, after being duly sworn (or affirmed) by me" indicates that the subscribing witness took an oath or affirmation.

The words "stated on oath (affirmation) that" begin the content of the subscribing witness's oath or affirmation. It follows with "he/she saw _____ (name of principal signer), the person who executed the foregoing instrument, subscribe the same (or acknowledge in his/her presence having executed the same)." This says that the subscribing witness saw the principal sign the document or took the principal's acknowledgment. The blank is to be completed with the principal's name. And "he/she had signed the same as a witness at the request of the person who executed the same," states that the witness signed the document as a witness at the principal's request.

EXECUTING A TYPICAL PROOF

With the following example, we will examine the steps required to execute a proof of execution by subscribing witness.

The Situation

On August 21, 2008, at 10 a.m., Anita A. Hamilton appears before Notary Roberta E. Bradley in Contra Costa County, California, and presents a services contract signed by her supervisor, David L. Shaw, on August 19, 2008.

Mr. Shaw cannot appear before a Notary himself, because he has been unexpectedly called out of the country on business. Ms. Hamilton was present at the signing, and has been instructed by Mr. Shaw to have the document "notarized."

The Notary works in the same office as Ms. Hamilton and Mr. Shaw and has been a close, personal friend of Ms. Hamilton for several years, inside and outside of the work environment.

Step 1: Personal Appearance

The principal signer, Mr. Shaw, does not personally appear before the Notary, but Ms. Hamilton, a witness to the signing, does. While this would not be acceptable for an acknowledgment or a jurat, it meets the personal-appearance requirement for a proof of execution.

Step 2: Determining the Type of Notarial Act

Ms. Hamilton asks to have Mr. Shaw's signature notarized. She explains that Mr. Shaw cannot personally appear because he is out of the country.

The Notary informs Ms. Hamilton that the notarization can be performed only in rare situations, provided that someone who witnessed the signing or who took Mr. Shaw's acknowledgment of having signed can serve as a subscribing witness.

Ms. Hamilton tells the Notary that she saw Mr. Shaw sign, and that he asked her to take the document to a Notary to have it notarized. Though she does not know what the notarial act is called, Ms. Hamilton has just asked the Notary to perform a proof of execution by subscribing witness.

Step 3: Identifying the Subscribing Witness

The Notary's long friendship with Ms. Hamilton in and outside the workplace sufficiently establishes her personal knowledge of Ms. Hamilton's identity.

Step 4: Witness Signs Document

The Notary instructs Ms. Hamilton to sign the document as a witness.

Step 5: Oath or Affirmation of Subscribing Witness

Next, an oath or affirmation must be administered. Ms. Hamilton prefers to take an oath.

Before administering the oath, the Notary tells Ms. Hamilton that lying under oath — perjury — is a criminal act.

Then, the Notary instructs Ms. Hamilton to raise her right hand and asks her. "Do you solemnly swear that you saw David L. Shaw sign his name to this document, so help you God?" Ms. Hamilton replies, "I do."

Step 6: Willingness and Awareness

With a proof of execution, there are two individuals whose willingness and awareness should be determined: the principal signer and the subscribing witness.

The willingness and awareness of Mr. Shaw, the principal signer, is determined through the subscribing witness. The Notary asks Ms. Hamilton if Mr. Shaw signed the document without apparent duress and if he appeared alert and aware when signing. Ms. Hamilton answers, "Yes."

As for Ms. Hamilton, the fact that she appeared before the Notary, signed the document as a witness and took an oath without hesitation reasonably establishes her willingness. Her awareness is determined throughout the notarization. Since she appears to the Notary to act reasonably and communicate effectively, she is considered aware.

Step 7: The Journal Entry

Next, the Notary begins the journal entry. She writes the date and

Month/Day/Year/Time of Notarization	Kind or Type of Notarization	Document Date (Month/Day/Year)	Document Kind or Type	Name and Address of Signer	
August 21, 2008 10:00 am.	Proof of Execution by Subscribe. Witness	August 19, 2008	services contract	Anita A. Hamilton (subscribing witness) 953 Sun Ray Avenue Anytown, US 00000 (510) 555-6975	Perso ID C

Identification of Signer	Additional Information	Notary Fee	Signature of Signer	Right Thumbprint of Signer	
☒ Personally Known by the Notary ☐ ID Cards — Describe each card below ☐ Credible Witness(es) — Include signature of each witness	Principal signer is David L. Shaw, who is out of the country. Attached loose certificate.	no charge	x Anita a. Hamilton	[thumbprint]	1
☐ Personally Known by the Notary					

Above is the journal entry for the proof of execution performed on Mr. Shaw's deed.

time of notarization, "August 21, 2008, 10:00 a.m."; the type of notarial act, "proof of execution"; the document date, "August 19, 2008"; and the document type, "services contract."

Then she records the name and address of the signer — who, in the case of a proof of execution, is the subscribing witness — Ms. Hamilton. She next records how she identified Ms. Hamilton by checking personal knowledge in the identification section.

The Notary then indicates in the additional information area the name of the principal signer, "David L. Shaw," and other pertinent facts, such as that Mr. Shaw is out of the country and that a loose certificate is used.

Next, she records the fee she charged, "no charge." Finally, Ms. Hamilton signs the journal and leaves her thumbprint.

Step 8: Completing the Certificate

The last step is the notarial certificate. While the document contains preprinted acknowledgment wording, this is not appropriate for a proof of execution. Instead, the Notary lines through the preprinted wording and provides a loose certificate with the following wording:

State of _____)
) SS.
County of _____)

On this _____ day of _____ (month), _____ (year), before me, the undersigned, a Notary Public for the state, personally appeared _____ (subscribing witness's name), personally known to me (or proved to me on the oath of _____ [name of person identifying the subscribing witness]) to be the person whose name is subscribed to the within instrument as a witness thereto, who, being by me duly sworn, deposes and says that he/she was present and saw _____ (name of principal), the same person described in and whose name is subscribed to the within and annexed instrument in his/her authorized capacity(ies) as a party thereto, execute the same, and that said affiant subscribed his/her name to the within instrument as a witness at the request of _____ (name of principal).

_____

(signature and seal of Notary)

First, the Notary completes the venue — the state and the county where the notarization takes place.

State of _California_____)
) SS.
County of _Contra costa_)

Then, the Notary fills in the date of notarization — the date that Ms. Hamilton appeared and requested a notarial act.

On this _21st_ day of _August_____ (month), _2008_ (year)....

Next, the subscribing witness's name, "Anita A. Hamilton," is inserted as the person who personally appeared before the Notary.

...before me, the undersigned, a Notary Public for the state, personally appeared _Anita A. Hamilton_ (subscribing witness's name)...

The Notary then indicates how Ms. Hamilton, the subscribing witness, was identified by lining through the inappropriate wording.

...personally known to me ~~(or proved to me on the oath of _____ [name of person identifying the subscribing witness])~~ to be the person whose name is subscribed to the within instrument as a witness thereto...

Next, the Notary selects the appropriate pronoun for the subscribing witness, Ms. Hamilton, by crossing out the inappropriate one.

...being by me duly sworn, deposes and says that he/she was present...

Then, the principal signer's name, "David L. Shaw," is written in and the appropriate pronoun for Mr. Shaw is indicated by, again, crossing out the inappropriate one.

...and saw _David L. Shaw_ (name of principal), the same person described in and whose name is subscribed to the within and annexed instrument in his/her authorized capacity(ies) as a party thereto, execute the same...

Then, the appropriate pronoun for the subscribing witness, Ms. Hamilton (here called "said affiant," because the witness has taken an oath or affirmation), is again indicated, and the principal signer's name, "David L. Shaw," is written in once more.

...and that said affiant subscribed his/her name to the within instrument as a witness at the request of _David L. Shaw_ (name of principal).

The final step in completing the certificate is the Notary's signature and official seal.

Roberta E. Bradley
(signature and seal of Notary)

SUMMARY

Only one notarial act — the proof of execution by subscribing witness — may be performed without the principal signer or a representative (such as an attorney in fact, guardian or conservator) for the principal appearing before a Notary. With proofs of execution, the principal's signature is notarized through a third party called a subscribing witness.

The subscribing witness watches a principal sign a document (or takes the principal's acknowledgment), signs his or her own name to the document, and then personally appears before a Notary on the principal's behalf. The subscribing witness must be personally known to the Notary and must swear or affirm before the Notary that the principal did sign (or acknowledge signing) the document. The ideal subscribing witness also personally knows the principal signer and has no interest in the document or transaction.

A proof of execution is usually an acceptable substitute for an acknowledgment on recordable documents. However, not every state allows proofs of execution. Some prohibit their use altogether, while others limit their use to cases in which the subscribing witness watched the principal sign. In addition, proofs may never be used for documents requiring a jurat.

Some persons, agencies and companies may not accept documents notarized with proofs because relying only on the word of a third party makes it impossible for a Notary to determine that the signature was not forged, coerced or incompetently made. Due to this potential for fraud, proofs of execution only should be performed as a last resort and not merely to avoid inconvenience.

As with other notarial acts, the Notary should record the details of the proof of execution in an official journal. The journal entry should include the date and time of the notarial act, the type of notarial act, the date and type of document, the name and address of the subscribing witness, how the subscribing witness was identified, the name of the principal signer, the fee charged and the signature of the subscribing witness.

Certificates for proofs of execution are fairly complex, with wording that describes an absent principal, a subscribing witness, identification and an oath or affirmation. ■

IMPORTANT TERMS

Proof: Abbreviation for proof of execution by subscribing witness.

Proof of Execution by Subscribing Witness: Notarial act where a person (called the subscribing witness) swears under oath or affirmation before a Notary that he or she either watched another individual (called the principal) sign a document or took that person's acknowledgment of an already signed document. The witness must affix a signature to the document in addition to the principal's.

Prove: Authenticate the signature of a principal signer not appearing before a Notary.

Subscribe: Sign.

Subscribing Witness: Person who either watches another (the principal) sign a document or takes that person's acknowledgment of an already signed document and appears before the Notary on behalf of the principal. The subscribing witness must sign the document in addition to the principal, must be personally known by the Notary, and must take an oath or affirmation stating that he or she witnessed the principal sign or took the principal's acknowledgment.

CHAPTER 11 TEST

In each blank, write the response — a, b, c or d — that best completes each of the following statements:

1. A subscribing witness _____.

    a. Vouches under oath or affirmation for the identity of a signer appearing before the Notary.

    b. Vouches under oath or affirmation for the genuineness of the signature of a person not appearing before the Notary.

    c. Proves the legality of a document before the Notary.

    d. Proves a signer is disabled and cannot appear before the Notary.

2. Proofs of execution are _____.

    a. Always acceptable alternatives to acknowledgments.

    b. Sometimes acceptable alternatives to jurats.

    c. Sometimes acceptable alternatives to acknowledgments.

    d. Always acceptable alternatives to representative acknowledgments.

3. Proofs of execution have a high potential for fraud because _____.

    a. The Notary must rely on the word of a third person to determine that a signature is genuine.

    b. The subscribing witness may rely on the principal for employment.

    c. The subscribing witness must rely on the Notary to determine that a signature is genuine.

    d. The Notary will only rarely know the principal signer.

4. For a proof of execution _____.

    a. Both subscribing witness and principal appear before the Notary.

    b. Only the principal appears before the Notary.

    c. Either the subscribing witness or principal appears before the Notary.

    d. The subscribing witness appears before the Notary.

5. The subscribing witness _____.

    a. Subscribes the principal's name to the document.

    b. Swears that the principal is unable to sign.

    c. Is typically personally known by the Notary.

    d. All the above.

Explain in your own words:

6. What are two characteristics for an ideal subscribing witness?

_____

_____

_____

Complete the journal entry and notarial certificate for the following notarization.

7. Today, at this hour, a coworker, Gayle M. Kramer, appears before you and asks you to notarize the signature of her supervisor, Donna E. Nunez, on a sales agreement. Ms. Nunez signed exactly a week ago today in Ms. Kramer's presence, but had to leave on emergency business overseas. Ms. Kramer lives at 4982 Euclid Street in your town and zip code. You are a personal friend of Ms. Kramer and charge no fee for the notarization. Complete the following journal entry:

	Month/Day/Year/Time of Notarization	Kind or Type of Notarization	Document Date (Month/Day/Year)	Document Kind or Type	Name and Address of Signer	
1						☐ Pers ☐ ID ☐ C
						☐ Pe

Identification of Signer	Additional Information	Notary Fee	Signature of Signer	Right Thumbprint of Signer	
☐ Personally Known by the Notary ☐ ID Cards — Describe each card below ☐ Credible Witness(es) — Include signature of each witness				Top of thumb here	1
		x			
☐ Personally Known by the Notary					

8. Complete the following certificate for the same notarization:

State of _____)

) SS.

County of _____)

On this _____ day of _____, _____, before me, the undersigned, a Notary Public for the state, personally appeared _____ (name of subscribing witness), personally known to me (or proved to me on the oath of _____ [name of personally known individual identifying the subscribing witness]) to be the person whose name is subscribed to the within instrument as a witness thereto, who, being by me duly sworn, deposes and says that he/she was present and saw _____ (name of principal), the same person described in and whose name is subscribed to the within and annexed instrument in his/her authorized capacity(ies) as a party thereto, execute the same, and that said affiant subscribed his/her name to the within instrument as a witness at the request of _____ (name of principal).

_____ L.S.

(Signature of Notary)

See pages 387–388 for correct responses.

CHAPTER 12

Protests, Depositions and Other Acts

In the preceding four chapters, we detailed the procedures and requirements for the four most often executed notarizations — acknowledgments, jurats with oaths and affirmations, copy certifications, and proofs of execution. Now we will touch upon some of the less common notarial acts, including the execution of protests and the taking of depositions.

PROTESTS

A protest is a written statement by a Notary or other authorized officer indicating that payment for a negotiable instrument — a check or promissory note, for example — has not been received. Failure to pay on a negotiable instrument is called dishonor.

Once common, protests are rarely performed today.

In the 19th century, protests were common notarial acts, but they are rarely performed today due to the advent of modern electronic communication and resulting changes in the banking and financial system. Antiquated statutes still give Notaries the power to execute protests in most states.

Notarial acts of protest are complicated and varied. They require

▼

187

special knowledge of financial and legal terms. Only a Notary who has this special knowledge or who is under the supervision of an experienced bank officer or attorney should execute a protest.

DEPOSITIONS

A deposition is a signed transcript of a person's oral statements, taken down (usually by a court reporter) for use in a lawsuit. The individual who gives the deposition is called a deponent.

Notaries have the power to take depositions in most states, but it is usually trained shorthand or court reporters — most of whom are also Notaries — that take depositions. Strict rules of procedure dictate how depositions are executed, so Notaries without appropriate training or supervision should not attempt them. Instead, the Notary should refer the request to a court reporter.

In executing a deposition, the deponent is first sworn to tell the truth, then asked a series of questions by attorneys. The deponent's answers are taken down and later transcribed in typed form. The deponent then signs the typed deposition before an official witness. Normally, the same court reporter-Notary swears in the deponent beforehand, writes down the testimony, and later witnesses the deponent's signing of the typed deposition.

However, in some situations, a Notary may be asked only to swear in a deponent and witness the signing of a deposition that is taken by a court reporter who is not a Notary. This is often the case when a court reporter travels from another state to take the deposition. Being from another state, the court reporter would not have notarial jurisdiction to swear in the deponent or officially witness the signature. In these circumstances, the local Notary merely administers an oath or affirmation then executes a jurat, so no special skill would be required.

The term "deposition" is often used interchangeably with "affidavit," but there are major technical differences. A deposition is associated with a lawsuit or trial (unlike an affidavit, which need not be) and requires that either side in the litigation be permitted to cross-examine the deponent, with the questions and responses included in the deposition's text.

Only trained court reporters should take depositions. Any Notary, however, may swear in the deponent and execute the jurat in conjunction with a deposition.

Notaries often will encounter previously-prepared documents containing the term "depose," which means in this context "testify under oath or affirmation." Such documents cannot precisely be described as depositions because the Notary has not sworn in the signer beforehand and written down the spoken testimony. They are more properly termed "affidavits" and may be executed by Notaries without any special expertise.

Oath or Affirmation for a Deposition

The following or similar wording is customary for a witness being sworn in by a Notary before giving testimony in a deposition:

> OATH: Do you solemnly swear that the testimony you will give in this matter will be the truth, the whole truth and nothing but the truth, so help you God?

> AFFIRMATION: Do you solemnly affirm that the testimony you will give in this matter will be the truth, the whole truth and nothing but the truth?

MARRIAGES

In Maine, South Carolina, Florida and West Feliciana Parish in Louisiana, Notaries have the authority to perform marriages. In all other states, the Notary Public may not perform marriages, unless the Notary is also a member of the clergy.

Notaries in Maine, South Carolina, Florida and West Feliciana Parish in Louisiana who wish to exercise their power to perform marriages should study their respective state's laws and check with local officials for customs and procedures.

Each of the three states and the Louisiana Parish have varying customs and legal procedures for performing the marriage, as well as for completing and filing the marriage certificate and charging a fee. There is one common procedure in all instances: the bride and groom must obtain the marriage license and present it to the Notary at the time of the ceremony.

An in-depth explanation of solemnizing nuptials is beyond the scope of this course. Before attempting to perform a marriage, the Notary should check with state and county officials for specific procedures.

LOUISIANA NOTARY LAWS

In Louisiana, Notaries have vastly different powers than in the 49 other states and the District of Columbia. This is due to Louisiana's

French heritage. Like Notaries in France and the Latin nations, Louisiana Notaries have authority not only to witness the signing and acknowledging of documents but also to draft and prepare many different documents. They carry out many of the functions that attorneys perform throughout the rest of the United States.

Louisiana Notaries are highly trained professionals who are attorneys in most cases. Aside from certain witnessing powers that they share with other U.S. Notaries, their duties in drafting and preparing documents are beyond the scope of this course.

Louisiana Notaries have greater authority than Notaries in other states.

ADDITIONAL POWERS

A few states give additional powers to Notaries. Some of these powers are antiquated and rarely used, others are commonly performed. The following sampling shows the scope of these additional powers:

- In Pennsylvania, Notaries may qualify to have certain ministerial functions in processing paperwork for the registration and conveyance of motor vehicles.

- Florida Notaries are authorized to verify vehicle identification numbers on applications for used motor vehicle titles. In addition, they may certify the contents of a safe-deposit box opened by a financial institution when the rental payment is overdue and the renter cannot be located after several attempts.

- Notaries in Washington may certify that an event has occurred or an act has been performed. Such certification is based on either the Notary's personal knowledge or on the oath or affirmation of a credible witness.

- Texas allows, in very limited situations, a proof of acknowledgment by handwriting, whereby two witnesses well acquainted with the handwriting of an unavailable principal signer swear or affirm in writing that the signature of the principal is genuine.

Many other states have similar, distinctive acts that may be performed by a Notary. Notaries in every state should read and understand their respective state's Notary handbook and statutes in order to fully understand the scope of their duties.

SUMMARY

In addition to the more common notarial acts — acknowledgments, jurats with oaths and affirmations, copy certifications, and proofs of execution — there are some less common ones. These include protests, depositions, marriages and certain other acts.

A protest is a written statement by a Notary indicating that payment for a negotiable instrument has not been received. Protests are rarely performed today because electronic communication and changes in the banking and financial system have made them less relevant. They are complicated notarial acts, and only Notaries with special knowledge or who are under the supervision of an experienced bank officer or attorney should attempt them.

A deposition is a signed transcript of a person's oral statements, taken down for use in a lawsuit. Strict rules of procedure dictate how depositions are executed, so it is usually court reporters — who also are often Notaries — who take depositions. Notaries without appropriate training should not attempt them. On occasion, a Notary may be asked to swear in a deponent and witness the signing of a deposition taken by a court reporter who is not a Notary. For this limited participation in a deposition, no special training is required.

Three states — Maine, South Carolina and Florida — give Notaries the authority to perform marriages. In addition, one county — West Feliciana Parish in Louisiana — also authorizes the act. Each state has varying procedures, so Notaries should check state laws and county regulations.

Due to its French heritage, Louisiana's Notaries have vastly different powers than those in other states and the District of Columbia. Louisiana Notaries are highly trained professionals who have authority to draft and prepare many different documents. They carry out many of the functions that attorneys perform throughout the rest of the United States.

A few states give Notaries additional, unique powers. Some are rarely used and others are commonly performed. All Notaries should read and understand their state's Notary handbook and statutes in order to fully understand the scope their duties. ■

IMPORTANT TERMS

Court Reporter: Person whose training in stenography qualifies him or her to transcribe spoken words into such form as a deposition. Also sometimes called a shorthand reporter.

Depose: To make a deposition; to testify under oath or affirmation orally or in writing.

Dishonor: Refusal to pay the sum of money promised or requested.

Notary-performed marriage: Act of uniting a couple as husband and wife. Performed by Notaries only in Maine, South Carolina, Florida and the West Feliciana Parish in Louisiana.

Ministerial Function: Function performed according to statute, established procedure or instructions from an authority, without exercising independent judgment.

Negotiable Instrument: Document containing a promise to pay a certain sum of money to the document's bearer.

Protest: Notarial act in which a Notary certifies that a person did not receive payment for a negotiable instrument.

Shorthand Reporter: Person whose training in stenography qualifies him or her to transcribe spoken words into such form as a deposition. More often called a court reporter.

CHAPTER 12 TEST

In each blank, write the response — a, b, c or d — that best completes each of the following statements:

1. Protests are _____.

    a. Simple notarial acts that any Notary may execute.

    b. Simple notarial acts executed only in certain states.

    c. Complicated notarial acts not authorized in any state.

    d. Complicated notarial acts executed by trained Notaries.

2. A deposition differs from an affidavit in that _____.

    a. An affidavit is associated with a lawsuit; a deposition is not.

    b. An affidavit allows cross-examining; a deposition does not.

    c. Court reporters usually execute depositions; any Notary can execute affidavits.

    d. Any Notary can execute depositions; court reporters usually execute affidavits.

3. Notaries with no special training _____.

    a. May swear in the deponent and witness the signing of a deposition taken by a court reporter.

    b. May swear in the deponent and take down the testimony in writing if a court reporter witnesses the signing.

    c. May not swear in the deponent and witness the signing of a deposition taken by a court reporter.

    d. May take down testimony in writing and witness the signing of a deposition if a court reporter swears in the deponent.

4. Marriages may be performed by Notaries _____.

    a. In most states provided neither the bride nor the groom are related to the Notary.

    b. In most states if the Notary is specially trained.

    c. In Maine, South Carolina, Florida and one parish in Louisiana.

    d. In all states if the Notary acts under the supervision of a judge, a justice of the peace or a member of the clergy.

See page 388 for correct responses.

PART IV:
SPECIAL
CIRCUMSTANCES

CHAPTER 13

Foreign-Language Signers and Documents

Foreign languages create special concerns for Notaries. Signers who do not speak a common language with the Notary and documents written in languages the Notary does not understand make performing a notarial act difficult and sometimes impossible.

State laws provide the Notary with little guidance for dealing with foreign-speaking signers and foreign-language documents. Laws may specify that only persons who can read and write the English language may be commissioned as Notaries. Or they may stipulate that only English-language documents may be accepted by a recorder. However, no law specifically prohibits a Notary from serving a foreign-speaking signer or from notarizing a foreign-language document. In fact, it may be considered discriminatory to refuse a lawful request for a notarization simply because the signer speaks, or the document is written in, a foreign language.

FOREIGN-SPEAKING SIGNERS

With foreign-speaking signers, the issue is not the language spoken, but communication. Direct communication between signer and Notary is

▼

197

essential in acknowledging a signature, reciting an oath or affirmation or in responding to a Notary's questions about identity. In addition, ascertaining willingness and awareness is all but impossible without direct communication. So, it is vital that the Notary and signer communicate in a common language — whether English, Spanish, French, Japanese, Arabic, sign language or any other language.

> The signer and Notary must be able to communicate directly in a common language.

The Notary never should rely on an intermediary or interpreter in performing a notarial act. The communication must be direct. Besides the possibility of misunderstanding, the interpreter may have a motive for misrepresenting the facts. For example, a dishonest interpreter might tell a signer who cannot understand English that an English-language document is a life insurance policy when it is actually a quitclaim deed transferring the signer's property to the interpreter.

If the Notary and signer cannot effectively communicate in the same language, the Notary must refuse to perform the notarization. The signer may be referred — through an interpreter or by other means — to a Notary who speaks the given language. Sometimes, foreign consulates, which normally have officers with notarial powers on staff, may be a convenient solution for the foreign-speaking signer.

FOREIGN-LANGUAGE DOCUMENTS

> Foreign-language documents may be notarized, but if the Notary cannot read the foreign language, the notarial certificate at least must be in a language the Notary understands.

Normally, there is no problem notarizing a foreign-language document, provided the Notary can read and write the language in which it is written and the requested notarial act may legally be performed by a Notary in the particular state. If the Notary understands the foreign language, he or she performs the notarial act like any other, ensuring that the foreign-language certificate wording is equivalent to wording required for the Notary's jurisdiction. The Notary should note the document's language in the "additional information" area of the journal record.

The difficulties occur when documents are prepared in a language the Notary does not understand.

Difficulties with Foreign-Language Documents

If a Notary cannot read and write the language of a document, he or she may not recognize an unauthorized notarial act or may not understand how to proceed with the notarization. In addition, gleaning data for the journal entry and completing the certificate correctly may be a problem, and blatant frauds may go undetected.

Understanding how to proceed. With documents the Notary cannot read, there very well may be a problem knowing how to proceed. Usually, it is the notarial certificate that instructs the Notary what act to perform. However, if the certificate is in a language the Notary cannot understand, he or she will have no instructions on whether to perform an acknowledgment, a jurat or other act. In addition, the Notary of a particular state might be prohibited from notarizing certain documents or may be required to follow specific procedures with certain types of documents. If the Notary cannot understand the document type, he or she may perform an improper act or may perform the notarization incorrectly. For example, California Notaries must obtain thumbprints in their journals for all signers of deeds they notarize, but if a Notary does not know the document is a deed, he or she will not know to request the thumbprint.

Gleaning accurate data for the journal entry. A Notary unable to read a document might not be able to extract accurate data to record in the official notarial journal. Such vital data as the type or title of the document might not be understandable to the Notary. Dates can pose a problem, too. For example, the term "5-12-08" means "May 12, 2008" in some areas of the world and "December 5, 2008" in others. A Notary's reliance on the signer to interpret the document, on a third-party interpreter or even on a written translation can present its own hazards.

Completing the certificate correctly. A Notary unable to read a document might fail to comply with instructions on placement of a seal, acceptable proof of identity or other important matters. This might possibly cause invalidation of the document. Such failure to comply is more likely when the document's notarial certificate itself is in a language unknown to the Notary and contains blank spaces for the Notary to complete.

Detecting blatant frauds. Notaries are not required to read the documents they notarize. But in extracting data for their journals and in completing certificates, they sometimes cannot help but notice that a document is fraudulent. Such would be the case with a document that makes clearly impossible promises about goods and services. The Notary cannot detect blatant frauds when the document is in a language the Notary cannot read. Any lawsuit resulting from a notarized fraudulent document might require the Notary to prove he or she was not involved in a conspiracy to defraud.

Misunderstanding the U.S. Notary's Function

Another consideration is when Notaries are asked to notarize not just foreign-language documents but also any document that will be sent to a non-English-speaking person. There is the likelihood that the U.S. Notary's function will be misunderstood.

Since Notaries in some other countries can draft documents and validate their facts, foreign-born document recipients may mistakenly believe that U.S. Notaries can do the same. For example, U.S. notarial seals on "affidavits of citizenship," in which signers state that they are U.S. citizens, may be misunderstood in Latin nations as official proof of the claimed citizenship.

Notarizing Foreign-Language Documents

Signers who want foreign-language documents notarized may have alternatives other than going to a Notary who cannot read and write the language: foreign consulates, bilingual Notaries and English translations.

Consulates. Many foreign countries have consulates in certain major U.S. cities, and one of the functions of these offices is to notarize documents that are bound for the particular consulate's home nation. Most of the larger foreign consulates in the United States will have officials with notarial powers. Consulates are listed in telephone directories. However, it may not be practical for a signer to travel to the city where a consulate is located.

Bilingual Notaries. Often, Notaries who speak English and a second language can be located to notarize documents written in the second language. In certain ethnic sections of large cities, it is not difficult to find such Notaries.

Translations. If acceptable to the document's recipient, Notaries may notarize signed, English-language translations of documents they cannot read. Sometimes on standard forms, English translations are provided along with the foreign writing.

"Certifying" Translations Prohibited

In no U.S. state is a bilingual Notary allowed to use a notarial seal to "certify" the accuracy of a translation. However, a Notary may notarize a signature on a translator's declaration — perhaps an affidavit — stating that a translation is accurate. Notaries, of course, cannot notarize their own signatures on translators' declarations.

Non-Roman-Letter Signatures

The Notary may encounter a situation in which an individual wishes to sign using characters other than the Roman alphabet used in English. For example, the signer may prefer to sign with Japanese, Chinese, Arabic, Hebrew or Cyrillic alphabetic characters. Whether on documents written in English or in a foreign language, Notaries should not notarize any signatures written in characters they cannot read, since the signed names could be different from the ones they are told.

Moreover, some public recorders will refuse to record documents bearing such signatures unless a translator's declaration is attached or other special procedures used. It is a good policy to check with the

Signatures in characters the Notary cannot read may not be notarized.

recorder first before notarizing a signature in non-Roman characters on a recordable document.

SUMMARY

Language differences create special concerns for Notaries, and state laws provide little guidance. No law specifically prohibits a Notary from serving a foreign-speaking signer or from notarizing a foreign-language document, but there are problems.

There must be direct communication between signer and Notary, so it is vital that the Notary and signer communicate in a common language, no matter what that language is. If the Notary and signer cannot directly communicate in the same language, the Notary must refuse the notarization. Notaries may not rely on a third party to interpret conversations with the signer.

Notaries may notarize foreign-language documents if they understand the language. Problems occur when documents are in a language the Notary does not understand. The Notary may not understand how to proceed or may not recognize an unauthorized act, gleaning data for the journal entry may be difficult, completing the certificate correctly may be a problem; and blatant frauds may go undetected.

A consideration with any document that will be sent to a non-English-speaking person is that the U.S. Notary's function may be misunderstood. Notaries in other countries have greater powers than U.S. Notaries, so foreign-born document recipients may mistakenly believe that U.S. Notaries have powers they do not.

Signers who want foreign-language documents notarized have a few alternatives: seeking help at a foreign consulate, going to a bilingual Notary or having an English translation of the document notarized.

Notaries are not allowed to use a notarial seal to "certify" the accuracy of a translation, though they may notarize a signature on a translator's declaration.

Occasionally, a signer will wish to sign using characters other than the Roman alphabet — Japanese, Chinese, Arabic, Hebrew or Cyrillic alphabetic characters, for example. Notaries should not notarize any signatures written in characters they cannot read. In addition, some public recorders will not accept documents bearing such signatures without a translator's declaration. ■

IMPORTANT TERMS

Affidavit of Citizenship: Written statement that may be notarized in which the signer declares that he or she is a U.S. citizen, as sometimes required for travel without a passport in Mexico and Caribbean nations.

Bilingual: Able to read, write and speak two languages.

Consulate: The office of an official, called a consul, appointed by his or her home country to reside in a foreign nation and care for the interests of that government's citizens through notarization, authentication of documents and other functions.

Interpreter: A person who explains or translates.

Roman Alphabet: Characters of the alphabet used in English and other European languages.

Translation: Conversion of written or spoken statements from one language to another.

Translator's Declaration: Written statement that a translation is accurate, signed by a person, known as a translator, who has made the translation.

CHAPTER 13 TEST

In each blank, write the response — a, b, c or d — that best completes each of the following statements:

1. Ability to read and write English is _____.

 a. Possessed by all U.S. residents.

 b. Required of all signers presenting documents to U.S. Notaries.

 c. Necessary before entering into a legal contract in the U.S.

 d. Required of applicants for a notarial commission in some states.

2. Notarizing a document the Notary cannot read is _____.

 a. Prohibited by law in almost all states.

 b. Seldom addressed by law but officially encouraged.

 c. Allowed but poses certain difficulties.

 d. Allowed if the Notary keeps a translation in the journal.

3. A translator's declaration _____.

 a. May not be notarized.

 b. May not be notarized by the translator.

 c. Is required when notarizing a non-English document.

 d. May be notarized only by a bilingual Notary.

4. An English document signed with Chinese characters may be notarized if _____.

 a. An interpreter explains the meaning to the Notary.

 b. The signer can at least understand spoken English.

 c. There is direct communication between Notary and signer.

 d. The Notary can read the Chinese characters.

Explain in your own words:

5. A Notary who cannot read and write a document's language could have difficulty in what three parts of performing a notarial act?

_____

_____

_____

_____

▼

6. What are three alternatives to notarization of a document by a Notary who cannot understand the language in which it is written?

_____

_____

_____

7. Complete the journal entry and notarial certificate for the following notarization.

Today at this time, a translator named Juan A. Martinez appears before you to sign and swear to a translator's declaration that is attached to an English-language translation of the Guatemalan birth certificate of a man named Jose Ruiz Rodriguez. You personally know Martinez, who resides at 8883 Hamilton Avenue in your town and zip code. You do not charge for the notarization. Complete the following journal entry:

	Month/Day/Year/Time of Notarization	Kind or Type of Notarization	Document Date (Month/Day/Year)	Document Kind or Type	Name and Address of Signer	
1						☐ Pers ☐ ID / ☐ C
						☐ Pe

Identification of Signer	Additional Information	Notary Fee	Signature of Signer	Right Thumbprint of Signer	
☐ Personally Known by the Notary ☐ ID Cards — Describe each card below ☐ Credible Witness(es) — Include signature of each witness				Top of thumb here	1
		x			
☐ Personally Known by the Notary					

8. Complete the following certificate for the same notarization:

Translator's Declaration

I declare that I made the attached English-language translation of the Guatemalan birth certificate of Jose Ruiz Rodriguez, which was in the Spanish language, and that to the best of my knowledge and belief it is an accurate and complete translation of its source document.

_____ (signature of affiant)

State of _____)

) SS.

County of _____)

Subscribed and sworn (affirmed) before me this _____ day of

_____, _____, by _____.

_____   L.S.

(Signature of Notary)

See pages 388–389 for correct responses.

CHAPTER 14

Meeting the Needs of Disabled Signers

Document signers with certain physical, learning or legal disabilities sometimes require special attention from Notaries. Some disabilities, such as those that physically prohibit a person from signing or impair an individual's understanding, may make notarization impossible. Others simply may require the Notary to apply special procedures.

TYPES OF DISABILITY

Generally speaking, there are three kinds of disability that might affect an individual's ability to sign a document and perform other actions necessary for a notarization: a physical disability, an intellectual disability or a legal disability.

A physical disability is one that prevents or inhibits writing (paralysis or a broken limb, for example) or impairs communication (as with seeing-, hearing- and speech-impaired signers).

An intellectual disability results either from illiteracy or a low IQ that can make signing or understanding a document difficult.

▼

A legal disability, including youthful age or proven insanity, can restrict or disqualify persons from signing on their own behalves.

SIGNATURE DIFFICULTIES

In all but a few states, Notaries may not perform notarizations for persons who are prevented by physical weakness or illiteracy from writing a signature or at least making a mark such as an "X" or a thumbprint. If a signer cannot write a signature but can make an "X" or leave a thumbprint — a procedure called a signature by mark — the document may be notarized.

In cases where a signer cannot even make a mark, some other arrangement may have to be made. Generally, a guardian, sometimes called a conservator, will be appointed by a court to handle the affairs of persons unable to sign or otherwise act on their own behalves.

The Notary does not have the authority to personally authorize or direct a disabled person to sign with a pen held in the mouth or to employ any other such extraordinary procedures. Only the person's attorney or another individual officially appointed to look after the person's legal affairs can sanction such procedures.

There are absolutely no circumstances where Notaries may allow another person to guide an individual's hand to "sign" a document. The signer may receive no assistance in making the signature.

> Individuals who cannot sign even by making a mark (an "X") usually must have a conservator appointed to handle their personal business affairs.

State Laws Vary

In a few states, Notaries have the authority to sign the name of a person who is unable to sign or make a mark. The disabled person must be competent, must personally appear before the Notary and must orally direct the Notary or a third party in the presence of the Notary to sign by proxy. In some states, a certificate of disability signed by the disabled person's physician must also accompany the document. This procedure helps disabled signers better handle their affairs.

Signature by Mark

When a signer, due to illiteracy or physical disability, cannot write a signature, he or she may sign by mark. However, if the signer can produce a legible signature, even if abnormal, such a signature is preferred, and the signature by mark is not necessary.

The customary mark is an "X," but other marks such as a thumbprint also may be acceptable. To be regarded as a signature under law, the mark must be witnessed by two persons.

Each witness should have no financial or beneficial interest in the document and actually must see the principal signer, or marker, make the mark on the document. An ideal witness must demonstrate honesty, awareness and impartiality. Generally, state laws allow a signer's relative to serve as a witness, but if the relative stands to gain or lose from the transaction, this person would not be an ideal witness.

The Notary need not personally know the two witnesses, nor is it necessary for the witnesses to personally know the signer by mark, but in both cases, there should be satisfactory evidence of identity.

The signature-by-mark witnesses sign the document near the principal's mark, and one witness also prints the signer's name next to the mark. Sometimes the words "his (or her) mark" also are included. The same procedure is followed for the journal signature: the principal signs with a mark, the two witnesses also sign, and one witness writes the marker's name near the mark. An example of this procedure follows:

> To be notarized, a signature by mark also requires the signatures of two witnesses. The Notary should not be one of these two witnesses.

X   mark of Karen A. Schulman   *John R. Burns*, witness
                                 Pat R. Jones, witness

NNA Recommendation

Though laws in some states allow the Notary to serve as one of the two required witnesses to a signature by mark, the National Notary Association strongly recommends that the Notary not be used as one of the two witnesses. This prevents confusion about the Notary's role.

The signature-by-mark witnesses' addresses should be recorded in the additional information column of the Notary journal, if space allows. Otherwise, additional journal-entry lines may be used to accommodate such information.

Because a mark witnessed by two persons is regarded as a signature under law, no special acknowledgment certificate need be used. Many Notaries, though, prefer to use special-purpose signature-by-mark forms that state the names and addresses of the witnesses who have signed the document. A typical signature-by-mark acknowledgment form follows:

State of _____)
) SS.
County of _____)

On this the _____ day of _____ (month), _____ (year), before me, the undersigned Notary Public, personally appeared _____ (name of signer by mark), personally known to me (proved to me on the basis of satisfactory evidence) to be the person who made and acknowledged his/her mark on the within instrument in my presence and in the presence of the two persons indicated below who have signed the within instrument as witnesses, one of whom, _____ (name of witness who writes signer by mark's name), also wrote the name of the signer by mark near the mark.

Witness my hand and official seal.

_____ (signature and seal of Notary)

_____ (first witness's name)
_____ (first witness's address)

_____ (second witness's name)
_____ (second witness's address)

IMPAIRED COMMUNICATION

There must be direct communication between the Notary and signer.

Just as with foreign-speaking signers, if the document signer cannot communicate directly with the Notary due to a hearing, speech and/or sight impairment, the Notary may not perform a notarial act for that person. Communication between signer and Notary may be achieved through written notes, lipreading, sign language or other means, but it must be direct. A third party may not serve as an interpreter.

Blindness

With a blind signer, the Notary should proceed carefully because there exists a potential for fraud. The sightless person may have been misled about the contents of a document he or she cannot see or read.

The Notary must determine whether the documents presented by blind persons are the ones they intend to sign. One way of doing this is to ask the individual to explain the document's purpose. If the individual is unsure of the purpose, the Notary may have to read — but not explain — the document to the signer.

Hearing- and Speech-Impaired Signers

Hearing- and speech-impaired document signers must communicate their willingness and awareness sufficiently to the Notary and, in the case of a jurat, indicate compliance with the oath or affirmation.

Many hearing-impaired signers read lips and speak clearly or communicate through written notes. A personal computer may prove helpful to the Notary in communication with a hearing- or speech-impaired signer and even can be used to administer required oaths.

Through limited speech, lipreading, written notes, gestures or any combination of these, most hearing- and speech-impaired signers are able to communicate with another person. If the Notary happens to be conversant in sign language, this would certainly help.

Once the Notary establishes the signer's understanding and awareness, and any special accommodations are noted in the Notary's journal, notarizations for the seeing-, hearing- and speech-impaired may be performed using regular notarial certificates.

AWARENESS

While the disabled signer may have certain physical or intellectual limitations, simply having a disability does not mean that the signer is uncomprehending. A disability does not mean a person cannot handle his or her personal affairs, sign documents and have a signature notarized. Disabled persons have legal rights as well as a legitimate need to execute legal documents, like any other person. However, some intellectual and legal disabilities may be associated with a lack of comprehension.

A disability might affect awareness, but the Notary must not assume that disabled persons are unable to comprehend.

Intellectual Disabilities

Certain mental conditions that are inborn or caused by accident or illness may deprive an individual of the judgment needed to handle his or her own legal affairs in a responsible manner. Such persons may be in the custody of an institution or guardian who has court-given powers to act on behalf of the mentally dysfunctional person.

Legal Disabilities

Signers who possess what is termed a legal disability are considered "incompetent" due to disqualifications imposed by law. Minors and those proven in court to be insane are considered legally disabled and are restricted or disqualified from signing for themselves. Being below legal age is by far the most common cause of legal incompetence and is the subject of the following chapter.

Determining Awareness of Disabled Signers

Determining the awareness of a disabled signer is done the same way as with any signer. As we learned in Chapter 5, the best tactic when confronted with any individual of questionable mental ability is to engage the person in simple conversation. It then should become apparent whether the person is capable of understanding the transaction and is a willing party to it.

Experts, such as the signer's physician or attorney, also may be consulted to determine awareness. If such an expert indicates a signer is comprehending, the Notary may proceed. (The expert's remarks should be recorded in the notarial journal.) However, the Notary always has the final determination whether to proceed with a notarization. If the comments of a physician or attorney about a signer's awareness are at odds with the Notary's personal observations and with common sense, the Notary must not proceed.

SUMMARY

Signers with certain physical, learning or legal disabilities sometimes require the Notary to use special procedures. Disabilities that physically prevent a person from signing or impair an individual's comprehension may make notarization impossible.

Three types of disability might affect a person's ability to sign a document and perform other actions necessary for a notarization. First, a physical disability that prevents or inhibits writing (paralysis or a broken limb, for example) or impairs communication (blindness, deafness, or muteness). Second, an intellectual disability such as lack of education (illiteracy) or intellectual incapacity (low IQ). Third, a legal disability, such as being under legal age or of proven insanity.

In all but a few states, Notaries may not perform notarizations for persons who cannot write their signatures or at least make a mark, such as an "X" or a thumbprint. If a signer cannot write a signature but can make an "X" or leave a thumbprint — which is called a signature by mark — the document may be notarized.

If a signer cannot make a mark, a guardian or conservator, may have to be appointed by a court to handle the signer's affairs. Notaries may not authorize a disabled person to sign using extraordinary procedures such as a pen held in the mouth, and Notaries may not allow another person to guide an individual's hand to "sign" a document. ■

IMPORTANT TERMS

Awareness: Being able to understand a document's significance.

Conservator: Guardian; person with the lawful power and duty to manage the affairs of another individual.

Disability: Physical, intellectual or legal condition that renders one incapable of performing certain functions such as writing, communicating and handling one's own affairs.

Guardian: Person with the lawful power and duty to manage the affairs of another individual; conservator.

Illiteracy: Inability to read and write.

Intellectual Disability: Incapacitating mental condition resulting either from lack of education (illiteracy) or intellectual incapacity (low IQ), that can make signing or understanding a document impossible.

IQ: Intelligence quotient; measure of intelligence.

Legal Disability: Legal status, including being under legal age or of proven insanity, that can restrict or disqualify persons from signing on their own behalves.

Marker: One who signs by mark.

Physical Disability: Incapacitating physical condition that can prevent writing (paralysis or a broken arm, for example) or impair communication (blindness, deafness).

Signature by Mark: An "X" or other symbol made in place of a signature by a person unable to write and witnessed by a Notary and two other persons.

Signature by Proxy: Signature made on behalf of a principal by a Notary or third party who is not an attorney in fact. Notary signatures by proxy are allowed only in a few states.

CHAPTER 14 TEST

In each blank, write the response — a, b, c or d — that best completes each of the following statements:

1. Document signers with disabilities _____.

    a. Cannot handle their affairs, so their signatures cannot be notarized.

    b. Sometimes require the Notary to employ special procedures.

    c. Make notarization impossible, so Notaries must refuse service.

    d. Have legal rights like every other person, so Notaries must always perform the requested act.

2. When a person cannot write a signature, the Notary _____.

    a. May allow another person to guide the individual's hand to sign the document, with appropriate witnesses.

    b. May instruct the person to sign with a pen held in the mouth.

    c. Must sign the document "by proxy" for the person.

    d. May notarize a signature by mark, with appropriate witnesses.

3. A signature-by-mark notarization involves _____.

    a. Two witnesses, including a Notary.

    b. Two Notaries, in addition to a witness.

    c. Two witnesses, in addition to the Notary.

    d. Two witnesses, in place of the Notary.

4. With a blind signer, the Notary should proceed carefully because _____.

    a. Sightless persons usually are not capable of acting responsibly.

    b. A potential for fraud exists.

    c. The blind are usually misled about the contents of a document.

    d. The Notary must read and explain the document to a blind signer.

5. A hearing-impaired document signer _____.

    a. Must communicate directly with the Notary through lip reading, sign language or written notes.

    b. Must communicate with the Notary through a third person.

    c. Must bring a court-appointed translator to ensure accurate communication.

    d. Must provide a certificate of comprehension, signed by a doctor.

6. Notarizations for disabled signers _____.

    a. Must be performed using special notarial certificates.

    b. Can be refused if there are not two witnesses.

    c. May be performed using regular notarial certificates.

    d. Must be performed using jurat certificates but not acknowledgments.

Complete the journal entry for the following notarization.

7. Today at this time, you visit a longtime friend, Marcel I. Benoit, in the hospital. You have been asked to take Mr. Benoit's acknowledgment on a power of attorney document giving his daughter, Rebecca Ross, authority to handle his affairs. Mr. Benoit has suffered a stroke and is unable to sign his name. However, he is able to make an "X." Available to witness Mr. Benoit's mark are Ms. Ross (residing at 5171 Dante Court in your city and zip code); her husband, Trevor C. Ross; a family friend, Morris R. Taylor (128 Elm Lane in your city and zip code); a hospital employee, Christy A. Burns (721 7th Street in your city and zip code); and yourself. You must decide who are best suited to serve as witnesses. Mr. Benoit's address is 4723 Santa Rosa Street in your city and zip code. You do not charge a fee.

	Month/Day/Year/Time of Notarization	Kind or Type of Notarization	Document Date (Month/Day/Year)	Document Kind or Type	Name and Address of Signer	
1						☐ Per ☐ ID ☐ Cred
2						☐ Per ☐ ID ☐ C
						☐ Per

	Identification of Signer	Additional Information	Notary Fee	Signature of Signer	Right Thumbprint of Signer	
	☐ Personally Known by the Notary ☐ ID Cards — Describe each card below ☐ Credible Witness(es) — Include signature of each witness			x	Top of thumb here	1
	☐ Personally Known by the Notary ☐ ID Cards — Describe each card below ☐ Credible Witness(es) — Include signature of each witness			x	Top of thumb here	2
	☐ Personally Known by the Notary					

See page 389 for correct responses.

CHAPTER 15

Notarizing for Minors

LEGAL AGE

In general, persons must reach the age of majority (18 to 21 years of age, depending on state law) in order to exercise all normal legal rights. Those under the legal age are called minors and are not considered "legally competent" to handle their own legal affairs, sign documents, contracts and deeds, or to conduct business for themselves. To put this in perspective with the preceding chapter, minors have a legal disability that disqualifies them from signing documents for themselves.

Usually a parent or guardian will sign for a minor.

Normally, parents or court-appointed guardians must sign on a minor's behalf. In certain rare instances, however, minors may lawfully sign documents and have their signatures notarized. Such circumstances would include minors approved by a court as reliable witnesses (who might sign affidavits and depositions) and emancipated minors engaged in business (who may sign valid contracts). An emancipated minor is an adolescent freed from the control and responsibility of his or her parents.

CONCERNS FOR THE NOTARY

A Notary should be particularly aware of the problems presented by younger signers. A Notary should not necessarily refuse to notarize for a minor, if the youth presents adequate identification, appears aware and willing to sign, and can satisfy the Notary's inquiries about having the authority to sign.

Identifying Minor Signers

What often poses the greatest problem in notarizing for minors is determining their identity.

The Notary identifies a minor using the same methods as for an adult: either personal knowledge, credible identifying witness(es) or identification documents. Since a minor signer may not be old enough to obtain a driver's license and may not possess any other type of acceptable identification document, such as a passport, identification must usually be based either on the Notary's own personal knowledge of the minor's identity or on a credible identifying witness (or witnesses) who can vouch for the identity of the minor signer.

Because credible identifying witnesses should be impartial and unaffected by the document, parents and other relatives should not be used to identify their own children or family members. Impartial means that the credible identifying witness should neither have a financial interest in the document nor be named in or affected by it. Usually, a parent will have a direct interest in any document his or her child may sign.

Determining Willingness and Awareness

Determining willingness and awareness for a minor signer is done in the same way as for an adult.

To determine a minor's willingness to sign, the Notary should simply ask the minor if he or she has signed or is about to sign the document voluntarily and then observe the minor's demeanor. In some situations, asking an influential third party, such as a parent, to leave the room during the notarization may assist the Notary in determining the minor signer's willingness. If the Notary suspects that the minor is being forced to sign, the Notary should refuse to perform the notarization.

Identifying a minor signer is just like identifying an adult. The problem often is that minors may not have suitable identification for notarization purposes.

The simple test for awareness, you will remember, is to engage the signer in a conversation about the document. If the minor can communicate coherently with the Notary about the purpose of the document, the Notary may consider the signer aware and comprehending. However, if the signer is unable to respond intelligibly to a Notary's basic questions, the Notary should refuse to notarize. Experts, such as the minor's attorney, also may be consulted to determine awareness. If an expert says the minor signer is aware, the Notary usually may proceed, recording the expert's remarks in the notarial journal.

Authority to Sign

The Notary should make a reasonable effort to determine that the minor does have the authority to sign the document presented for notarization. This can be accomplished by asking the minor (as well as any adult present) what agency or person directed the minor to sign. It also may be prudent and useful to ask if the agency or person accepting the document is aware that the signer is not of legal age and if the person or agency will accept a minor's signature.

NNA Recommendation

To alert a document's recipient to the signer's age, it is a good idea to require minor signers to write their ages after their signatures. The Notary is not required to verify the minor signer's age.

SUMMARY

Minors are generally considered "legally incompetent." To handle one's own affairs and sign contracts, deeds and other documents, a person must typically reach legal age — 18 to 21 years of age, depending on the state. Otherwise, it is usually a parent or guardian who signs for a minor.

In some situations, minors may lawfully sign documents and have their signatures notarized. If a minor presents valid identification, appears aware and willing to sign and can satisfy the Notary about having the authority to sign, the Notary may perform the notarization.

Often, identification poses a problem for minors. Since a minor may not possess any type of acceptable ID such as a driver's license or passport, identification must usually be based on personal knowledge or credible identifying witness(es).

To determine a minor's willingness to sign, the Notary asks if the minor has signed or is about to sign the document voluntarily and observes the youth's demeanor. The simple test for awareness is to engage the signer in a conversation about the document. If the minor can communicate coherently about the purpose of the document, the Notary may consider the signer aware and comprehending.

The Notary also should question the minor (as well as any adult present) about having the authority to sign. ■

IMPORTANT TERMS

Age of Majority: Age at which persons can exercise all normal legal rights — varying from 18 to 21 years, depending on state law. Also called legal age.

Awareness: Being able to understand a document's significance.

Emancipated Minor: Person under the age of majority who has been freed from the control and responsibility of his or her parents, usually applying to adolescents who leave the parents' household by agreement.

Guardian: Person with the lawful power and duty to manage the affairs of another individual.

Legal Age: Age of majority.

Minor: Person under the age of majority.

Natural Guardian: Parent of a child.

CHAPTER 15 TEST

In each blank, write the response — a, b, c or d — that best completes each of the following statements:

1. Normally, to sign contracts and legal documents, one must _____.

    a. Reach the age of majority.

    b. Be a citizen of the United States.

    c. Possess a state-issued driver's license.

    d. Be registered to vote.

2. A Notary should _____ refuse to notarize for a minor, if the youth is aware and willing to sign, has authority to sign, and presents adequate identification.

    a. Normally.

    b. Always.

    c. Never.

    d. Not necessarily.

3. Normally, the greatest problem in performing notarial acts for signers who are minors is determining _____.

    a. Their willingness and awareness.

    b. Their identity.

    c. Their authority to sign.

    d. Their age.

4. A Notary should require a minor to write his or her _____ next to the document signature.

    a. Parents' names and addresses.

    b. Social Security number.

    c. Age.

    d. School.

5. The ideal credible identifying witnesses for identifying minor signers are _____.

    a. Nonrelatives who are unaffected by the document.

    b. Their own parents.

    c. Relatives who are unaffected by the document.

    d. Other minors.

6. Minors have a _____ that may disqualify them from signing documents on their own behalf.

    a. Mental disability.

    b. Legal disability.

    c. Maturity disability.

    d. Physical disability.

See page 389 for correct responses.

CHAPTER 16

Troublesome Documents

Certain documents commonly pose questions for Notaries that are generally not answered by state laws and rarely are addressed by handbooks provided by Notary-regulating officials.

Such questions can arise with any document presented for notarization that has missing or incomplete parts, is a photocopy, or bears a signature that differs from the name on the signer's identification. In addition, two particular document types — wills and immigration papers — cause Notaries dilemmas.

INCOMPLETE OR BLANK DOCUMENTS

Documents should not be notarized unless they are complete and have no blank spaces. Notarizing an incomplete or blank document is a very bad idea. In fact, laws in several states (California, Colorado and Florida) explicitly prohibit a Notary from doing so, and officials in many other states discourage the practice. In New York, an Attorney General's opinion (No. 319, of 1939) holds that notarizing an incomplete or blank document is improper.

Common sense would prevent most Notaries from notarizing a

Documents with unfilled blanks or that are incomplete should not be notarized.

signature on a completely blank sheet of paper, because a fraudulent document later could be created on the sheet above the notarial certificate. Also, it would be impossible to make a journal record of a document without such features as a title or date.

Notaries would be wise to regard the signing of a certificate on a blank or incomplete document just like the signing of a blank or incomplete bank check. In both cases, it is asking for trouble.

What Makes a Document Complete?

To be considered complete, a document must have three elements:

1. A statement by the signer. This personal written statement forms the document's text and details terms with which the signer has agreed.

2. A signature. The signature indicates the signer's agreement with and willingness to be obligated by the terms of the document text.

3. A notarial certificate. This wording describes the facts the Notary is requested to certify.

Incomplete Text

Documents that are complete except for blank spaces that will be filled in later also have great potential for fraudulent misuse. A borrower, for example, might sign an incomplete promissory note, trusting the lender to fill it out, and then later find that the lender has written in twice the amount actually borrowed or twice the agreed interest rate. Incomplete spaces are a danger for the document signer, who may be victimized; and for the Notary, who may be required to testify in a subsequent lawsuit.

Ironically, the signer who is the potential victim often insists that an incomplete document be notarized. It may be inconvenient to obtain data needed to complete the document and the signer may decide to "get the notarization out of the way first."

The prudent Notary will decline to notarize a blank sheet of paper and ask any signer to fill in the blank spaces of an incomplete document before notarizing. If the spaces are inapplicable and intended to be left blank, the signer should be asked to line through each space in ink or write "Not Applicable" or "N/A" in the blank.

Acceptable Blanks

In rare situations, a space may be left blank. Documents requiring multiple signers and adoption papers requiring confidentiality are examples.

On rare occasions, there may be an acceptable reason for leaving a space blank on a notarized document. Sometimes, for example, a paper requiring more than one signature must be circulated to collect the separate signatures and notarial certificates. Such a document's "Date of Signing" space may be left blank until the final signature is affixed. On any such occasion, a Notary should record in the journal the reason the space was left blank.

In addition, to preserve confidentiality in adoptions, it is generally acceptable for the names of birth mothers or adoptive parents to be filled in after certain adoption forms are signed and notarized.

A recordable document should not be regarded as incomplete just because the box labeled "Reserved For Use By Recorder" has not been filled out. This information only can be completed after the notarized paper has been recorded. Also, large recordable parcel maps may include several separate documents on the same sheet of paper (such as, Statement by Purchaser or Statement by Surveyor). These may be signed and notarized separately, even though other documents (or statements) printed on the same sheet have not been completed.

Photographs, Birth Certificates, Checks, Artistic Works

Signers sometimes request notarization of papers that do not have all of the three necessary elements. For example, Notaries at times are asked to "notarize a photograph," in order to identify the person in the picture. However, a photograph by itself has neither a signer's personal statement, a signature nor a notarial certificate and should not be notarized.

Some individuals sign a copy of their birth certificate and request notarization in an attempt to prove U.S. citizenship. However, such a document should not be notarized because two elements, the personal statement and notarial certificate, are missing. This is also true of signatures on the back of bank checks or on paintings.

Sometimes persons will try to protect their rights to inventions or artistic works, such as songs and plays, by asking a Notary to sign, seal and date their design plans or actual creations. In these cases, all three necessary elements may be missing. A Notary's signature and seal without jurat, acknowledgment or other appropriate wording do not constitute a certificate. Persons wishing to protect their ownership of an invention should contact a patent attorney or the U.S. Patent and Trademark Office in Washington, D.C. Similarly, those who want to protect their right of authorship to a literary work should contact a copyright attorney or the U.S. Copyright Office, also in Washington, D.C.

PHOTOCOPIES AND FAXES

Photocopies may be notarized so long as the signature is original and not a copy.

A photocopy or fax copy may be notarized if its signature is original and not itself photocopied. That is, the signer must have signed the photocopy or fax with pen and ink. A photocopied or faxed copy of a signature may never be notarized.

However, public recorders sometimes will not accept notarized photocopies because they will not adequately reproduce in microfilming.

Since many faxed documents fade, it is suggested that they be photocopied and then the photocopy signed and notarized.

It is usually not a good idea to notarize a carbon copy, since the carbon writing may be brushed off later and replaced with unauthorized writing. (See "Conformed Copies" in Chapter 10, page 158.)

WILLS

Wills should be notarized only if instructions and a notarial certificate are provided.

Wills are such sensitive and important documents that there are certain dangers for Notaries who execute them. Some holographic (handwritten) wills may be invalidated by notarization. Notaries who make the mistake of helping prepare a will may be sued by would-be or dissatisfied heirs. (See "Unauthorized Practice of Law" in Chapter 19, page 268.)

A document presented to a Notary as a will should be notarized only if clear instructions and a notarial certificate are provided for the Notary. Ideally, the signer should be following the precise directions of an attorney.

Often, misguided individuals will prepare their own wills and bring them to Notaries to have them "legalized." They will depend on the Notaries to know what kind of notarization is appropriate. Of course, Notaries have no authority to offer such advice. Whether notarized or not, these supposed "wills" may be worthless.

In many states, notarization of a will is rarely done and is unnecessary if other witnessing procedures are used. In some states, wills don't need to be notarized at all. Often, it is not the signature of the testator or testatrix (maker of the will) that must be notarized, but the signatures of witnesses on affidavits appended to the will.

Living Wills

Documents popularly called living wills may be notarized without the special attention required by wills. Living wills are not actually wills but written statements of a signer's wishes concerning medical treatment in the event the signer has an illness or injury and is unable to give instructions on his or her own behalf.

IMMIGRATION DOCUMENTS

Many Notaries are reluctant to notarize documents issued by or filed with the U.S. Citizenship and Immigration Services due to concern about the severe penalties for photocopying naturalization certificates and a few other critical USCIS forms. This reluctance is unfounded, however, and there are no laws that prohibit the notarization of immigration documents.

Immigration forms may be notarized, but naturalization certificates may not be photocopied.

The most common USCIS forms that a Notary may be requested to notarize are the Affidavit of Support (Form I-134/I-864) and certain other nonstandard documents, such as translators' declarations, that may be submitted in support of USCIS petitions. All may be notarized.

Another commonly seen USCIS document that must be notarized is Form I-171H, needed for the preapproval of an orphan visa. The National Notary Association recommends that only experienced Notaries who customarily work with agencies specializing with international adoptions notarize these forms, because a missing or incomplete document in the adoption dossier can jeopardize the adoption. In addition, this form does not include notarial wording, so the signer, adoption agency or attorney must provide wording or instruct the Notary as to the type of notarization (acknowledgment or jurat) to perform. Signers asking the Notary questions should be directed to their adoption agency or attorney for answers.

SIGNATURE AND IDENTIFICATION DISCREPANCIES

Notaries occasionally are asked to notarize a document bearing a signed name that differs from the name on the signer's current identification document.

This is not unusual. People commonly change their names legally due to marriage, divorce or other reasons, and some use casual or formal variations of their names for different circumstances. For example, the driver's license presented to the Notary may say "Sandra A. Williams" (the signer's current married name), but the document requires "Sandra A. Buchanan" (her maiden name). Or, the Notary (or credible identifying witnesses) may personally know the signer as "Gayle McGuire" (the name she commonly uses), but the document calls for the signature of "Patricia Gayle McGuire" (her full, legal name).

To prevent invalidation or rejection of a document, a Notary must pay particular attention to the signed name that is being notarized. While a signer may be directed by an escrow or title company to sign a former name on a real estate document, the Notary must be able to identify the signer by the name that is signed on the document. This is the Notary's challenge with signature and ID discrepancies.

In cases where the document name and ID name do not agree, to perform the notarization, the Notary must either: 1) determine if the difference is acceptable; 2) have the signer provide additional identification; or 3) have the signer sign with "AKA" ("also known as"). If none of these three solutions can be met or is satisfactory, then the Notary has no choice but to refuse to perform the notarial act.

Acceptable Differences — Less but Not More

Some signature and ID name discrepancies are acceptable for the purposes of notarization. But the Notary must not allow the signer to take excessive liberties with the differences.

When the names on the document and on the ID differ, the Notary should first apply the less-but-not-more test first outlined in Chapter 4. Under this test, the signature name required on the document may be less, but not more, than the name appearing on the ID (or by which the Notary or credible identifying witnesses know the signer). In addition, the names may not be substantially different. If, for example, the ID name reads "John David Hunt," the Notary might accept a signature using certain abbreviations, such as "John D. Hunt," "J.D. Hunt" and "John Hunt." However, if the ID name reads merely "John D. Hunt," the Notary should not accept the signature "John David Hunt," since "D" could stand for a multitude of other names (Donald, Dale, Duane, etc.).

Following are examples of acceptable and unacceptable document and ID name differences:

The signature may be shorter (less) than the name on the ID, but it may not be longer (more).

ACCEPTABLE

Name on Document/Signature	Name on ID
Kevin J. White	Kevin James White
M. E. Kohl	Marissa Ellen Kohl
Pat Johnson	Patricia Johnson
Roberta E. Sanchez	Roberta E. Sanchez-Lopes

UNACCEPTABLE

Name on Document/Signature	Name on ID
David Edward Bernstine	David E. Bernstine
Jane K. Douglas-Smith	Jane K. Douglas
Byron John Burns, III	Byron John Burns
Cynthia Anne Greene	Cynthia Anne Summers
Charlie Kim	Chan Ho Kim

It is not unheard of for unscrupulous persons to exploit name similarities to steal valuable property. The victim sometimes will be the exploiter's similarly named parent, son or daughter. Thus, suffixes such as "III" and "Jr." should not be ignored. The safest policy for the Notary is to insert on the notarial certificate the exact full name appearing on the ID, allowing the less-but-not-more rule to apply to the signed name.

If the name differences are substantial and do not pass the

less-but-not-more test, the next step is for the Notary to ask for some form of alternate identification to verify the name as required by the document or to have the person sign using "AKA" or "also known as."

Additional Identification

In some cases, the signer may be able to provide some other form of additional, acceptable identification that agrees with the name as it appears on the document. For instance, if the signer's driver's license name is different than the name on the document, perhaps credible identifying witnesses might know and be able to identify the signer by the document name. Or maybe the signer's passport has the same name as the document while the more recent driver's license does not.

AKA — Also Known As

Another solution for document and ID name discrepancies is for the signer to sign both names, linking the two with the phrase "also known as," "AKA" or other wording to that effect. First, the signer signs the document using the name as it appears on the ID, next writes "AKA," and then signs the name as required on the document. The Notary notarizes only the name that appears on the ID, and this is the only name that appears on the notarial certificate, since this name is the only one which can be proven to the Notary. Typically, the signature format would be as follows:

> Beverly C. Peterson, also known as Beverly C. Eisman

Or this alternate:

> Beverly C. Peterson, AKA Beverly C. Eisman

Or this alternate:

> Beverly C. Peterson, who took title to property in the name of Beverly C. Eisman

Signing both the document name and the ID name linked by "AKA," the signer satisfies the requirements of the document as well as of the Notary.

A similar procedure can be used when the signer wants to use a professional name in addition to the real name. Here, the phrase "professionally known as" ("PKA") would replace "AKA."

When two names are signed, it is critical that the Notary only print the ID name in the blank space on the notarial certificate ("...personally appeared before me _____, who acknowledged..."), because that is the only name the Notary can verify through the identifying document. Unless the signer is personally known to the Notary by both names, it is the signer who must link the two names when signing the document, not the Notary when completing the certificate.

In general, signers can write any other name or title (Treasurer, Vice President, etc.) they want after their signatures, but the Notary's certificate must bear only documented names and titles that appear on the signer's ID. And a Notary cannot advise a signer to use "AKA."

Important

The signer should check with the document's receiving agency to make sure that the use of "AKA" or "PKA" is acceptable. Some agencies may not accept the document signed in this manner. If not, the only options to the signer are either to locate a Notary who can identify the signer in the required name through personal knowledge or to bring a credible identifying witness to the Notary to verify the name.

SUMMARY

Blank or incomplete documents, photocopies, wills, immigration papers and documents with name discrepancies can cause dilemmas for Notaries that generally are not addressed in state laws.

Documents should not be notarized unless they are complete and have no blank spaces. The Notary should ask the signer to fill in the blank spaces of an incomplete document. If the spaces are intended to be left blank, the signer should be asked to line through each space or write "Not Applicable" or "N/A" in the blank. In rare cases, it may be acceptable to leave a space blank on a notarized document. For example, when a document needing multiple signatures needs to be routed for individual signing and notarization, the "Date of Signing" space may be left blank until the final signature is affixed.

Signers sometimes request notarization of documents that do not have all three necessary elements — a signer's personal statement, a signature and a notarial certificate. Thus, a photograph, birth certificate, check, design or work of art should not be notarized.

A photocopied or faxed document may be notarized if its signature is original and not itself copied. It usually is not a good idea to notarize a carbon copy, since the carbon writing may later be brushed off and replaced with unauthorized writing.

Wills should be notarized only if clear instructions and a notarial certificate are provided. Ideally, the signer should be following the directions of an attorney. Some individuals draft their own wills and depend on Notaries to know how to proceed. Notaries have no authority to offer such advice. Wills are sensitive documents, and some actually may be invalidated by notarization. Notaries who make the mistake of helping prepare a will may be sued by dissatisfied heirs.

There are no laws that prohibit the notarization of immigration documents. The most common U.S. Citizenship and Immigration Services forms that a Notary may be requested to notarize are the Affidavit of Support (Form I-134/I-864) and certain nonstandard documents that may be submitted in support of USCIS petitions, such as translators' declarations.

Notaries occasionally are asked to notarize a document that requires a person to sign with a name that differs from the name on the signer's current identification documents. The signature name required on a document may be less, but not more, than the name appearing on the ID, and the names may not be substantially different. In some cases, the signer may be able to provide another form of additional identification that agrees with the name as on the document. Another solution is for the signer to sign both names, linking the two with the phrase "also known as," "AKA" or other wording. But a Notary cannot advise a signer to do this. ∎

IMPORTANT TERMS

AKA: Abbreviation for also known as; otherwise named.

Holographic: Handwritten.

Immigration: Entering a country to become a legal resident, permanent or temporary.

Living Will: Written statement of a person's wishes concerning medical treatment in the event the signer has an illness or injury and is unable to give instructions on his or her own behalf.

N.A.: Not applicable. Also "NA" or "N/A."

Naturalization: Becoming a citizen.

PKA: Abbreviation for professionally known as; name one uses for professional business purposes; professional alias.

Testator, Testatrix: Maker of a will. Testator is male; testatrix is female.

U.S. Citizenship and Immigration Services, USCIS: U.S. government agency having authority over immigration.

Will: Legal document containing a person's wishes about disposition of personal property after death; short for last will and testament.

CHAPTER 16 TEST

In each blank, write the response — a, b, c or d — that best completes each of the following statements:

1. Blank spaces on a document _____.

   a. Need not concern the Notary.

   b. Make notarization illegal.

   c. Should be completed or lined through by the signer in most instances.

   d. Are acceptable if noted in the journal.

2. To be notarized, a document must have _____.

   a. A statement by the signer, a signature and a notarial certificate.

   b. A statement by the signer and a signature.

   c. A statement by the signer and a notarial certificate.

   d. A signature and a notarial certificate.

3. An acceptable blank space on a document submitted for notarization might be _____.

   a. The address of property on a deed.

   b. Personal financial information.

   c. The date of signing on a document with multiple signers.

   d. The yet-to-be-determined interest rate on a variable-rate mortgage.

4. A photocopy may be notarized only if _____.

   a. The Notary has made the photocopy.

   b. The photocopy has been conformed.

   c. Its signature is a photocopy and not an original.

   d. Its signature is an original and not a photocopy.

5. Valid wills _____.

   a. Require notarization without exception.

   b. If handwritten, may be invalidated by notarization.

   c. Are any notarized document stating the wishes of a testator.

   d. Are never notarized.

6. Notarization of immigration documents _____.

    a. Is authorized in some cases.

    b. Is permitted only for naturalization certificates.

    c. Carries severe criminal penalties.

    d. Is never necessary.

7. A person identified as M. Jean Trudeau may sign and have his signature notarized as _____.

    a. Marcel J. Trudeau.

    b. M.J. Trudeau.

    c. Marcel Jean Trudeau.

    d. M. John Trudeau

8. A common solution when document and ID names differ is for the signer to _____.

    a. Sign both names linking the two with the phrase "also known as."

    b. Submit the document without notarization.

    c. Sign both names and have the Notary notarize both.

    d. Return the document unsigned.

9. With an AKA signature, the Notary notarizes _____.

    a. The undocumented name first and the identification name second.

    b. The identification name first and the undocumented name second.

    c. Only the undocumented name.

    d. Only the identification name.

Explain in your own words:

10. Why should Notaries not notarize wills without clear instructions and a notarial certificate provided?

_____

_____

_____

See page 390 for correct responses.

CHAPTER 17

Accommodating the Recorder

ADAPTING TO THE REQUIREMENTS

Notarization is an important step leading to the public recording of deeds and other valuable documents. When such papers are placed in the public record, the rights of private individuals, particularly in regard to ownership of real property, are safeguarded.

In notarizing documents and in performing certain other statutory duties, Notaries often have to adapt to the requirements of public recording officials.

Usually, recording documents is the responsibility of a county official called a recorder, registrar or auditor. Like the Notary, a recorder is a ministerial officer who must follow written rules closely. These rules dictate the type and format of documents that may be recorded and may vary from state to state and county to county.

Since notarization is necessary to record a document in the public record, the Notary and signer must be concerned with the requirements of the recording official or the document may be rejected.

Averting Document Rejection

A recorder cannot accept deeds or certain other signed documents unless they have been acknowledged before a Notary or other official with notarial powers first. The recorder relies on the Notary to verify that a document's signature is genuine. If the Notary does not properly complete the notarization or if there are significant discrepancies, the recorder has no choice but to reject the filing of the document.

Four problems commonly cause recorders to reject notarized documents: an improper seal impression, an improper signature, an improper notarial certificate and improperly made corrections.

Improper Seal Impression

Missing, illegible (unreadable), overprinted and expired notarial seals are the most frequent causes of document rejection. Even a legible seal impression can be unacceptable if it is stamped over wording. Notaries never should touch up an illegible impression with pen and ink, as this is a certain cause for rejection by many recorders. If a seal impression is unreadable, another impression that is readable should be affixed nearby. When there is no room for another impression, a loose notarial certificate may have to be attached.

Improper Signature

A missing signature of the Notary or document signer is a common cause for document rejection, as is a signature that differs from the Notary's name in the seal or from the signer's name in the document text or notarial certificate.

Sometimes, a person with a new name will be required to sign a deed or other property conveyance paper in a former name. As discussed in the previous chapter, one possible solution for such signers is to find a Notary or credible identifying witness who personally knows them by both names. Another solution allowed by recorders in most states is for the Notary to write the signer's present new name (the one the Notary can identify the signer by) on the notarial certificate, while the signer signs this present name on the document and adds after the signature "also known as (former name)" or "who took title as (former name)."

Improper Notarial Certificate

Notarial certificate wording that is not appropriate for the particular notarial act or that does not comply with state requirements is another cause for document rejection. If the wording included on the document is not appropriate or does not comply with state law, the Notary may be asked to correct the wording or attach a loose notarial certificate containing the correct wording.

Inappropriate or improperly completed notarial certificates often prompt recorders to reject documents. When, for example, a person has signed a deed as a corporate officer, the deed will not be accepted for recording if it bears an acknowledgment certificate for an individual. Notarial certificates with dates preceding the document's date of signing also may cause rejection of the document, as may changes to a certificate not initialed by the Notary and/or in writing different from the Notary's.

Improper Corrections

Improperly made corrections on the document or notarial certificate frequently cause rejection of a document. In general, correction fluid, nontransparent tape or any material that would cover up wording should not be used on a recordable document or its notarial certificate, since recorders may be suspicious about what was covered.

Whenever a Notary corrects any wording in a notarial certificate (such as the wrong venue) or a signer corrects any wording in a document, the following steps should be taken, using dark ink:

- Line or type through the incorrect wording;
- Print or type the correct wording above the line-out; and
- Initial and date the correction.

If excessive corrections or changes are necessary on a certificate, the Notary should consider starting over with a brand new certificate.

AUTHENTICATION

Authentication proves a Notary's authority.

When a notarized document is sent out of the state or out of the country, the recipient may require proof that the notarial signature and seal are genuine. This verification of the genuineness of the signature and seal of a Notary is called authentication or legalization.

The customary proof is a certificate of authority (also called a certificate of capacity, a certificate of prothonotary or a "flag"). It is issued and attached to the notarized document by the local or state official with custody of notarial bonds and oaths. This certificate states that the signature and seal on the document to which it is attached belong to a legitimate Notary.

Anyone wanting proof that a particular individual holds a notarial commission may request a certificate of authority from the official with custody of notarial bonds and oaths.

Documents Sent to Another State

Normally, for a document recipient elsewhere in the United States or its territories, a single certificate of authority from a county clerk, prothonotary or other designated local official is sufficient proof of a Notary's authority.

Obtaining the certificate of authority is the responsibility of the signer or document recipient, not the Notary. However, Notaries may have to direct signers to the certificate-issuing offices where their bonds and oaths are filed. Usually, anyone bearing a notarized document and paying the required fee can have a certificate of authority attached to the document. Sometimes this procedure may be carried out through the mail.

 State Laws Vary

Since authenticating procedures vary by state, the office of the Notary-regulating official for the Notary's state or a reference book such as the *U.S. Notary Reference Manual* (published by the National Notary Association) should be consulted for information on authentication procedures.

Documents Sent to Another Country

For a notarized document sent abroad, the authentication procedure may be quite complicated and time-consuming. It can involve attachment of as many as five or six separate certificates of authority, typically starting with the clerk of the Notary's county and continuing in succession to the state secretary of state, the U.S. Secretary of State, the particular foreign consulate in Washington, D.C., and finally to a ministry in the foreign nation. Each certificate validates the authenticity of the preceding one.

As can be imagined, this traditional process of chain certification often takes months. Many nations have devised shortcuts. For instance, in some American cities, foreign consulates may ask nearby Notaries for examples of their seals and signatures. The consulates may then refer signers of foreign-bound documents to these Notaries and, through the samples, authenticate the notarizations themselves, shortening the time of going through U.S. officials.

Important

Frequently, notarial certificates on documents notarized in the United States and sent abroad have been drafted in compliance with foreign notarial laws. Notaries should ensure that their state laws authorize them to perform notarial acts described in these certificates.

Apostilles

More than 90 nations, including the United States, participate in a treaty that streamlines authentication of notarized documents sent between any two of the participating nations. Called the *Hague Convention Abolishing the Requirement of Legalization for Foreign Public Documents*, this treaty permits one-step authentication through use of a standard certificate of authority called an *apostille* (French for "notation").

Designed state officials — the secretary of state in most cases — are authorized to attach an *apostille* to a foreign-bound notarized document as the only needed proof of a valid notarial commission. The attached *apostille*, which usually may be obtained through the mail, will be honored in any of the other nations subscribing to the Hague Convention.

As with authentication, procedures for obtaining *apostilles* vary from state to state. The office of the Notary-regulating official for the Notary's state or a reference such as the *U.S. Notary Reference Manual*

Apostilles streamline the authentication process between nations that have subscribed to the Hague Convention.

(published by the National Notary Association) should be consulted for instructions.

Nations participating in the Hague treaty are listed in Appendix 3, "Hague Convention Nations," on pages 379-380. Since this list of participating nations will change as time passes, up-to-date information about the Hague Convention may be obtained through the U.S. Department of State in Washington, D.C. (See page 379 for this address.)

SUMMARY

Notaries often have to adapt to the requirements of the public recording officials who are charged with safeguarding documents in the public record, particularly those documents regarding ownership of real property. A recorder cannot accept deeds or other signed documents unless they have been acknowledged before a Notary or other authorized official. If the Notary does not properly complete the notarization, the recorder will reject the document.

A missing, illegible, overprinted or expired notarial seal impression is the most frequent cause of document rejection. If a seal impression is unreadable, another should be affixed nearby. The recorder also may reject the document when the signature of the Notary or document signer is missing or is different than required. Notarial certificate wording that is not appropriate for the particular notarial act or that does not comply with state requirements is another cause for document rejection, as is an improperly completed notarial certificate. And corrections to the document or notarial certificate that are improperly made frequently cause rejection of a document. Correction fluid, nontransparent tape or any material that would cover up wording should not be used on a recordable document or its notarial certificate.

Documents sent out of state or to another country may require proof that the notarial signature and seal are genuine. This proof is called authentication or legalization. A certificate of authority is issued by the local or state official with custody of notarial bonds and oaths. Obtaining the certificate of authority is the responsibility of the signer or document recipient, not the Notary. Usually, anyone presenting a notarized document can obtain a certificate of authority.

For documents sent to other countries, the authentication procedure may involve attachment of as many as five or six certificates of authority from different government agencies, each validating the authenticity of the preceding one. The *Hague Convention Abolishing the Requirement of Legalization for Foreign Public Documents* simplifies this chain certification with a one-step process using a standard certificate of authority called an *apostille*. More than 90 nations abide by the treaty. Designated officials — usually the Secretary of State — in each U.S. state may issue *apostilles* to foreign-bound notarized documents as the only needed proof of a valid notarial commission. ■

IMPORTANT TERMS

Apostille: Certificate of authority required by Hague Convention on authentication that replaces a traditional chain of certificates of authority.

Authentication: Process of proving the genuineness of the signature and seal of a Notary or other official, usually through attachment of a certificate of authority.

Certificate of Authority: Paper stating that the signature and seal on an attached document belong to a legitimate Notary or other official.

Certificate of Capacity: Certificate of authority.

Certificate of Prothonotary: Certificate of authority issued by a prothonotary.

Chain Certification: Traditional authentication procedure that requires sequential attachment of certificates of authority, each validating the genuineness of the preceding one.

County Auditor: County Recorder, in some states.

County Clerk: Official whose duties may include keeping a file of the bonds and signed oaths of office of Notaries, issuing certificates of authority for those Notaries, and accepting custody of journals surrendered by those Notaries upon retirement.

County Recorder: Official who registers deeds and certain other documents in the public record.

Deed: Document transferring ownership of property and requiring notarization.

Flag: Jargon term for certificate of authority.

Hague Convention: *Hague Convention Abolishing the Requirement of Legalization for Foreign Public Documents*, a treaty signed by more than 90 nations, including the United States, that simplifies authentication of notarized documents sent between nations.

Legalization: Authentication.

Prothonotary: County clerk, in some states.

CHAPTER 17 TEST

In each blank, write the response — a, b, c or d — that best completes each of the following statements:

1. Typically, it is the duty of a county recorder to _____.

    a. Take custody of notarial journals.

    b. Issue certificates of capacity.

    c. Issue certified copies of deeds.

    d. Keep notarial bonds and oaths on file.

2. A smudged seal impression may be corrected by _____.

    a. Tracing over the illegible words with pen and ink.

    b. Reaffixing the seal nearby.

    c. Reaffixing the seal over the smudged impression.

    d. Covering the impression with correction fluid.

3. The process of authentication _____.

    a. Assures that all facts stated in a notarized document are true.

    b. Is the responsibility of the Notary.

    c. Is required for all notarized documents.

    d. Proves the genuineness of the signature and seal of a Notary.

4. Obtaining a certificate of authority _____.

    a. Is an official notarial act in most states.

    b. Is the responsibility of the document signer.

    c. Must be done before the document is notarized.

    d. May be done only by the Notary.

5. An *apostille* _____.

    a. May be issued by any county clerk or prothonotary.

    b. Must be completed and attached by the Notary.

    c. May be issued by some foreign consulates located in the U.S.

    d. May be issued by the secretary of state in most states.

6. The Hague Convention _____.

    a. Streamlines traditional procedures of authentication.

    b. Institutes the procedure called chain certification.

    c. Regulates all notarized documents sent between nations.

    d. Regulates all notarized documents sent out of state.

Explain in your own words:

7. What are the four general types of discrepancy that commonly cause recorders to reject notarized documents?

_____

_____

_____

_____

8. What three steps would a signer take in correcting a document or a Notary in correcting a notarial certificate?

_____

_____

_____

See page 390 for correct responses.

PART V: COMMON PITFALLS

CHAPTER 18

Detecting Fraudulent Identification

While not expected to have a crime investigator's expertise, the Notary nonetheless is relied upon to exercise commonsense judgment and not accept questionable identification in performing notarial acts. The public depends on the Notary to screen out many forgers presenting false IDs.

Every identification document should be carefully examined for evidence of fraud, since it is possible that any document signer could be an impostor presenting phony IDs. While there is no foolproof method to detect them, many fraudulent identification documents can be easily spotted through attention to detail, common sense and awareness of common telltale discrepancies.

Fraudulent IDs help impostors get phony documents notarized and recorded, allowing them to sell, take control of or take out loans on property they do not own.

HOW PHONY IDENTIFICATION IS CREATED

Unfortunately, fraudulent identification documents can be created or obtained fairly easily by enterprising swindlers. Through imposture, counterfeiting or alteration, these crooks can obtain identification documents to aid in their criminal endeavors. The resulting phony IDs will vary in quality. Some are virtually indistinguishable from real ones, while others readily can be detected as fakes. The key to spotting phony IDs is understanding what to look for.

Imposture

Imposture occurs when an individual secures an ID from a genuine issuing agency by posing as another person and falsely submitting that person's name. Typically, the impostor will use the birth certificate of a deceased individual to acquire false identification documents issued in the name of that person.

Because it was issued by a genuine agency, this is the most difficult type of fraudulent ID to detect. About the only way a Notary can discover an ID created through imposture is by testing the signer's knowledge of the information on the ID. There is a strong likelihood that a signer is an impostor if he or she does not know the birth date or street address on identification presented.

Counterfeiting

When a false ID is made from scratch, it is called counterfeiting. Fancy and official-looking seals are no problem for the resourceful counterfeiter and, therefore, no guarantee of an ID's authenticity. Tip-offs to a possibly counterfeit ID are:

Card wear inconsistent with the date of issuance. A four-year-old driver's license normally will show the wear and tear of use over four years. It certainly will not appear brand new. Counterfeiters may try to artificially age their creations, but the aging often is across the whole card and not concentrated at the edges, as with actual wear.

Misspelled words in the standard printed part of IDs. While not always the case, government agencies generally can be relied upon not to have misspellings in the printed portion of the IDs they issue.

Unlikely similarities among cards, such as identical photographs or type faces. Even when ID photos are not identical, the same clothing or background among photos on different cards can be a giveaway.

Inappropriate patterns and textures or lack of official imprints. Many cards have intricate patterns and beaded or grainy surfaces that are hard to duplicate. Increasingly, state driver's licenses bear imprinted patterns that are visible when exposed to infrared or ultraviolet light.

Inappropriate typewriting. The name of the ID's issuing state or agency should be graphically printed on the card, not typed or handwritten.

Alteration

Alteration is a method whereby an identification document that usually has been lost or stolen is changed to conform to an unauthorized person. Clues indicating a possibly altered ID are:

Raised edges around a photograph, resulting from placement of a second picture over an original.

Covered official seals and signatures, which often are placed intentionally over a genuine photo but which may be partially hidden by a fraudulent photo.

Inconsistencies in color or texture, smudges and erasures which may indicate tampering. Ultraviolet light can reveal interruptions in an otherwise invisible card pattern to indicate tampering.

Inappropriate dissimilarities in a single ID, such as different styles of printed or typed characters in a physical description. The tamperer may not have been able to duplicate the original type.

Inappropriate laminations (plastic coverings), possibly holding new photographs in place. An ID stating "do not laminate" should never be laminated.

Signatures varying between that on the ID card and that on the document or in the Notary's journal.

DETECTING FALSE IDENTIFICATION

Ideally, the Notary should be familiar with the type of identification document used to identify a signer. This familiarity makes it easier to spot discrepancies and screen out fakes.

Also helpful are books such as the *U.S. Identification Manual* and the *I.D. Checking Guide* that contain sample IDs from all states.

In addition to looking for the already listed tip-offs, the Notary often can detect an impostor by taking the ID and testing the signer's knowledge of the data on the card. Whether a phony ID has been obtained through imposture, counterfeiting or alteration, an impostor may be unfamiliar with vital data on a particular card, especially if the impostor has several false identities. Individuals who do not know the birth date or street address on IDs they carry are probably impostors.

Notaries should never be afraid to ask questions if something does not seem right about a person's ID, since one of the Notary's most important functions is to guarantee identity.

SUMMARY

Every ID presented to the Notary should be carefully examined for evidence of fraud. There is no certain method to detect fraudulent IDs, but many can be spotted through attention to detail, common sense and awareness of common telltale discrepancies.

Fraudulent identification documents are created through imposture, counterfeiting or alteration. Imposture happens when a person obtains an ID from a genuine issuing agency by posing as another and providing a false name. Counterfeiting is when a false ID is made from scratch. Alteration is a method whereby an identification document is changed to conform to an unauthorized person.

The Notary only should accept identification documents with which he or she is familiar.

Ideally, the Notary should be familiar with the type of identification document used to identify a signer. Notaries often can detect an impostor by testing the signer's knowledge of vital data on the ID. Those who cannot recall the birth date or street address on IDs they carry are likely impostors. ∎

IMPORTANT TERMS

Alteration: Method of creating a false identification document by tampering with a valid ID.

Counterfeit: False document made from scratch in imitation of an authentic one.

Fraudulent: Deliberately false or deceptive.

Impostor: Person with false identity.

Imposture: Pretending to have another identity.

Lamination: Plastic, protective covering.

Type Face: Style of typed letter characters.

Ultraviolet Light: Light source that produces radiation just short of visibility causing otherwise invisible markings to be seen. Also known as UV light or black light.

CHAPTER 18 TEST

In each blank, write the response — a, b, c or d — that best completes each of the following statements:

1. In screening IDs for fraud, Notaries are expected to _____.

    a. Check every ID against an official reference manual.

    b. Leave counterfeit detection to the experts.

    c. Consult the police and FBI.

    d. Exercise commonsense judgment.

2. An ID that appears to be brand new but has a four-year-old date of issue might be a phony obtained through _____.

    a. Counterfeiting.

    b. Alteration.

    c. Tampering.

    d. Imposture.

3. Raised edges around the photograph of an ID might indicate a fraudulent card obtained through _____.

    a. Counterfeiting.

    b. Alteration.

    c. Photocopying.

    d. Imposture.

4. Ideally, the Notary should be familiar with the type of identification document used to identify a signer because _____.

    a. Familiarity makes it easier to spot phony IDs.

    b. A familiar ID will never be fraudulent.

    c. Unfamiliar IDs are more than likely phony.

    d. Reliance on unfamiliar ID is prohibited by law.

5. Notaries often can detect an impostor _____.

    a. By asking a supervisor to determine if the ID is legitimate or not.

    b. By asking the signer to provide two local character references.

    c. By testing the signer's knowledge of information on the ID.

    d. By noting whether the signer has shifty eyes.

See page 390 for correct responses.

▼

CHAPTER 19

Notarial Misconduct

Notarial misconduct occurs when a Notary purposely or negligently violates a law, regulation, official directive or expected standard of honesty, care or good judgment in the execution of a notarial act. The misconduct may result from performing a prohibited action or from failing to perform a mandatory action.

Because a Notary is a public official held to a high standard of conduct, he or she may be subject to certain penalties (i.e., commission suspension or revocation), even when an infraction had nothing to do with a notarization but nonetheless casts doubt on the Notary's integrity.

Because they are expected to uphold high personal standards of integrity, Notaries may be punished for acts having nothing to do with notarization.

State Laws Vary

Notary laws differ markedly from state to state in defining notarial misconduct. Some states, for instance, prescribe stiff criminal penalties for mishandling a Notary journal, while others do not even require Notaries to keep journals. (Of course, wise Notaries in every state keep journals, even if not required to do so by law.)

There are two major forms of notarial misconduct that every state prohibits: false certificates and the unauthorized practice of law.

FALSE CERTIFICATES

In every state, it is a criminal offense for a Notary to knowingly make false statements in a notarial certificate.

Important transactions in commerce and law depend on the truthfulness and accuracy of the Notary's certificate. Making a notarial certificate, the Tennessee Supreme Court said in 1917 (*Figuers v. Fly*):

> [I]s an act which must in the nature of things be relied on with confidence by men of business. Those buying or taking security by way of liens on real estate ought not to be required to look with suspicion on such a certificate.

Mistakes in notarial certificates are caused by a failure to understand the notarial duties required by the certificate, conscious criminal intent or simple carelessness. All are unacceptable, and all comprise notarial misconduct. Falsehoods or misstatements in notarial certificates most often involve one of three matters: the personal appearance of the signer before the Notary, the identity of the signer or the date of the notarial act.

False Personal Appearance

Virtually every certificate completed by a Notary contains a statement that the signer signed or acknowledged signing "before me" or "in my presence." Yet, sometimes misguided Notaries will not require signers to appear before them. They might perform a notarial act merely on familiarity with a signature or on the unsworn word of a third party. Such practices are illegal and dangerous. Not only is the Notary potentially guilty of a criminal act in making a false statement about appearance, but there is a strong possibility that the nonappearing person's signature was forged.

The signer must be required to personally appear before the Notary at the time of notarization.

False Identity of Signer

Notarial certificates, particularly those for acknowledgments, often

Positive identification means that the Notary has no reasonable doubt that the signer has the claimed identity.

indicate how a signer's identity was established to the Notary, whether by personal knowledge or satisfactory evidence. However, Notaries sometimes will state that a stranger or barely-known acquaintance is "personally known." Or, they might allow an introduction by a third party to suffice as personal knowledge. This is particularly dangerous. Too often, signers identified to Notaries through casual introduction by friends prove to be impostors. A Notary only should rely on the word of a third party if that individual is personally known to the Notary, disinterested in the transaction and willing to be formally sworn in as a credible identifying witness.

False Date of Notarization

It is not uncommon for a Notary to be asked to falsify the date of a notarial act. A signer, for instance, may have neglected to observe an important deadline. He then may ask the Notary to put an earlier date on a certificate attached to the tardy papers than the actual date of appearance before the Notary. Of course, such falsification by the Notary is improper and, most likely, illegal.

Other Certificate Errors

There are many other occasions when a Notary might be prompted to falsify information on a certificate. For example, a Notary may have no knowledge that a signer is vice president of a corporation yet be asked to complete a corporate acknowledgment certificate stating the person is "known to me to be vice president." Or, a Notary may fail to administer an oath or affirmation yet complete a jurat certificate stating a document was "subscribed and sworn to before me."

Important

Even when false information on a certificate does not in itself seem harmful, it can be used as evidence in a civil lawsuit or administrative proceeding to prove a Notary's general negligence and lack of care. Such evidence could contribute to loss of a commission or having to pay damages in a lawsuit. It is imperative that Notaries carefully read and adhere to every word in the certificates they officially sign and seal. In the performance of notarial acts, false statements and deception of any kind are not tolerated.

UNAUTHORIZED PRACTICE OF LAW

In serving the general public, nonattorney Notaries sometimes get into trouble by being too helpful. Even when pressured by a persistent client, Notaries must resist the temptation to give legal advice. Every state prohibits Notaries and all other persons not licensed by its bar association from practicing law. When a nonattorney gives legal advice, it is called the unauthorized practice of law.

Only those licensed to practice law may give legal advice.

Notaries may be tempted more often to practice law without authority than perhaps any other public or private officer. This is because document signers often misunderstand the powers of Notaries and assume they can give advice about a document that requires notarization.

But the basic role of Notary as a ministerial officer is to follow legal directions, not give them. Notaries may not help other persons draft, prepare, complete, select or understand documents.

Most Notaries who engage in the unauthorized practice of law do so innocently and unknowingly in an attempt to help out a friend, client or employer.

 ## State Laws Vary

Part of the problem is that the practice of law has no clear-cut and universal definition. In one state, for example, certain nonattorney professionals may be allowed to prepare real estate documents; in another, they may not.

There are three rules that Notaries in all states should obey to avoid the unauthorized practice of law: do not choose notarial certificates, do not prepare documents and do not give advice.

Do Not Choose Certificates

Nonattorney Notaries should not determine what type of notarial

It may seem odd that the Notary cannot determine the type of notarial act to perform, but such a decision has important legal considerations.

certificate a document requires, since this decision can have important legal ramifications. If the Notary chooses the wrong certificate, a document could be delayed in processing or invalidated altogether, and the Notary could be liable for any resulting damages.

An exception is professionals certified in a given field, such as real estate. Such professionals may prescribe notarial certificates and give advice for documents within their field, but only if state law and their professional training and expertise permit.

Do Not Prepare Documents

A nonattorney Notary should not prepare or complete documents for others unless state law allows him or her to do so as a professional certified in a pertinent field.

Otherwise, the Notary is not only criminally prosecutable for the unauthorized practice of law, but also financially liable for advice that proves damaging. In a 1958 case (*Biakanja v. Irving*), the California Supreme Court ruled that a Notary who helped prepare a will — and did so incorrectly — was liable for the difference between the amount the will actually paid and the amount the beneficiaries would have received had the will been properly prepared by an attorney.

This prohibition against preparing documents applies to the documents of friends and employers, as well as the Notary's clients.

Do Not Give Advice

Even seemingly innocent questions like, "What does this mean?" or, "Where do I sign?" or, "Am I the grantor or the grantee?" are loaded with potential liability. Notaries who indicate the wrong place to sign or give an inaccurate explanation of a document clause can be held liable for any resulting damages. A Notary who is not an attorney or a professional certified in a relevant area of expertise never should advise a signer on any matter relating to a document.

Areas Prone to Trouble

Notaries in certain businesses are more apt to wander unintentionally into the unauthorized practice of law than those in other fields. Paralegals must be particularly cautious because they are permitted to prepare and advise clients about certain standard legal forms. Technically, however, paralegals must work under the direct supervision of an attorney and must refrain from offering advice outside the limits of their allowed discretion.

Notaries who provide secretarial and translation services also may be tempted to help clients prepare or complete documents. They should be cautious in the following instances:

Translating. When a translator assists a signer not fluent in English in filling out a legal document, the translator should literally translate both the document and the signer's responses without offering advice or significantly paraphrasing. A translator who is also a Notary may not certify a translation and also notarize the certification.

Supplying Forms. Supplying a standard document or certificate upon request is allowed, but recommending a document or certificate is not.

Typing Dictated Words. When typing language for a document as it is dictated by the signer, this role is strictly secretarial. The signer's exact words must be typed.

How Notaries Can Help

One way to help signers seeking advice is to refer them to attorneys. However, this is not always necessary. Another way the Notary can help is by suggesting that the signer contact the person or agency who issued or will receive the document. Usually, the document's issuer or eventual recipient has the expertise and authority to answer such questions as, "What goes in this blank space?" and, "What kind of notarization do I need?"

Everyone likes to be helpful, especially to clients, supervisors and friends. However, the best way for Notaries to avoid the unauthorized practice of law is to know the limits of their helpfulness.

PENALTIES FOR MISCONDUCT

Notaries who clearly understand the penalties that the law may impose for their misconduct will view the performance of any notarization with heightened seriousness.

Notaries are liable for their misconduct in performing any notarization. This means Notaries are subject to administrative, criminal and civil penalties for any wrongdoing. Any or all of these may be imposed for a single impropriety, although each may require a separate hearing or trial. For a given act of misconduct, a Notary could lose his or her commission and be fined and imprisoned and have to compensate a financially-injured person for damages.

Administrative Penalties

The Notary regulating official may revoke, suspend or deny a Notary commission due to misconduct.

Revocation, suspension and denial of a commission are administrative penalties imposed by state officials who regulate Notaries.

Revocation voids the Notary's commission, stripping the individual of all notarial powers and making it unlikely that a commission will be issued to that person again. Suspension restricts the Notary from notarizing for a certain length of time, such as six months. It can be imposed as a punishment or as a precautionary measure while the Notary's conduct is under investigation. Denial prevents a Notary from getting a new commission.

In some states, specified fines or mandatory education may be imposed on the Notary for certain forms of misconduct.

The range of misconduct that can warrant administrative penalties is broad and varies from state to state. Punishable misconduct need not be directly related to notarization, but it must reflect on the Notary's ability to perform a proper notarization.

Dishonesty. Any act that shows dishonesty or moral turpitude may bring an administrative penalty. The Notary's integrity and incorruptibility must be beyond question. For example, an applicant

▼

or Notary who is found to have lied on a commission application form likely will have the commission denied or revoked. A Notary who loses a professional license, such as a real estate credential, for lying to clients, may have a notarial commission denied or revoked as a result.

Loss of Eligibility. Failure to maintain commission eligibility standards can cause revocation. Notaries found to have moved out of state or to have become unable to read or write will have their commissions revoked by most states. It is considered an act of misconduct for a Notary to hide disqualifications from state officials.

Disobedience of authority. Failure to follow instructions from authorities can result in administrative penalties. For example, a state may prohibit Notaries from making certified copies, ask them to report changes of business address or mandate other actions not specified by law. Typically, such instructions to the Notary are contained in official Notary guidebooks or in letters from the commissioning official.

Disobedience of law. Failure to comply with statute can result in administrative penalties. The noncompliance can be a violation of a state's notarial law, such as failure to keep a journal or overcharging for notarial services. Or, it can be a violation of any state or federal law, particularly if the offense shows blatant dishonesty, as in counterfeiting.

Negligence. Failure to use a degree of care that is expected of a person of ordinary prudence and intelligence also can result in administrative penalties. The most common act of negligence is not properly identifying document signers.

Criminal Penalties

A crime is a serious violation of law for which the penalty is a fine,

Some misconduct by a Notary may be criminal, and the Notary may have to stand trial and be subject to fines and even jail time for his or her misdeeds.

imprisonment or both. Less harmful crimes, called misdemeanors, are punished by a small fine and/or incarceration in a local jail. More harmful crimes, called felonies, are in most cases punished by longer imprisonment in a penitentiary.

Most acts of criminal misconduct by Notaries are classified as misdemeanors and are punishable by fines of less than $1,000 and/or jail terms of less than one year. Although state laws differ in defining criminal misconduct by a Notary, laws in virtually every state make it at least a misdemeanor for a Notary to knowingly fill out a notarial certificate with false information. In addition, each of the acts in the following list are crimes in some states:

- Destroying, defacing or concealing a Notary journal.
- Failing to hand over a Notary journal to officials upon resignation or removal from office.
- Charging excessive fees for notarial services.
- Failing to post a schedule of fees.
- Performing notarizations after commission expiration.

Making a false certificate and failing to surrender notarial records are regarded by some states as felonies.

Even when a violation is a misdemeanor or less, the Notary can be guilty of a felony if the violation is part of a criminal conspiracy. For example, it may only be a misdemeanor to fill out a false certificate, but if the Notary knows the certificate is part of a scheme to cheat a person out of property, the Notary may be subject to felony penalties for criminal conspiracy.

Notaries most often are criminally prosecuted when their misconduct is part of a more comprehensive violation. Law enforcement officials may be reluctant to prosecute an isolated offense resulting from a Notary's ignorance of the law rather than from criminal intent. However, this is not always the case.

In addition, many state laws impose criminal penalties on non-Notaries for such acts as impersonating a Notary, unlawfully possessing a notarial seal and soliciting a Notary to perform an unlawful act.

Civil Penalties

Potentially one of the most severe penalties involves a civil lawsuit against an offending Notary by a person who suffered financial loss as a result of the Notary's improper conduct. The object of such a suit is to recover the financial loss from the Notary. Civil penalties are the subject of Chapter 20, "Financial Liability."

SUMMARY

When a Notary violates a law, regulation, official directive or expected standard of honesty, care or good judgment — intentional or not — he or she may be subject to certain penalties for misconduct. Misconduct may result from performing a prohibited action or from failing to perform a mandatory action.

In all states, it is a criminal offense to make false statements in a notarial certificate. The false statement may be caused by failure to understand notarial duties, criminal intent, or carelessness; all are misconduct. Most often, certificate misstatements concern the signer's personal appearance, the signer's identity and the notarization date.

Nonattorney Notaries may not help other persons draft, prepare, complete, select or understand documents. Anyone not licensed to practice law may not give legal advice. To do so is considered the unauthorized practice of law. To avoid such misconduct, Notaries must not choose notarial certificates, prepare documents or give advice. However, professionals certified in a given field may prescribe notarial certificates, prepare documents and give advice within their field if law and their professional expertise permit.

Notaries are subject to administrative, criminal and civil penalties for wrongdoing. Any or all may be imposed for a single act of misconduct. Administrative penalties that may be imposed by state officials include revocation, suspension and denial of a commission, as well as specified fines. Most criminal acts of misconduct by Notaries are classified as misdemeanors and are subject to fines of less than $1,000 and/or jail terms of less than one year. Felonies are punished by longer imprisonment. Civil penalties result from a lawsuit against a Notary by a person who suffered financial loss due to Notary's misconduct. The object of the suit is to recover the financial loss from the Notary. ∎

IMPORTANT TERMS

Administrative Penalty: Punishment imposed by authorities who regulate Notaries, in the form of revocation, suspension or denial of a notarial commission and, in some states, fines or mandatory education.

Civil Penalty: Payment of funds by a Notary resulting from a lawsuit to recover financial losses that were claimed to have been caused by the Notary's misconduct.

Commission Revocation: Voiding the notarial powers of a Notary.

Commission Suspension: Voiding the notarial powers of a Notary for a set period of time.

Conspiracy: Association of persons to commit a crime; unlawful plot.

Crime: Law violation that is punishable, in the case of a misdemeanor, by a fine and/or confinement in a jail, or, in the case of a felony, usually by confinement in a penitentiary.

False Certificate: Untruthful notarial certificate or other written official statement by a public officer.

Liability: Obligation to suffer the penalties for misconduct.

Moral Turpitude: Conduct contrary to expected standards of honesty, morality, justice or modesty; depravity.

Negligence: Failure to use a degree of care that is expected of a person of ordinary prudence and intelligence.

Notarial Misconduct: Notary's violation of a law, regulation, official directive or expected standard of honesty, care or good judgment, usually in executing a notarization.

Paralegal: Trained professional who, under the supervision of an attorney, prepares documents and performs certain other standard functions within a narrow area of discretion; legal assistant.

Secretarial Service: Function of typing or otherwise transcribing another person's speech or writing verbatim, without altering, paraphrasing or advising.

Unauthorized Practice of Law: Illegal act of a nonattorney in helping another person to draft, prepare, complete, select or understand a document or transaction.

CHAPTER 19 TEST

In each blank, write the response — a, b, c or d — that best completes each of the following statements:

1. A Notary's knowing completion of a notarial certificate containing a false statement _____.

    a. Is a criminal act.

    b. Is acceptable if the signer agrees.

    c. Is not the Notary's responsibility if ordered by an employer.

    d. Is never punishable if unintended.

2. Notaries may _____.

    a. Advise use of a particular certificate but not supply it.

    b. Not advise use of a certificate but supply it upon request.

    c. Neither advise use of a certificate nor supply it upon request.

    d. Advise use of a certificate but only if they are able to supply it.

3. _____ is not the unauthorized practice of law by a Notary.

    a. Explaining the meaning of a paragraph in a document.

    b. Telling the signer how to fill in a document's blanks.

    c. Typing wording on a document as instructed by a signer.

    d. Recommending that a document's text be changed.

4. Notaries are liable for _____.

    a. Only their advice given to signers without a fee.

    b. Only their advice given to signers with a fee.

    c. Their notarial acts and any advice given to signers.

    d. Their notarial acts and nothing else.

5. Lying in a commission application would likely _____.

    a. Be a forgivable error in most states.

    b. Show dishonesty and result in denial of the commission.

    c. Be a criminal offense, punishable by imprisonment.

    d. Result in a civil suit for damages.

6. A change in a Notary's status that would cause termination of a Notary commission would be _____.

    a. Marriage or divorce.

    b. Passing the state bar examination.

    c. New employer.

    d. Moving out of state.

Explain in your own words:

7. In their certificates, Notaries most often err in making false statements about what?

_____

_____

_____

8. To prevent the unauthorized practice of law, what three practices should Notaries avoid?

_____

_____

_____

9. What are the three kinds of punishment for misconduct by a Notary?

_____

_____

_____

10. What is the most common act of negligence by a Notary?

_____

_____

_____

See page 390 for correct responses.

CHAPTER 20

Notarial Liability

GETTING SUED

For many Notaries, the most intimidating penalty for misconduct is payment of personal funds as a result of a civil lawsuit. This is understandable. Not only do lawsuits threaten court verdicts or out-of-court settlements that require the Notary to pay for damages, they also bring about attorney fees and other legal defense costs for which the Notary is responsible.

A civil lawsuit results when a private person, corporation or other legal entity seeks to recover losses caused by a Notary's alleged misconduct. In a lawsuit, the injured party initiating the suit is called the plaintiff; the party being sued is called the defendant.

LIABILITY OF THE NOTARY

Notaries can be held financially liable for damages caused by their misconduct.

A Notary is personally liable for the full amount of damages caused by any misconduct in performing a notarization.

Suppose, for example, that a forged and notarized trust deed is used as collateral for a $50,000 home-equity loan. If the lending company cannot find and recover from the impostor who borrowed the money, it likely would sue the Notary for the $50,000. If the Notary had performed the improper notarization during employment, the lending company also could sue the Notary's employer.

The misconduct may be intentional or unintentional, but the Notary is equally liable. The fact that a mistake was "honest" cannot prevent a lawsuit. For example, if a Notary's failure to affix an official seal results in a deed's rejection by a recorder, causing a real estate transaction to fall through, the sales agent could sue the Notary for the lost sales commission.

Liability Considerations

Many considerations affect the outcome of a civil lawsuit against a Notary. Following are three of which every Notary should be aware:

Statute of limitations. Normally, a lawsuit must be filed against a Notary within a specific period, typically three years from the date of the improper act. In some cases, though, the period may extend from the date of discovery of the improper act.

Liability to all parties. Increasingly, courts are ruling that a Notary is liable to all persons who rely on a notarized document — not just to a person or entity named in the document.

Notary not sole cause. The Notary's misconduct does not have to be the only or direct cause of damages. For example, a false Notary certificate (notarial error) and a false document (forger's crime) together may cause a lender to accept a phony deed as collateral.

Settling Out of Court

Most lawsuits against Notaries never get to the trial stage. In many cases, out-of-court settlements are arranged by attorneys representing the plaintiff and defendant after all facts have been gathered through interrogatories and depositions. If there is a strong case against a Notary, his or her attorney may advise settling out of court.

THE NOTARY BOND

The potential for a Notary's error causing monetary loss is real enough that most states require Notaries to be bonded in order to protect the public. A Notary bond is a guarantee that a person financially damaged by a Notary's misconduct will be reimbursed (up to the limit of the bond) in the event the Notary fails to do so.

Depending on state law, the required Notary bond guarantee ranges from $500 to $15,000. The issuer of the bond is called a surety and is usually a bonding company licensed to do business within the Notary's state. In some states, the surety may be an individual.

How a Bond Functions

It is a common misunderstanding that the bond protects Notaries from civil lawsuits. It does not. The Notary bond protects only the public — those individuals or entities who suffer a financial loss due to a Notary's error. The Notary bond does not "insure" the Notary from claims; whatever money is paid out on the Notary's behalf, the Notary is obligated to pay back to the surety.

A bond assures injured parties that they have some protection from damages caused by a Notary's error. But a bond is not an insurance policy; the Notary is responsible for repaying the bond company any money it pays out on the Notary's behalf.

Suppose a Notary is bonded for $10,000 and sued for $5,000. If the Notary is shown to be liable and cannot pay the $5,000, the bonding company (surety) would pay this amount to the injured party. Then, the bonding company would seek repayment from the Notary. If the Notary did not respond, the bonding company would sue the Notary to recover the $5,000.

If the Notary were found to be liable for $15,000 and could not pay, the Notary would be obligated to the surety for the $10,000 it paid to the injured party and also to the injured party directly for the remaining $5,000.

Obtaining and Filing a Bond

To purchase a bond, a Notary pays the surety a premium — usually amounting to less than one percent of the bond's dollar guarantee. The bond term is written to coincide exactly with the Notary's term of office. Before or shortly after the commission starting date, depending on state law, the Notary must file the bond with a designated public agency, normally the county clerk.

ERRORS AND OMISSIONS INSURANCE

There is insurance available for protection against lawsuits targeting a Notary's personal assets. While the bond protects the public, this insurance, called Notary errors and omissions insurance (or E&O insurance), protects the Notary by absorbing the costs of lawsuits resulting from the Notary's unintentional errors, up to the policy's limit. Not only will E&O insurance pay out damages to an injured party after a court verdict or out-of-court settlement, but most policies also will absorb attorney's fees and other defense costs. In a sense, E&O insurance is kind of a "malpractice insurance" for Notaries.

E&O insurance differs from a bond in two major ways. First, unlike the Notary bond that is mandatory in most states, E&O insurance is not required by law; it may be purchased or cancelled by the Notary at any time. Second, although all bond funds paid out by the surety must be paid back by the Notary, the Notary does not reimburse the E&O insurance company for any payments it makes.

Although vulnerability to lawsuits is an occupational hazard of the Notary's office, errors and omissions insurance offers some protection.

E&O Coverage

Coverage limits for E&O policies generally vary from $10,000 to $25,000. Should a lawsuit be decided against the Notary, the insurance company will pay all damages up to the coverage limit. The Notary is obliged to pay any damages over this limit.

In general, errors and omissions insurance will cover the insured Notary for all unintentional damaging actions performed during the term of the policy. As long as the disputed notarial act occurred within an E&O policy's effective term, it is not unusual for the policy to honor resulting claims made after its expiration date.

However, E&O policies usually do not cover non-notarial acts and notarial acts that are dishonest, fraudulent, illegal, criminal, malicious, libelous or slanderous.

E&O insurance provides liability protection for the Notary. It is something like malpractice insurance.

E&O coverage and policy provisions may vary considerably from insurer to insurer. Some policies require deductibles. Some can be written to cover Notary and employer.

Attorney's Fees

An advantage of most E&O policies is that they arrange for and absorb the costs of a sued Notary's defense. The Notary need not go to the trouble of finding an attorney, since the specially skilled attorneys of the insurance company will handle the defense. Often these attorneys are able to have lawsuits dismissed or to negotiate out-of-court settlements for considerably less than the claimed damages. Many Notaries purchase E&O insurance mainly to avoid out-of-pocket expenses in having a groundless lawsuit legally dismissed.

REASONABLE CARE

The Notary's best defense against a lawsuit is use of reasonable care. Legal definitions of reasonable care vary from state to state, but, in general, it is defined as the degree of attentiveness and precaution that would widely be expected of a person of ordinary prudence and intelligence. The opposite of reasonable care is negligence.

Reasonable care means taking every precaution expected of an ordinary person.

Ordinary Prudence Not "Average" Practice

If a notarial act results in a lawsuit and the Notary can show that he or she took every precaution that would be expected of a person of ordinary prudence and intelligence, a jury would be strongly compelled to find the Notary blameless. In fact, convincing evidence of reasonable care by the Notary often prevents a lawsuit.

Reasonable care is not necessarily the same care that an average person might take. For example, a Notary accused of identifying a signer based on an informal introduction unsuccessfully argued in court that the average Notary in the local area followed the same unlawful practice (*Transamerica v. Green*, 11 Cal. 3rd 693 89 CR915 1970). It is not enough that the Notary be average. The Notary must be law-abiding.

Since an ordinarily prudent person abides by the law, reasonable care means, above all, following whatever notarial duties the law and official instructions may dictate, such as identifying a document signer and affixing an official seal.

Yet, determining exactly how to follow the law, especially a vague law, often is difficult. When the law provides inadequate direction, Notaries should be guided by good business practices and by high standards of honesty and common sense.

In using reasonable care, there are three duties to which Notaries should be particularly attentive: 1) requiring document signers to appear before them, 2) identifying document signers, and 3) keeping a journal record of all notarial acts. The overwhelming majority of lawsuits against Notaries result from a Notary's failure to exercise reasonable care in these three areas.

Requiring personal appearance. Notarizations should not be based on telephone calls, recognition of a signature or on the word of a third party who is not willing to be put under oath as a subscribing witness. The signer must appear face to face before the Notary. Whether required by law or not, the signer should be asked to sign the Notary's journal.

Identifying the signer. This is the most critical of all notarial duties. Notaries must identify strangers using only legally allowed methods. They should carefully examine all ID cards relied on as identification and never identify a stranger on the word of a third party who is not willing to be put under oath as a credible identifying witness.

Keeping a journal record. A detailed and accurate notarial journal is the Notary's best evidence in court that reasonable care was used. Particularly important to record are descriptions of ID cards and signatures of all document signers and witnesses. A meticulously kept journal that shows the Notary's care can prevent a lawsuit.

No list of reasonably careful steps could be all-inclusive. The best way for Notaries to protect themselves is to take precautions greater than those required by law and, when the law is vague, to bend over backward in their prudence.

Since the protection of errors and omissions insurance is limited by the coverage ceiling, use of reasonable care is the closest a Notary can come to absolute protection.

SUMMARY

A Notary is personally liable for the full amount of damages caused by any misconduct in performing a notarization. A civil lawsuit results when an individual or entity legally seeks to recover losses caused by a Notary's misconduct. The misconduct may be intentional or unintentional, and the penalty is payment of personal funds as a result of a civil lawsuit.

Most states require Notaries to be bonded to protect the public from loss due to a Notary's mistake. The Notary bond guarantees that a person financially damaged by a Notary's misconduct will be reimbursed. A common misunderstanding is that the bond protects Notaries from civil lawsuits. It does not. Whatever money is paid out on the Notary's behalf, the Notary is obligated to pay back to the surety.

There is insurance protection available for Notaries. Notary errors and omissions insurance protects the Notary by absorbing the costs of lawsuits resulting from the Notary's unintentional errors. Unlike the bond, E&O insurance is not required by law, and the Notary does not reimburse the E&O insurance company for any payments it makes.

The Notary's best protection and defense against civil lawsuits is use of reasonable care. Reasonable care is the degree of attentiveness and precaution that would widely be expected of a person of ordinary prudence and intelligence. This means, above all, following whatever notarial duties the law and official instructions dictate. The Notary should be particularly attentive in requiring document signers to personally appear, in identifying document signers and in keeping a journal record of all notarial acts. The overwhelming majority of lawsuits against

Notaries result from a Notary's failure to exercise reasonable care in these three areas. ■

IMPORTANT TERMS

Bond, Notary: Written guarantee that money up to a limit will be paid by a surety to a person financially damaged by a Notary's misconduct in the event the Notary fails to do so.

Civil Lawsuit: Legal action taken by a private person, corporation or other legal entity to recover losses caused by a Notary's alleged misconduct.

Defendant: Person accused of causing damages and from whom compensation is sought in a lawsuit.

Errors and Omissions Insurance: Contract between a Notary and an indemnity company whereby, in the event of a lawsuit against the Notary resulting from certain acts in performing a notarization, the company absorbs the Notary's costs and financial liabilities up to an agreed limit.

Out-of-Court Settlement: Agreement between the two sides of a lawsuit to end the dispute without imposition of an official ruling.

Plaintiff: Person or entity initiating a lawsuit to seek compensation for damages; the suer.

Reasonable Care: Degree of attentiveness and precaution that would be expected of a person of ordinary prudence and intelligence.

Statute of Limitations: Law setting a time limit on filing a lawsuit to recover damages or on prosecuting for criminal misconduct.

Surety: Person or company obliged to pay money up to a limit in the event a bonded individual fails to do so; guarantor.

CHAPTER 20 TEST

In each blank, write the response — a, b, c or d — that best completes each of the following statements:

1. Court judgments requiring payment to a victim result from _____.

    a. Lawsuits filed by Notary-regulating officials in order to remove a Notary from office.

    b. Criminal investigations into wrongdoing.

    c. Lawsuits filed to recover damages caused by misconduct.

    d. Administrative hearings.

2. When a Notary is sued, _____.

    a. The suer is called the defendant and the Notary the plaintiff.

    b. There is a $1 million ceiling on damages that may be claimed.

    c. The Notary is protected if the damage was unintended.

    d. An out-of-court settlement often is arranged.

3. A Notary bond _____.

    a. Protects Notaries against all lawsuits.

    b. Offers Notaries no protection at all against lawsuits.

    c. Protects Notaries against suits for unintentional misconduct.

    d. Protects Notaries against suits for intentional misconduct.

4. E&O insurance for Notaries typically provides coverage for _____.

    a. Damages of any amount claimed in a lawsuit.

    b. Acts done in the policy term but after commission expiration.

    c. A claim made after policy term expiration if the act was performed during the policy term.

    d. A criminal act by the Notary.

5. If a bonding company pays out $2,000 for a Notary who is liable for damages of $5,000, _____.

    a. The Notary owes the company $2,000 and the suer $3,000.

    b. The Notary owes the company nothing and the suer $3,000.

    c. The Notary owes the company $2,000 and the suer nothing.

    d. The company owes the Notary $3,000.

6. The bond protects the _____.

    a. Public and E&O protects the Notary.

    b. Notary and E&O protects the public.

    c. Surety and E&O protects the Notary.

    d. Public and E&O protects the surety.

Explain in your own words:

7. What are two other major differences between a bond and E&O insurance, besides that described in #6, preceding?

_____

_____

_____

8. In using reasonable care, what are three duties to which Notaries should be particularly attentive?

_____

_____

_____

See pages 390–391 for correct responses.

▼

PART VI: PROFESSIONAL RESPONSIBILITY

CHAPTER 21

Impartiality

Impartiality is the quality that makes Notaries indispensable as official witnesses. An impartial Notary has no motive for ignoring a discovered illegality, such as a counterfeit ID card.

High ethical standards dictate that impartiality must rule the Notary, not only in reporting illegalities, but also in offering notarial services to all and in refusing to interfere with a signer's chosen, lawful action.

DISCRIMINATION

Notaries are public officials who must never act out of personal bias.

As an official commissioned to serve the public, a Notary should not, out of personal bias, discriminate against any person by refusing notarial service, providing inadequate service or by charging unequally.

The ethical Notary constantly strives to deal equally with all people.

Signers

Any lawful and reasonable request for a notarial act must be honored by the Notary. A signer's race, national origin, lifestyle, sexual orientation, religion or political belief should never in itself be a reason for refusing to notarize.

Customers and Noncustomers

A person's status as a noncustomer is not an ethical basis for refusing to notarize. A Notary is not commissioned to serve just the clients of any one business, even when the employer has paid for the commissioning fees and notarial supplies. There is no such official as a "Notary Private."

Furthermore, the offer of free Notary services to customers while charging noncustomers for the same service is discriminatory and ethically inappropriate.

Document Contents

A Notary should not refuse to notarize a lawful document because he or she personally disapproves of its contents. A Notary, for example, would be ethically bound to notarize a circulator's affidavit for a ballot petition even when personally opposed to the petition.

Unreasonable Requests

The obligation to service all lawful requests without discrimination does not mean that a Notary must honor unreasonable requests. It is not reasonable to expect a Notary to provide services beyond normal business hours or to expect the Notary to travel great distances without reimbursement for expenses. Neither is it reasonable to expect a Notary to drop everything when a signer walks in unannounced; however, the Notary should accommodate such requests within a reasonable time.

UNDUE INFLUENCE

There is another ethical facet to the Notary's role as an impartial witness: avoidance of undue influence. In general, undue influence is an attempt to cause a person to do what he or she would not do if left to act freely. In regard to notarized documents, undue influence can be a case of a Notary improperly influencing a signer, a third party imposing influence on a signer, or a signer or other party influencing the Notary.

Influence by Notaries

Notaries must not influence a person to sign or not sign a legal document.

Notaries might violate the ethical restraint against undue influence by trying to persuade a signer to sign a ballot petition to recall a public official or not to sign a deed transferring title to property. Of course, a Notary would be fully justified in influencing a signer not to perform an illegal act.

The Notary's personal motive to influence a signer might be financial, philosophical or emotional. A Notary, for example, might have a financial reason for not wanting a deed signed, a philosophical reason for wanting a signature on a recall petition or an emotional reason for not wanting a son or daughter to sign a contract resulting in a family separation.

Although a personal interest does not automatically mean that a Notary will exert undue influence, in any such cases it may be best for Notaries to disqualify themselves from notarizing. This removes any doubt about a signer's free will.

Influence by Third Parties

Another part of the ethical duty to avoid undue influence is preventing undue influence on a signer by a third party. The Notary's very presence will normally prevent signings influenced by open force or threat.

However, there are less blatant forms of influence that may be attempted in the Notary's presence. The signers most often manipulated in this manner are the elderly and the hospitalized. The manipulator in many cases is a close relative or friend who will deceive or browbeat a person into signing a deed or power of attorney. In such instances, ethical Notaries will refuse to notarize if they feel a signer is not signing freely.

A manipulated signer does not necessarily have to be a person of weak mental ability, although this is often the case. A competent homeowner, for example, may be persuaded by a salesman to purchase a home improvement — unaware of a clause buried in the notarized contract that forfeits the house to the contractor if payment is late. To deter such abuses, all Notaries can reasonably do is ask willing signers if they have carefully read their documents.

Ethical Notaries never allow themselves or others to sway signers from doing what they would voluntarily do on their own.

Influence by Signers

It is often forgotten that undue influence has another side. While Notaries should not unduly influence signers, neither should they be unduly influenced themselves to forsake normal standards in performing notarizations.

Notaries must never allow themselves to be persuaded by a client, employer or other third party to compromise their official responsibilities and professional ethics in any way. For example, if a client attempts to persuade the Notary to abandon proper procedures by not requiring proof of identity of an unknown signer presented as the client's wife, the Notary must refuse.

> Notaries must not allow themselves to be influenced by a signer or third party to act improperly.

SUMMARY

Being impartial means the Notary cannot ignore a discovered impropriety.

A Notary should not discriminate against any person. Any lawful and reasonable request for a notarial act must be honored. The document signer's ethnicity, lifestyle or beliefs must never be reasons for refusing service. The status of the signer as a noncustomer also is not a proper basis for refusing to notarize. There is no such official as a "Notary Private." The subject matter or purpose of a document is not acceptable grounds for refusal to notarize.

However, the Notary is not obligated to honor unreasonable requests such as services beyond normal business hours, traveling great distances without reimbursement or immediately serving a signer while engaged in another task.

Notaries must make sure they avoid undue influence, which is any attempt to cause a person to do what he or she would not normally do if left to act freely. In regard to notarized documents, a Notary may not influence a signer to sign or not sign; a third party may not unduly influence a signer; and a signer or other party may not influence a Notary to act improperly. ■

IMPORTANT TERMS

Discrimination: Unequal treatment without due and lawful cause.

Impartiality: State of being unbiased; specifically, having no motive but to perform notarial duties legally and ethically.

Undue Influence: Attempt to cause a person to do what he or she would not do if left to act freely.

CHAPTER 21 TEST

In each blank, write the response — a, b, c or d — that best completes each of the following statements:

1. A reasonable request would be asking a Notary to _____.

    a. Notarize for a noncustomer of the Notary's employer.

    b. Drop everything and travel 50 miles to notarize without reimbursement of expenses.

    c. Drive across town at once before a signer loses consciousness.

    d. Be on call day and night until an important document arrives.

2. A Notary may refuse to notarize documents _____.

    a. Signed by non-natives of the United States.

    b. Whose signers have political beliefs that are "un-American."

    c. Containing a statement known by the Notary to be false.

    d. Whose signers have an "immoral" lifestyle.

3. If an employer does not require a client to show IDs, a Notary _____.

    a. May take the client's acknowledgment without identification.

    b. May notarize if the employer is personally known to both and sworn in as a credible identifying witness.

    c. May notarize if the client swears to his own identity.

    d. May notarize under no circumstances.

4. For the Notary, undue influence by a third party on a signer _____.

    a. Is unacceptable if coercive.

    b. Is unacceptable in any form.

    c. Is acceptable in any form.

    d. Is acceptable in any form if the third party is a relative.

5. A Notary's personal interest in a notarized transaction _____.

    a. Means that undue influence will be exerted by the Notary.

    b. Is not important.

    c. Is prohibited by statute in all cases.

    d. Should prompt the Notary to disqualify himself or herself.

6. If a friend of the Notary requests notarization of a phony deed to sell land the friend does not own, the Notary should _____.

    a. Influence the friend not to proceed.

    b. Not even mention the illegality to the friend.

    c. Mention it, then perform the notarization.

    d. Tell the friend to find another Notary.

7. An ethical Notary will _____.

    a. Charge noncustomers but not customers for notarial services.

    b. Advise a signer against signing a lawful contract.

    c. Not notarize for a woman bullied into signing by her husband.

    d. Notarize a ballot initiative while trying to persuade a signer to sign it.

8. If a Notary is very busy when a person requests a notarization, _____.

    a. The person should be turned away.

    b. The Notary should drop everything at once to serve the person.

    c. The person should be told, "Come back when I am not busy."

    d. The Notary should serve the person in a reasonable amount of time.

Explain in your own words:

9. What are the two sides of undue influence for Notaries?

_____

_____

_____

See page 391 for correct responses.

▼

CHAPTER 22

Notarial Ethics

BEYOND THE LAW

How can a Notary Public "do the right thing" if the law does not say what the right thing is? Certainly this can make notarizing difficult.

May Notaries refuse to notarize because the signer is not a customer? May they notarize for a family member? May they notarize for a client who pays the Notary a fee for services other than the notarial act?

Rarely are these and other practical questions answered by state law. That is because laws are seldom specific or comprehensive enough to describe fully the duties of a public official or publicly-regulated professional. Ethical guidelines must fill the void.

Where laws and official guidelines leave off, ethics take over.

This is especially true with Notaries. In the United States, the laws, regulations and official directives that define the Notary's role universally fail to address numerous common dilemmas that perplex and confound every Notary. State laws that govern Notaries are often so vague or incomplete that Notaries must rely on rules of ethics for guidance.

UNIVERSALLY ACCEPTED STANDARDS

In general, rules of ethics are based on widely accepted standards of honesty, fairness and common sense. There are certain common denominators among all professional ethical codes. Usually, for example, such codes urge practitioners to increase their knowledge and skill and thereby upgrade their profession.

NOTARY PUBLIC CODE OF PROFESSIONAL RESPONSIBILITY

Guided by input received over four decades from tens of thousands of Notaries and by a drafting panel of concerned Notary-regulating officials, attorneys and representatives of groups with large numbers of Notaries, the National Notary Association has developed the *Notary Public Code of Professional Responsibility* to guide Notaries when laws, regulations and official directives fall short.

This *Code* — finalized May 1, 1998 after many years of input and development — is printed in its entirety in Appendix 1 (*Notary Public Code of Professional Responsibility*, page 331).

It is based upon 10 widely-accepted principles that define the Notary's unique function:

1. The Notary is a government officer and a public servant.
2. Impartiality is fundamental to the integrity of any notarial act.
3. Personal appearance and identification are essential.
4. Deterrence of fraud is the Notary's basic function.
5. The Notary may be a public officer and a private employee.
6. The Notary is a ministerial officer without independent discretion.
7. The Notary seal is the official symbol of the Notary.
8. The journal of notarial acts is an important public record.
9. The Notary must preserve confidentiality.
10. Education is crucial to the Notary's effectiveness.

Each *Code* principle generates particular standards of professional and ethical practice for the Notary. All of these standards serve the dual function of maximizing the public utility of the Notary office, while protecting the Notary from liability by preventing misconduct.

The National Notary Association's Notary Public Code of Professional Responsibility provides standards of practice to guide the Notary when law and official directives do not.

Following is a summary of the *Notary Public Code of Professional Responsibility*:

Government Officer and Public Servant

Because the Notary Public is a government officer and is appointed to serve all of the public without discrimination, the Notary must not refuse to perform a lawful and proper notarial act without due cause or a reasonable suspicion that can be explained. Conversely, a Notary must refuse to notarize when he or she has a reasonable suspicion that the transaction is fraudulent or illegal.

A signer's status as a nonclient or noncustomer of the Notary or the Notary's employer does not constitute due cause, nor does the signer's race, nationality, ethnicity, citizenship, religion, politics, lifestyle, age, disability, gender or sexual orientation.

Similarly, notarial fees must be charged fairly. The Notary must not base the charging of fees, or the amount of the fee, on the signer's race, nationality, ethnicity, citizenship, religion, politics, lifestyle, age, disability, gender or sexual orientation, nor on the signer's status as a client or nonclient, customer or noncustomer.

A Notary must refrain from advertising that he or she has powers not actually given by law. In addition, the Notary must not use the Notary seal or the title "Notary Public" to endorse or oppose any product, service, program, proposal, individual, candidate, organization or contest. Finally, the Notary must prevent others from using or reproducing the Notary's seal or title in an advertisement.

Ultimately, if the Notary finds that he or she is no longer able to carry out the functions of a Notary Public — due to personal incapacitating impairments (e.g., deteriorating eyesight or hearing) — he or she has a professional responsibility to resign the commission.

Impartiality

To uphold the integrity of the notarial act, the Notary must be personally disinterested in and unaffected by the transaction at hand.

Notaries must decline to notarize any document which might result in a financial gain or any other advantage other than the fee for a notarization. The Notary must never notarize his or her own signature or a document which names the Notary or bears the Notary's signature.

In any transaction that would call into question the Notary's impartiality, the Notary must decline to notarize. Likewise, if the Notary has a personal interest in the document, such as when notarizing for relatives or cosigning with a spouse, an impartial third-party Notary should be sought.

Notaries must avoid influencing any person to act or not act in a lawful transaction in which they will notarize, but they should always attempt to influence a person not to act in any unlawful transaction.

Personal Appearance and Identification

The Notary always should require a signer to personally appear at the time of notarization. Personal appearance allows the Notary to screen the signer for three things: identity, willingness and awareness. Ascertaining the identity of the signer is a fundamental function of a Notary. A Notary always must ensure that a signer has not been unduly influenced or pressured into signing a document, especially a document the signer may not understand. Direct communication between the signer and the Notary is always crucial.

In cases where a Notary cannot establish identity through one of the acceptable methods — personal knowledge, identification documents or the sworn word of a qualified, impartial, credible witness — or suspects that a signer does not understand the content or ramifications of the document, the Notary should refuse to notarize.

Fraud Deterrence

Detecting and deterring document fraud is a basic purpose of a Notary Public. The Notary must refuse to perform any notarial act that is illegal, dishonest, improper or contrary to the *Notary Public Code of Professional Responsibility*. Any illegality involving a notarial act must be reported to appropriate law enforcement authorities.

A Notary never should provide a pre-signed notarial certificate to another person to complete and/or attach to a document outside of the Notary's presence. A Notary never may knowingly issue a notarial certificate containing information that is false, inaccurate or incomplete. A Notary is personally responsible for verifying and preparing all information on a notarial certificate and for affixing the official signature and seal. The certificate should not be attached until the document is complete (without blank spaces) and signed with an actual pen-and-ink signature. Faxed signatures are unacceptable.

Public Officer and Private Employee

While the Notary may be both a public officer and a private employee, the Notary must always follow and give precedence to any law, regulation or official directive when it conflicts with the instructions of an employer, client, customer, coworker, friend or relative or other person or entity. When it comes to notarization, the Notary is responsible, first and foremost, to the state.

The Notary cannot be required by an employer to surrender or resign the commission upon termination of employment, even if the employer paid for the commission. An employer cannot cancel a Notary's bond, even if the Notary leaves that employer. Once purchased, the bond remains in effect for the entire term of the Notary's commission.

Ministerial Officer

Because the Notary is a ministerial official, the Notary's actions are limited by law and do not entail use of significant independent judgment or discretion. A Notary who is not an attorney or a professional trained in a pertinent field must not determine the type of notarial act or notarial certificate that is required, must not prepare a document for another person or provide advice on how to complete a document, and must not provide advice on how to proceed in a given matter involving a notarial act.

Unless the Notary is also an attorney, these types of "how-to" questions should be answered by an attorney. In all cases, the Notary should avoid the unauthorized practice of law.

Official Notary Seal

As the universally recognized symbol of the office of Notary Public, an impression of the Notary's official seal should be affixed on every document notarized. The seal should be manually affixed each and every time; a preprinted, reproduced or computer-generated image of the seal is not permitted.

The official seal always must be safeguarded to prevent its misuse by others and may never be lent for use by another person, even if the other person is a Notary. The Notary never should lend or offer the seal for use in a commercial advertisement or solicitation.

When the Notary's term of office ends, the Notary must destroy or deface the official seal unless law prescribes another disposition, such as submitting the seal to a Notary-regulating authority. Notaries should check with the appropriate Notary-regulating office in their state to determine the correct disposition of the notarial seal and other records.

Journal of Notarial Acts

The journal of notarial acts is a public record intended to benefit society by reducing fraud and groundless lawsuits and by protecting individual rights. Notaries should maintain complete, sequential records of every notarial act performed in a bound journal with numbered pages. Each journal entry should be made at the time the notarial act was performed — not before, not after.

The Notary's journal should be safeguarded and not surrendered to any person without lawful authorization. When presented with a written request specifying the approximate date, nature of the transaction and signer's name, the Notary should show or provide a copy of a specific journal entry to any person. The requester also should show adequate identification. The Notary must protect other individuals' privacy by not allowing random or unsupervised examinations of the journal by persons without official authority.

Unless there are official procedures for disposal of the journal, a person who ceases to be a Notary should safeguard any notarial records for at least up to the statutory deadline for civil lawsuits.

Confidentiality

The Notary has a responsibility to act as an impartial witness and respect the confidentiality of documents and their signers. However, it is also the Notary's responsibility to scan the document for blank spaces and to extract necessary information for the journal.

Further, the Notary should not allow anyone to inspect a journal entry unless that individual can provide the approximate date, type of notarization and document, and the names of the parties involved.

Education

The Notary's effectiveness in protecting the public from fraud is directly related to the quality of the Notary's initial and continuing education and training.

Notaries must know and understand all laws, regulations, official directives, standards and guidelines relative to the performance of notarial acts in their jurisdictions. All pertinent official pamphlets, handbooks, manuals and other literature should be studied. The Notary must keep current on new laws and regulations and on any other developments that affect the performance and validity of notarial acts in the Notary's jurisdiction.

The Notary also should freely provide notarial expertise and assistance to less-experienced Notaries in order to uphold the standards of the public office and report Notaries who consistently fail to uphold those standards to commissioning authorities.

NO FORCE OF LAW

In some jurisdictions, the standards of the *Notary Public Code of Professional Responsibility* are actually requirements of law, such as the requirement to keep a record of all notarial acts performed. In most cases, however, the *Code's* standards of practice do not carry the force of law but rather are guidelines of professional conduct.

Following the *Code's* ethical rules can prove helpful when a Notary is faced with a lawsuit. Adhering to the standards will demonstrate that the Notary took all of the necessary steps to exercise reasonable care.

▼

However, violators of ethical rules in some professions may face punishment by a licensing authority. For instance, attorneys who violate the American Bar Association's *Code of Professional Responsibility* risk loss of their licenses to practice law. With Notaries, however, these ethical standards usually do not carry the force of law.

SUMMARY

State laws that govern Notaries are often vague or incomplete, so Notaries often must rely on rules of ethics and professional responsibility for guidance. Such rules are widely accepted standards of honesty, fairness and common sense.

The National Notary Association has developed the *Notary Public Code of Professional Responsibility* to guide Notaries when laws, regulations, state manuals and other official directives fall short. The *Code* is based upon widely accepted principles that define the Notary's unique functions.

The Notary Public is a government officer and must serve all of the general public without discrimination. The Notary must remain impartial when performing notarial acts. Detecting and deterring document fraud is the basic function of the Notary. Any notarial act that is illegal, dishonest, improper or contrary to the *Notary Public Code of Professional Responsibility* should be refused.

A Notary may be a public officer and a private employee, but the Notary always must give precedence to any law, regulation, state manual or official directive when it conflicts with the wishes of an employer, client, customer or other person. The Notary's actions are limited by law and do not require or allow the use of independent judgment, especially when that judgment involves the preparation of legal documents.

As the symbol of the office of Notary Public, the Notary's official seal should be affixed to every single document notarized. Notaries should maintain complete, sequential records of every notarial act performed in a bound journal. Notaries must know and understand all laws, regulations, official directives, standards and guidelines relative to their performance of notarial acts.

In some jurisdictions, the *Code's* standards are requirements of law, but in most cases, the standards of professional and ethical practice do not carry the force of law. ■

IMPORTANT TERMS

Ethics: Principles of good conduct; moral values.

Notary Public Code of Professional Responsibility: Code of conduct for Notaries. Developed by the National Notary Association based on input received over four decades from numerous Notaries and a drafting panel of Notary-regulating officials, attorneys and representatives from groups with a large consistency of Notaries. Printed in its entirety in Appendix 1 ("Notary Public Code of Professional Responsibility").

Rules of Ethics: Widely accepted standards of honesty, fairness and common sense.

CHAPTER 22 TEST

In each blank, write the response — a, b, c or d — that best completes each of the following statements:

1. When laws are not specific or comprehensive enough to describe fully the duties of a Notary, _____.

    a. The Notary must defer to his or her employer for instructions.

    b. Ethical guidelines fill the void.

    c. Only an attorney can properly provide guidance.

    d. The notarial act requested is illegal.

2. Ethical rules for Notaries _____.

    a. Are often vague or incomplete.

    b. Have never been defined.

    c. Are not enforceable through the legal system.

    d. Are of no use to the average Notary.

3. A Notary is a government officer and _____.

    a. Must serve all of the public evenhandedly.

    b. Has the authority to refuse to perform a notarial act without due cause or reasonable suspicion.

    c. Must not refuse to perform any notarial act, lawful or unlawful.

    d. Receives special, official privileges.

4. In any transaction that would call into question the Notary's impartiality, the Notary _____.

    a. May proceed if the signer declares that it is OK.

    b. May proceed if sure no one will find out.

    c. Must decline to accept a fee for performing the act.

    d. Must decline to notarize.

5. Detecting and deterring document fraud is _____.

    a. The basic function of the Notary Public.

    b. Admirable, but should be left to law enforcement officials, not Notaries.

    c. Not the concern of the Notary.

    d. Too specialized a field for the Notary to be involved in as a ministerial official.

6. When conflicts between the instructions of an employer and the responsibility of a Notary arise, the Notary _____.

    a. Must yield to the employer.

    b. Must immediately resign the Notary commission.

    c. Must always follow and give precedence to any law, regulation or official directive.

    d. Must immediately resign as an employee.

7. Only a Notary who _____ may prepare a document for another person or provide advice on how to complete a document.

    a. Was commissioned by a federal judge.

    b. Is an attorney or a professional trained in a pertinent field.

    c. Has been authorized by a client.

    d. Possesses a college degree.

8. Notaries must know and understand _____.

    a. Most laws, regulations, official directives, standards and guidelines relative to their performance of notarial acts.

    b. All laws, regulations, official directives, standards and guidelines relative to their employer's business.

    c. The laws, regulations, official directives, standards and guidelines relative to the particular transaction being notarized.

    d. All laws, regulations, official directives, standards and guidelines relative to their performance of notarial acts.

See page 391 for correct responses.

CHAPTER 23

Beneficial Interest

Beneficial interest is the most common cause of undue influence. Usually, beneficial interest means a financial gain, but it can mean any gain or advantage, financial or otherwise.

Most state laws prohibit Notaries from acting in transactions in which they have a direct beneficial interest. However, these laws rarely completely state what does and does not constitute a disqualifying beneficial interest.

DISQUALIFYING INTEREST

Statutes almost never definitively address three common and potentially disqualifying situations: 1) notarizing for family members, 2) notarizing corporate papers as a corporate officer and 3) notarizing as an agent receiving a commission.

Notarizing for Family Members

Most state laws do not expressly prohibit notarizing for a relative but are increasingly doing so. Notaries who do so in many instances will violate the statutes prohibiting a direct beneficial interest. For instance, if a Notary is asked to witness her husband's signature on a loan document for the purchase of a home they will share, she will directly benefit from the transaction and should disqualify herself.

The likelihood of a direct beneficial interest is usually greater with immediate family members — spouse, mother, father, son, daughter, sister or brother — than with nonimmediate family such as in-laws, cousins, nieces, nephews, aunts and uncles. The matter of interest in an inheritance is more often a consideration with lineal descendants (children, grandchildren, etc.) and ascendants (parents, grandparents, etc.) than with nonlineal relatives.

In many instances, a Notary will have no beneficial interest in notarizing for a relative and will not be prevented by law from doing so. However, to avoid later questioning of the Notary's impartiality, as well as accusations of undue influence, it is always safest for a signer to find a Notary who is not related.

Notarizing as a Corporate Officer

Occasionally, state laws will prohibit a Notary who is a corporate director, president, vice president, secretary, treasurer or other officer from notarizing papers involving the particular corporation, since the personal fortunes of such officers often can be directly linked to those of the corporation.

In the absence of specific prohibitions in the law, Notaries who are corporate officers should consider each situation carefully before deciding whether they have a disqualifying interest. For example, a corporate president whose income varies directly with corporate profits may have a direct interest in any sales agreement adding to corporate income. On the other hand, a corporation's treasurer who happens to be a salaried employee might not have a direct beneficial interest in the same documents.

Regardless of whether a corporate officer's beneficial interest in a transaction is perceived as direct or remote, it is always safest for that person not to notarize corporate papers. A salaried employee who is not an officer, such as a clerk or administrative assistant, can serve as a

Notaries generally should avoid notarizing for relatives due to the potential for beneficial interest. This is especially true for immediate family members.

Corporate officers should not notarize corporate documents.

Notary. Such a policy can prevent later questions about the officer's impartiality.

In the case of partnerships, a Notary who is a partner normally has a disqualifying interest in any document or transaction affecting the partnership.

Notarizing as an Agent on Commission

Is a sales agent's commission a disqualifying interest that should prevent the agent from notarizing a sales agreement? Does an attorney paid by a client to act as advocate have a disqualifying interest that should prevent the attorney from notarizing papers prepared for the client?

These questions seldom are addressed specifically by law. In many states, the usual prohibition against a direct beneficial or financial interest is interpreted to disqualify sales agents, attorneys and other professionals from notarizing for clients who are paying them. (A notable exception is California, whose law allows sales agents and attorneys to notarize for clients.) Regardless of state law, a good policy in any sales or law office is to have a person other than the directly benefiting agent or attorney act as Notary. This other individual would be strictly salaried or have no direct stake in the payment of a commission or fee.

Common sense and honesty should serve as ethical guides for the Notary when state law is noncommittal about disqualifying interest. Notaries who have any doubt at all about whether their interest in a transaction is disqualifying should not perform the notarization. This can prevent later challenges to the transaction on grounds that the Notary was biased and used undue influence to compel the signer to sign.

ALLOWED INTEREST: FEES

State laws allow Notaries to charge a statutory fee for performing a notarial act. Most laws are very explicit about the maximum fee that may be charged for a particular type of notarization. In different states, for example, the fee for executing an acknowledgment ranges from 25 cents to $10 per signature. Normally, states permit Notaries to charge any amount less than the maximum or to not charge at all.

A person who will receive a commission from a transaction should not notarize documents relating to that transaction.

State laws usually are strict in prescribing penalties for overcharging. Such penalties can range from criminal (fines, jailing) to administrative punishment (revocation of a commission).

Fees for Clients and Nonclients

Clients and nonclients must be treated equally in charging fees.

Ethical issues sometimes arise for Notaries in regard to fees. One issue is whether it is proper to waive notarial fees for clients while charging nonclients for the same services. This policy is ethically at odds with the Notary's role as an impartial public servant. To avert charges of discrimination, Notaries should be consistent in charging all persons the same amount or in not charging at all.

Travel Fees

Travel fees must be reasonable and agreed to beforehand.

Another ethical issue is whether and how to charge for travel. A few states prescribe mileage fees that may be charged for a Notary's travel, but most do not address the matter in law or regulation. Generally, Notary-regulating officials do not object to reimbursement for travel expenses, as long as the charge is reasonable and the signer both agrees to it beforehand and understands that it is not required by law. What constitutes a reasonable travel fee is left to the good judgment of the Notary. Here again, the Notary's common sense, honesty and fairness must serve as ethical guides.

SUMMARY

Most states prohibit Notaries from acting when they have a direct beneficial interest, such as a financial gain or other advantage.

Notarizing for a relative has the potential to involve beneficial interest. Beneficial interest is usually more likely with immediate family members such as spouses, mothers, fathers, sons, daughters, sisters or brothers.

A Notary who is a corporate officer or partner should consider each situation carefully to determine if there is a disqualifying interest, since the individual's income may be directly linked to a particular document requiring a notarial act. It is always safest for an officer or partner not to notarize corporate or partnership papers. An employee who is not an officer can serve as a Notary.

In many states, sales agents, attorneys and other professionals are disqualified from notarizing for clients who are paying them. An exception is California. A good policy in any sales or law office is to have a person other than the directly benefiting agent or attorney act as Notary.

Common sense and honesty should guide the Notary when state law is not specific about disqualifying interest. Notaries who have any doubt at all should not perform the notarization.

States allow Notaries to charge a fee for notarizations. Most laws specify a maximum fee, and states permit Notaries to charge any amount less than the maximum or to not charge at all. It is not proper to waive notarial fees for clients while charging nonclients for the same services. Notaries may charge for reasonable travel expenses, as long as the signer agrees to it beforehand and understands that it is not required by law. ■

IMPORTANT TERMS

Agent's Commission: Fee for performing as a representative or advocate on behalf of another person.

Beneficial Interest: Advantage.

Corporate Officer: Agent appointed to conduct business for a corporation.

Disqualifying Interest: Advantage or potential advantage resulting in ineligibility to perform a notarial act.

Lineal Relatives: Family members of previous and subsequent generations in a direct line, such as parents, grandparents, great-grandparents and so on, and children, grandchildren, great-grandchildren and so on.

Statutory Fee: Charge prescribed by law for services.

CHAPTER 23 TEST

In each blank, write the response — a, b, c or d — that best completes each of the following statements:

1. Notarizing for a spouse _____.

    a. Is specifically prohibited by law in most states.

    b. May violate law prohibiting a direct financial interest.

    c. Is proper if the Notary is not also a signer of the document.

    d. Is never improper.

2. Corporate sales agreements are best notarized by _____.

    a. A salaried clerical employee.

    b. The corporate vice president.

    c. The agent executing the sale.

    d. The corporate president.

3. A sales commission _____.

    a. Is a financial but not a beneficial interest.

    b. Disqualifies agents from notarizing sales papers in some states.

    c. Never disqualifies agents from notarizing sales papers.

    d. May be collected in place of the Notary's statutory fee.

4. In most states, travel fees are _____.

    a. Set by law.

    b. Prohibited by law.

    c. Officially allowed, though not addressed by law.

    d. Ethical violations even when officially allowed.

5. The signer least likely to pose a disqualifying interest is _____.

    a. A purchaser of the Notary's property.

    b. The mother of the Notary.

    c. A friend of the Notary.

    d. A partner of the Notary.

6. Notaries unsure if they have a disqualifying interest should _____.

    a. Notarize but note their doubts in the journal.

    b. Notarize only if the signer does not object.

    c. Notarize if they waive the fee for notarial services.

    d. Not notarize.

7. To avoid discrimination, the safest course for Notaries is _____.

    a. Not to charge members of minority groups for notarial services.

    b. To charge all persons for notarial services.

    c. Not to charge all persons for notarial services.

    d. To be consistent in charging or not charging all persons.

Explain in your own words:

8. What three common and potentially disqualifying situations for Notaries do laws seldom address?

_____

_____

_____

See page 391 for correct responses.

CHAPTER 24

Advertising and Notaries

Until recent years, state laws provided little guidance on advertising by and involving Notaries. But increasingly, laws are being enacted to deter misleading advertising that involves Notaries. One thrust of these laws is to prevent misrepresentation of the powers of a Notary. Another is to prevent commercial endorsements by Notaries.

Still, there are many questions related to advertising that are not addressed by law. In these areas, the Notary's common sense and good judgment should offer direction.

ADVERTISING NOTARIAL SERVICES

There are no statutory or ethical restraints against simply advertising notarial services. In a sign, newspaper ad, telephone book listing or business card, it is not illegal or unethical to print such notices as: "Lisa Romano, Notary Public," "Ali Morad, Notarial Services," or "Notary Public on Premises."

As long as the references to a Notary's title and function are honest, dignified and in keeping with the Notary's role as a public official, there is usually no impropriety.

False or Misleading Ads

Some states' laws contain general prohibitions against false or misleading ads in which Notaries claim to have powers that they are not given by law. For example, an ad for "Notary-Certified Translations" falsely indicates that Notaries have the power to certify translations.

Even in states without specific bans on false or misleading advertising by Notaries, it would be ethically improper — if not illegal under other laws — for a Notary to imply that he or she has powers not provided by law.

Advertising by Notaries must not mislead the public into believing the Notary has authority not granted.

Immigration Service Advertising

Some states expressly prohibit persons who claim to be immigration "consultants," "specialists," "experts" or "counselors" from also advertising as Notaries. These laws attempt to prevent self-styled and unscrupulous immigration counselors (who are also Notaries) from misrepresenting their authority.

This deters abuse of uninformed non-U.S. residents who think that Notaries are attorneys who may prepare legal documents, as Notaries do in their home countries.

Advertising in Foreign-Languages

Some state laws specifically prohibit use of non-English variations of the term "Notary Public" — such as the Spanish *notario publico* — because such foreign officials essentially are attorneys.

In addition, these laws usually require any non-English-language ads for notarial services to contain a statement that the Notary is not an attorney, as well as a list of the statutory notarial fees in English and the foreign language.

TESTIMONIALS AND ENDORSEMENTS

Opportunistic Notaries have been known to use their seals and titles to endorse commercial products, services and contests in advertising and mail solicitations. These Notaries offer testimonials in praise of a product or service or serve as an "official" judge.

Notaries may never use their seal or title to endorse a product or service.

Many states' laws prohibit use of the Notary seal and title for any purpose other than performing a notarial act. Even when such use does not violate a law, it breaches high ethical standards and compromises the office of Notary Public.

Widespread misunderstanding of the Notary's role causes such ads and solicitations to be a dangerous disservice to the public. Many people mistakenly believe that a Notary's involvement means governmental endorsement, and this misunderstanding is exploited by many promoters. Sadly, a Notary's testimonial to the benefits of a particular product may deceive many persons into believing that an otherwise unremarkable, or even shoddy, product is better than others.

Ethics and good judgment, if not law, should prevent all Notaries from intentionally using their titles and seals — or allowing their titles and seals to be used by others — for any purpose other than to indicate that a lawful notarial act has been performed.

SUMMARY

Law and ethical standards prohibit misrepresentation of the powers of a Notary and commercial endorsements by Notaries.

Notaries may advertise their services as long as the references to their title and function are honest, dignified and in keeping with the Notary's role as a public official.

Many states specifically prohibit false or misleading ads in which Notaries claim to have powers they are not given by law. Some states prohibit so-called immigration consultants from also advertising as Notaries to prevent exploitation of uninformed immigrants. Some states prohibit use of non-English variations of the term "Notary Public" in advertising and require any non-English-language ads to contain a statement that the Notary is not an attorney, because notarial officers in foreign countries are essentially attorneys.

Many states have laws expressly disallowing use of the Notary seal and title for any purpose other than performing a notarial act. Notaries may not issue testimonials or endorse products, services and contests. ■

IMPORTANT TERMS

Advertisement: Paid public announcement intended to sell a product, service or idea.

Endorsement: Public expression of approval.

Immigration Consultant: One who advises and assists another in the legal process of immigrating to the United States, especially in preparing the necessary paperwork. Also called an immigration specialist, immigration expert and immigration counselor.

Solicitation: Enticement; advertising with an offer.

Testimonial: Expression of praise; endorsement.

CHAPTER 24 TEST

In each blank, write the response — a, b, c or d — that best completes each of the following statements:

1. The following in an ad is ethically questionable: _____.

    a. "Pamela Hill, Notary."

    b. "Pamela Hill, Notarial Services."

    c. "Pamela Hill, Notarization Performed Here."

    d. "Pamela Hill, Most Qualified Notary in Town."

2. Notaries may serve as official government judges in contests _____.

    a. At no time.

    b. If they are not paid.

    c. If the contests are run honestly.

    d. If the proceeds will go to a worthy cause.

3. Many non-natives of the United States _____.

    a. Will expect Notaries to act for free, as in their native lands.

    b. Are unfamiliar with Notaries, since they are not found abroad.

    c. May resent being asked for IDs as an invasion of privacy.

    d. Believe that Notaries may prepare documents, like attorneys.

4. A Notary's seal in an ad is a disservice to the public since _____.

    a. Seldom does the Notary actually test the product or service.

    b. It means official endorsement to many people.

    c. Usually it appears without the Notary's knowledge.

    d. Changes may be made in the ad without the Notary's knowledge.

5. A Notary who takes dictation may ethically advertise _____.

    a. "Stenographic & Notarial Services."

    b. "Notary-Certified Stenography."

    c. "Certified Notary/Stenographer."

    d. "Official Stenography by Notary."

6. References to a Notary's title and function should _____.

    a. Praise the importance of the office of Notary.

    b. Downplay the role of the Notary whenever possible.

    c. Be truthful and in keeping with the role of a public official.

    d. Never be made.

▼

Explain in your own words:

7. What are the two purposes of laws that regulate advertising by Notaries?

_____

_____

_____

See page 391 for correct responses.

APPENDICES

APPENDIX 1

Notary Public Code of Professional Responsibility

INTRODUCTION

Purpose of the Code

The Notary Public's key role in lending integrity to important transactions of commerce and law necessitates sound standards for the performance of notarial acts.

While many occupations pose professional and ethical norms for their practitioners, the need for guidelines is particularly acute with persons holding the office of Notary because of their unusual status as both public and private functionaries. In few offices is the practitioner more subject to conflicting pressures. Yet, in few offices are the guiding statutes so scant and inadequate.

The purpose of the *Code of Professional Responsibility* is to guide Notaries Public in the United States when statutes, regulations and official directives fall short.

The standards in this *Code* are of two types. The majority are principles, policies and practices that have proven over the years to be effective in helping Notaries perform their primary function of detecting and deterring fraud; in minimizing fraud, these standards also work to reduce the Notary's exposure to lawsuits. The remainder are standards derived from the conviction that a public officer in a democracy must serve all persons equally, without regard to such distinctions as race, nationality, ethnicity, citizenship, religion, politics, lifestyle, age, disability, gender or sexual orientation.

Because the acts of Notaries affect individual rights and property under both civil and criminal law, it is imperative that professional standards for Notaries be widely acknowledged as just, fair and well-developed. To that end, the standards in this *Code* were drafted with input from representatives of occupational fields with a large constituency of Notaries Public. Also contributing were state and local officials who regulate the activities of Notaries, as well as legal, business and surety experts.

Organization of the Code

This *Code of Professional Responsibility* is based upon 10 widely accepted "Guiding Principles" that clarify the multiple roles of the Notary Public in the United States. They are general rules for responsible conduct.

Each Principle in turn embraces particular "Standards of Professional and Ethical Practice" for the Notary. Each Standard works to maximize the public utility of the notarial office, while minimizing the Notary's exposure to liability.

The Standards of Professional and Ethical Practice are exemplified by "Illustrations" posing problematic situations that are common or typical for Notaries. Details are provided to help the reader visualize each situation.

For each Illustration, "The Ethical Imperative" or "The Professional Choice" indicates the course of action best exemplifying the pertinent Guiding Principle and Standard of Professional and Ethical Practice.

The Ethical Imperative identifies an action that, if not taken, would constitute a clear and serious violation of the Notary's fundamental role as an impartial witnessing official, as defined in the Guiding Principles.

The Professional Choice identifies an action that, if not taken, would undermine or lessen the Notary's effectiveness as a fraud-deterring public servant.

The 10 "Commentary" sections supplement the *Code* by explaining the drafters' views, concerns and rationales in shaping important provisions, and by discussing certain pertinent other matters not directly addressed by the *Code*.

Basis of the Code

The Guiding Principles and Standards of Professional and Ethical Practice are the distillation of decades of interaction between the National Notary Association and thousands of Notaries from every walk of life and from every state and U.S. jurisdiction. They address the

INTRODUCTION

common problems, issues and questions encountered by Notaries, particularly matters of conflicting interest.

The Principles and Standards reflect the conviction that Notaries must operate in a businesslike fashion, basing their actions on proven practices of business and government, and always carefully documenting their official activities.

Statutory Requirements

In some jurisdictions, a particular Standard of Professional and Ethical Practice may already be a requirement of statute, such as the common but not universal legal mandate to keep a record of all notarial acts performed. In most cases, however, the Standards do not carry the force of law. Therefore, throughout the *Code*, the word "shall" does not necessarily denote a legal obligation for the Notary, but it always constitutes a compelling recommendation.

In rare cases, the Standards may contradict provisions in a state's Notary statutes or administrative regulations, particularly when these rules stipulate procedures for disposal of the seal or journal upon termination of the Notary's commission. In these instances, of course, pertinent statutes and regulations must be obeyed by the Notary.

For the overwhelming majority of Notaries, no statute or administrative rule will prevent adherence to any and every Standard of Professional and Ethical Practice in the *Code*.

Employer Expectations

The Standards frequently will contradict not the provisions of law but the policies or expectations of the Notary's employer. This is often the case when an employer wishes to discriminate between customers and noncustomers by providing or withholding notarial services that the *Code* stipulates should be available to all.

Notaries should understand that the *Code* is a model for preferred conduct and not a gauge of unlawfulness or criminality.

Uses and Benefits of the Code

This *Code* may serve as a tool to guide and educate not only Notaries Public, but also lawmakers, public administrators, private employers and any users of notarial services.

It is a moral imperative for progressive change, and a catalyst for improving notarial statutes and conventions in commerce and law.

Widespread implementation of the *Code* will reduce fraud and litigation.

Any Notary's adherence to the *Code's* Standards brings confidence that he or she is acting in accord with the highest professional and ethical traditions of the notarial office.

Widespread adherence to the Standards by Notaries in the United States will engender heightened respect and recognition for their notarial office in the enterprises of government and business, both in this nation and abroad.

Revision of the Code

The *Notary Public Code of Professional Responsibility* is not intended to be static and unchangeable. Its organization allows the separable Standards to be added, deleted or amended with little or no disruption of other elements in the *Code*.

While the 10 Guiding Principles of the *Code* are sufficiently general to embrace considerable change in the duties and practices of the Notary office without amendment to their current form, it is likely that the *Code's* 85 Standards may in time need revision or supplement to accommodate technological developments.

Periodic review and revision of the *Code* are intended.

NOTARY PUBLIC CODE OF PROFESSIONAL RESPONSIBILITY

Guiding Principles

I

The Notary shall, as a government officer and public servant, serve all of the public in an honest, fair and unbiased manner.

II

The Notary shall act as an impartial witness and not profit or gain from any document or transaction requiring a notarial act, apart from the fee allowed by statute.

III

The Notary shall require the presence of each signer and oath-taker in order to carefully screen each for identity and willingness, and to observe that each appears aware of the significance of the transaction requiring a notarial act.

IV

The Notary shall not execute a false or incomplete certificate, nor be involved with any document or transaction that is false, deceptive or fraudulent.

V

The Notary shall give precedence to the rules of law over the dictates or expectations of any person or entity.

VI

The Notary shall act as a ministerial officer and not provide unauthorized advice or services.

VII

The Notary shall affix a seal on every notarized document and not allow this universally recognized symbol of office to be used by another or in an endorsement or promotion.

VIII

The Notary shall record every notarial act in a bound journal or other secure recording device and safeguard it as an important public record.

IX

The Notary shall respect the privacy of each signer and not divulge or use personal or proprietary information disclosed during execution of a notarial act for other than an official purpose.

X

The Notary shall seek instruction on notarization, and keep current on the laws, practices and requirements of the notarial office.

GUIDING PRINCIPLE I

The Notary shall, as a government officer and public servant, serve all of the public in an honest, fair and unbiased manner.

Standards of Professional and Ethical Practice

Article A: Refusal to Notarize

I-A-1: Refusal without Due Cause
The Notary shall not refuse to perform a lawful and proper notarial act without due cause.

> **Illustration:** The Notary is asked by a stranger to notarize that person's signature on a document. However, the Notary is hesitant to notarize for any unknown individual because of a presumed increased likelihood of fraud and liability.

> *The Ethical Imperative:* As a public officer and servant, the Notary notarizes the stranger's signature if no improprieties are requested or detected.

I-A-2: Refusal for Reasonable Suspicion
The Notary shall refuse to notarize if the Notary has knowledge, or a reasonable suspicion that can be articulated, that the transaction is unlawful or improper.

> **Illustration:** The Notary is asked by a stranger to notarize that person's signature on a document. As proof of identity, the stranger presents a single identification card, a state driver's license. The Notary notices that the photograph on the license is raised from the surface of the card and appears to overlay a state seal and the signature of a DMV official.

> *The Ethical Imperative:* The Notary refuses to notarize the stranger's document, since there is strong evidence that the ID has been tampered with and bears a false photograph, and that the stranger is an impostor.

I-A-3: Undue Cause for Refusal
The Notary shall not refuse to perform a lawful and proper notarial act because of the signer's race, nationality, ethnicity, citizenship, religion, politics, lifestyle, age, disability, gender or sexual orientation, or because of disagreement with the statements or purpose of a lawful document.

> **Illustration:** The Notary is asked by a stranger to notarize that person's signature on a document. The Notary notes that the stranger is a member of an ethnic minority group. The Notary has heard that most persons in this ethnic group are untrustworthy, through stories that family and friends have told over the years. The Notary hesitates to perform the notarization.

> *The Ethical Imperative:* The Notary notarizes the stranger's document, if no improprieties are requested or detected. Ethnicity here is irrelevant and, by refusing, the Notary may become liable for violating the stranger's civil rights.

I-A-4: Improper Refusal Due to Nonclient Status
The Notary shall not refuse to perform a lawful and proper notarial act solely because the signer is not a client or customer of the Notary or the Notary's employer.

COMMENTARY

GENERAL
Guiding Principle I sets the tone for the entire *Code*. By identifying the Notary as a public official, the Principle makes clear that a Notary Public has certain obligations to the general public, and must fulfill those obligations in a fair, honest and constitutionally acceptable manner. Consequently, many of the *Code's* 85 Standards direct Notaries to execute their official duties consistent with the demands put upon public officers.

PUBLIC OFFICIAL STATUS
Notaries have the power to impart an official imprimatur to a document or transaction. There are a plethora of judicial opinions that declare Notaries are "public officers." *(See, e.g., Britton v. Nicolls,* 104 U.S. 757, 765 (1881); *Werner v. Werner,* 526 P.2d 370, 376 (Wash. 1974); and *Commercial Union Ins. Co. v. Burt Thomas-Aitken Const. Co.,* 230 A.2d 498, 499 (N.J. 1967).) But public official status is different for a Notary than for many other public officials. Unlike some public officials, *e.g.,* elected officers, appointed administrators or policemen, a Notary is not a government employee, *per se.* This distinction can have far-reaching ramifications, especially in the area of personal liability. Usually Notaries are not afforded the sovereign immunity protection routinely available to public officials acting within the scope of their authority. Indeed, in some jurisdictions the enabling statute identifies the Notary as a quasi-public official *(see, e.g.,* KAN. STAT. ANN. § 53-101; and MO. REV. STAT. § 486.220.3) and in others the same result has been reached by court decision *(see, e.g., Transamerica Ins. Co. v. Valley Nat'l Bank,* 462 P.2d 814, 817 (Ariz. Ct. App. 1969); and *Ely Walker Dry Goods Co. v. Smith,* 160 P. 898, 900 (Okla. 1916)). These classifications, however, are primarily for liability purposes, and do not detract from the central thesis that a Notary is a public official empowered by the states to perform specified duties.
The Principle identifies the Notary as a public servant because notarial services are rendered to the public at large under the authority of state statutory rules. The Principle uses the public servant designation to reinforce the view that Notaries are important functionaries who are obligated to serve individual members of the public. Although notarial acts benefit the public at large by fostering reliance on various types of documents and acts, Notaries nevertheless are distinguishable from other public servants whose primary obligations are to the public as a whole, instead of individual members. Additionally, the drafters recognize that a substantial majority of state-commissioned Notaries are employees whose notarial services are only incidental to their principal job duties. For some of these Notaries, obligations to their employers, job site locations removed from public access, or both, raise important issues concerning their ability to serve members of the public at large. The *Code* addresses this problem consistent with the view that, absent special state legislation to the contrary, Notaries are public and not private servants. (*See* Standard I-4-A and accompanying Commentary.)

ARTICLE A: Refusal to Notarize
The Standards interpret the Principle consistent with the role expected of a public official. They are drawn from the *Model Notary Act,* Section 3-103(b), which reads, "A Notary shall perform notarial acts in lawful transactions for any requesting person..." Consequently, I-A-1 states the overarching proposition that a Notary should never refuse to act based upon the Notary's personal inclination or bias. As a public servant, the Notary is obligated to perform notarial services for all members of the public, regardless

Illustration: The Notary operates a business. A stranger walks in and requests notarization of a document. The Notary is reluctant to take time away from business to notarize for anyone but customers.

The Ethical Imperative: The Notary notarizes the stranger's document, if no improprieties are requested or detected. Notaries are commissioned to serve the public at large, not just the patrons of a particular business. While no document signer is justified in demanding that a Notary "drop everything" to perform a notarial act, the Notary should try to accommodate the request for notarial services within a reasonable time. However, for any sudden request that would be particularly time-consuming or disruptive to business (*e.g.,* notarize 100 documents immediately), it is reasonable for the Notary to reschedule the services to a more convenient time or to refer the signer to another nearby Notary available to perform the acts at once. Accommodating the public's need for notarial services is paramount for the publicly commissioned Notary.

Article B: Fees

I-B-1: Improper Assessment of Fee

The Notary shall not base the charging or waiving of a fee for performing a notarial act, or the amount of the fee, on the signer's race, nationality, ethnicity, citizenship, religion, politics, lifestyle, age, disability, gender or sexual orientation, or on agreement or disagreement with the statements or purpose of a lawful document.

Illustration: The Notary is asked by a stranger to notarize that person's signature on an affidavit for a ballot initiative the Notary opposes. The Notary is inclined to "punish" this proponent of the initiative by charging for the notarization, even though the Notary has never before charged for notarizing.

The Ethical Imperative: The Notary notarizes the stranger's affidavit without charging a fee. If it has been a consistent policy not to charge for performing notarial acts, the ethical Notary will not assess a fee as a punitive measure against a political opponent. The publicly commissioned Notary must strive to serve the public evenhandedly; thus, the best policy is for all to be charged the same, or for none to be charged. However, the Notary may waive the fee for ill or impoverished persons or for other charitable or *pro bono* causes.

I-B-2: Improper Assessment Due to Nonclient Status

The Notary shall not base the charging or waiving of a fee for performing a notarial act, or the amount of the fee, on whether the signer is a client or nonclient, or a customer or noncustomer, of the Notary or the Notary's employer.

Illustration: The Notary operates a business. A stranger walks in and requests notarization of a document. The Notary performs the notarization but wants to discourage future notarial services for noncustomers that take time away from business. Though never before charging for notarizations, the Notary ponders whether to charge the stranger and to impose a policy of charging noncustomers but not charging regular customers for notarial services.

The Ethical Imperative: The Notary does not charge the stranger for the notarization. Because Notaries are commissioned to serve the public evenhandedly, the ethical Notary does not "punish" persons who do not patronize a particular business by charging a fee for notarial services that are offered free to patrons of the same business. All should be charged the same, or none should be charged.

Article C: Dignity of Office

I-C-1: Dignity Befitting Public Office

---

of any signer's beliefs or personal attributes. Most state statutes are silent on this issue. Many jurisdictions merely authorize or empower Notaries to perform specific acts *(see, e.g.,* ARK. CODE ANN. § 21-14-104; COLO. REV. STAT. 12-55-110; and TEX. GOV'T CODE § 406.014), which can be interpreted to mean Notaries are not required to honor all requests. There are, however, notable exceptions. (*See, e.g.,* UTAH CODE ANN. § 46-1-8(2), providing "a notary shall perform notarial acts in lawful transactions for any requesting person..."; and CAL. GOV'T CODE § 8205(a), imposing "the duty of a Notary Public, when requested" to perform acts authorized in the section.) Sometimes Notaries are specifically given discretion in exercising their authority. (*See* IOWA CODE § 9E.8, allowing a Notary to exercise "reasonable discretion" in deciding whether or not to perform notarial services; and CONN. GEN. STAT. § 3-94f, providing that a Notary shall not "unreasonably refuse" to perform a notarial act. *And compare* N.M. STAT. ANN. § 14-12-1 and § 14-12-10, the former section authorizing the Notary to perform various notarial acts and the latter requiring the Notary to perform "protests.")

Although Notaries serve the public, Standard I-A-2 makes clear that a paramount function of the Notary is to deter fraud. Thus, if the Notary knows or has reason to believe that a transaction is illegal or improper, he or she should refrain from providing notarial services. (*Accord* GA. CODE ANN. § 45-17-8(b)(1).) The Illustration of Standard I-A-2 applies the Standard to an impostor-signer situation. (*Note,* if the Notary proceeds, he or she may be liable to third parties injured by the fraudulent transaction. *See, e.g.,* VA. CODE ANN. § 47.1-26; and *Tutelman v. Agricultural Ins. Co.,* 25 Cal.App.3d 914 (1972). If the Notary actually knows the transaction is fraudulent, providing notarial services constitutes a criminal act. *See, e.g.,* N.C. GEN. STAT. § 10A-12; and N.M. STAT. ANN. § 14-12-18.)

The *Code* takes the position that the Notary cannot use personal bias as the basis for deciding whether or not the transaction is tainted with an irregularity. The Standard is written to be as expansive as possible in identifying potential biases. Of particular note is the proscription against using statements made in or the purposes for an otherwise lawful document as the basis for refusing to provide notarial services. Notwithstanding the goal of deterring fraud, the Standard does not anticipate that a Notary will make an independent investigation of the transaction. The *Code* merely posits that a Notary should refuse to put his or her official seal of approval on a transaction that the Notary has reason to believe is fraudulent or otherwise illegal. The Notary is expected to exercise the same care as would an ordinary, reasonable person under like circumstances. Thus, the *Code* neither imposes a special standard of care nor requires legal training for Notaries. This position has statutory support. (*See* IDAHO CODE § 51-111(1), providing Notaries are to use "reasonable care" in fulfilling their general duties.)

Perhaps the most troublesome issue concerning a Notary's decision either to render or withhold services arises in the case of the employee-Notary. Quite often employers dictate that the employee-Notary only provide notarial services for the employer's clients or customers. Arguably this practice has been approved by statutory rule (*see* CAL. GOV'T CODE § 8202.8), but it is not a universally accepted position (*see* IOWA CODE § 9E.8).

Absent statutory authority to the contrary, the *Code* adopts the view that Notaries as public servants are required to serve all individuals who request notarial service. Understandably this position raises a number of difficult logistical problems. As demonstrated in the Illustration for Standard I-A-4, there is no expectation that a Notary either be "on-call" or at the "beck and call" of the public. The operating principle is "reasonable availability." (*See* 14 Op. Att'y. Gen. 250 (Cal. 1949).)

The thornier side of this issue is whether or not the public has access to the Notary-employee. The *Code's* position is well-suited to situations wherein the Notary-employee works in an establishment conveniently open to the public for other commercial purposes, such as a drug store, stationery supply shop or supermarket. But in quasi-public (*e.g.,* banks or real estate offices) or private (*e.g.,* law firms or business offices) venues, application of the Standard is more problematic. The drafters understand that Notary-employees are not at liberty to establish business policy. Therefore, they cannot be reasonably expected to jeopardize their jobs by disobeying employer directives that

The Notary shall conduct himself or herself with a dignity befitting a public officer and in a manner that does not bring disrepute or discredit upon the notarial office.

> **Illustration:** The Notary is employed in an office with one other Notary, both notarizing affidavits for coworkers. Each affidavit requires administration of an oath to the affiant. The Notary has heard the colleague say to affiants at the start of an oath, "I know this is stupid, but will you please raise your right hand..."; jokingly, the colleague may also have the signer "swear" by placing a hand on a magazine. The Notary considers whether to be similarly flippant about notarial duties in order to fit in better with coworkers.

> *The Ethical Imperative:* The Notary refrains from adopting the officemate's attitude toward notarization. The Notary cautions the colleague that such improprieties undermine the effectiveness of the notarial act, discredit the office of Notary and may jeopardize or invalidate the document. The Notary decides to report any further such improper liberties with official duties to a supervisor and, if the actions persist, to the state Notary-commissioning authority.

Article D: Advertising and Endorsement

I-D-1: Undignified Advertisement

The Notary shall not advertise notarial services in an undignified or excessively commercial manner.

> **Illustration:** The Notary advertises in the telephone book a willingness to notarize "Anytime, Anywhere." To compete against other traveling Notaries, the Notary considers running a new ad that would state, "I Will Not Be Undersold!" and, "I'm Crazy — I'll Go Anywhere At Any Hour!"

> *The Ethical Imperative:* The Notary does not place the new advertisement, since it treats the public office of Notary in both an undignified and an excessively commercial manner.

I-D-2: Misrepresentation

The Notary shall not misrepresent the notarial office; claim or advertise powers, authority, advantages or rights that the office does not give; nor use language that is likely to mislead non-natives of the United States about the powers of the office.

> **Illustration:** The Notary owns a shop in an area with a large concentration of Latin-American immigrants. The Notary wants to put a sign in the shop window to advertise notarial services, but ponders whether it should read "Notary" or "Notario."

> *The Ethical Imperative:* The Notary does not advertise using the Spanish term *Notario Publico* or *Notaria Publica* because this is the title of an attorney-like officer in Latin nations and it may mislead immigrants into thinking that U.S. Notaries have the same powers and are entitled to the same fees.

I-D-3: Endorsement Improper

The Notary shall not use or allow use of the Notary's seal or title ("Notary Public") to endorse, extol or denigrate a product, service, program, proposal, individual, candidate, organization or contest, or to corroborate or disprove claims about them.

> **Illustration:** The Notary is a volunteer for a charity that will raffle off a new car to raise funds. So that the raffle is perceived as honest and aboveboard, the president of the charity wants to advertise that the contest will be "Notary-Supervised and Guaranteed," using the name of the Notary.

> *The Ethical Imperative:* The Notary does not allow the

---

include providing notarial services only for the employer's customers. The *Code* does not encourage Notary-employees to disregard their employers' policies, even ones that may seem inappropriate, though such employees are urged to try tactfully to "educate" their employers. Also, in those instances where the Notary-employee works in a restricted area, it will be either impossible or impracticable for the public to gain access to the Notary-employee. Through its silence, the *Code* does not seek to interfere in these situations. Indeed, the Introduction states that the *Code* is designed to be a model, not a mandate, for preferred conduct. Nonetheless, the *Code* adheres to the general view that Notaries are public servants and should be available to perform their services for the public at large. By focusing on this problem, the drafters hope appropriate state authorities will act to clarify the situation in their respective jurisdictions.

ARTICLE B: Fees

Most state Notary statutes establish a schedule that sets out the allowable charges for the different notarial services that may be provided. Generally there is no requirement that a Notary charge for providing a notarial service. (*Accord* GA. CODE ANN. § 45-17-11(c).) Charging excessive fees, however, can be grounds for having one's commission revoked. (*See* OHIO REV. CODE ANN. § 147.13.) Although not addressed in the *Code*, preferred practice suggests that a fee schedule be posted in the vicinity where notarial services are provided. (*Accord* 5 ILL. COMP. STAT. 312/3-103(b); and DEL. CODE. ANN. tit. 4, § 310(c).)

Sometimes a Notary's decision on whether to charge a fee may carry an improper bias. Standard I-B-1 posits that personal bias should never be used as a basis for determining whether or not a fee should be charged. This is consistent with the view that a Notary may not use personal bias in determining whether or not to render notarial services. (The Illustration demonstrates the application of the Standard on this matter.)

Standard I-B-2 addresses a different type of discriminatory practice, that of basing the decision to charge a fee on whether or not the signer is a client of either the Notary or the Notary's employer. This is a common problem because Notaries tend not to be exclusively in the trade or business of being a Notary. Consistent with the view that a Notary is a public servant, the *Code* adopts the position that the Notary should treat all members of the public evenhandedly. If the Notary's primary business customers are not charged for notarial services, then non-customers should be treated similarly.

Again, as is the case with providing notarial services, Notary-employees may be subject to employer policies that preclude them from following the Standard. The Illustration of Standard I-B-2 specifically addresses Notaries who can control or set policy. These Notaries are admonished not to discriminate on the basis of "customer" status. By not providing a corresponding Illustration for Notary-employees subject to their employers' dictates, drafters of the *Code* tacitly accept that discriminatory practices imposed upon the Notary are an unfortunate reality and that imposing an ethical obligation on Notary-employees in such sensitive and tenuous positions may be unfair. Each such Notary-employee must decide whether to tolerate such discrimination, attempt to "educate" the employer, defy the policy, or voluntarily terminate employment.

In developing Article B, the drafters were not unmindful of the rationale supporting "customer" status fee discrimination. There are costs associated with providing notarial services that must be paid (*e.g.*, licensing fees, supplies and lost business time). Businesses must absorb these costs and account for them in some way. It is not unreasonable to consider the expenses and cost of doing business and allocate them to the general business overhead. These costs are then built into the pricing of goods and services offered by the business. Thus, customers in a sense "pay" for the Notary-related fees, but non-customers do not. From this perspective, it may be regarded as both appropriate and fair to charge non-customers for the notarial services. Failing to do so could be argued as discriminatory to the customers who are paying for the non-customer's otherwise notarial office to be used to lend seeming integrity or credibility to a contest, regardless of the nobility of its cause. Guaranteeing and certifying the integrity of contests is not an authorized notarial act. Further, the Notary should not notarize any document (*e.g.*, an affidavit signed by the president of the charity) with knowledge that the notarial seal or title will be used in a solicitation or endorsement, since some persons associate any involvement by a Notary with official government certification.

Article E: Ability and Availability to Serve

I-E-1: Resignation if Impaired

The Notary shall resign from office if any permanent change in the Notary's physical status would prevent or significantly impair the proper performance of notarial duties.

> **Illustration:** The Notary is a retiree whose eyesight has deteriorated considerably in recent years. Even with glasses, the Notary is only able to read if the letters are unusually large and bold; distinguishing faces is very difficult.

> *The Ethical Imperative:* The Notary must immediately resign the commission, since such poor eyesight prevents the careful scrutinizing of ID cards and faces required for proper performance of notarial duties and protection of the public from document fraud. Any physical condition that prevents a Notary from directly and personally gleaning information about a signer's identity and about the circumstances of a particular notarization, without reliance on an assistant or intermediary to make such determinations, is a disqualifying one.

I-E-2: Refusal for Lack of Knowledge

The Notary shall decline to notarize if the Notary does not feel sufficiently knowledgeable or competent to perform properly any requested notarial act.

> **Illustration:** The Notary is asked to execute a protest by a stranger who presents a technically-worded notarial form. When the Notary admits to having no idea how to complete the form, the stranger says, "Don't worry, I'll walk you through it."

> *The Ethical Imperative:* The Notary declines to notarize without the knowledge to proceed competently and confidently. Only a specially trained or experienced Notary who is familiar with pertinent provisions of the Uniform Commercial Code should undertake the technically complex notarial act of protest.

I-E-3: Reporting Pertinent Change

The Notary shall report to the commissioning agency any pertinent change in personal status — including change of name or address, conviction of a felony, or adjudicated liability in a lawsuit involving a notarial act — affecting the Notary's availability to the public and the repute of the Notary as a person of integrity.

> **Illustration:** The Notary is planning a permanent move to live and work in another state. There are two years remaining in the commission term.

> *The Ethical Imperative:* The Notary reports the move to the state Notary-commissioning authority and resigns the commission. State officials must know the whereabouts of all Notaries and be kept apprised of their availability to serve the state's citizenry.

---

free receipt of the notarial services. Notwithstanding the economic appeal of this argument, the *Code* falls back on its general position that Notaries are public servants and should deal with all members of the public similarly. Additionally, it can be argued that a private business that has a Notary available for its own uses at all times should pay for the convenience by treating all users equally. The Standard does not suggest the employer should provide free notarial services for the public; it only asks that all members of the public be treated in the same manner.

ARTICLE C: Dignity of Office

The Standard adopts the view that Notaries are obligated to comport themselves in a professional manner. Notaries often play an essential role in validating documents or transactions. It is imperative that the Notary understand that those actions that tend to denigrate the office may ultimately impact the efficacy of a document or transaction. A flippant attitude or disrespect for the office should not be countenanced.

ARTICLE D: Advertising and Endorsement

The *Code* does not disapprove of Notary advertisements, but frowns upon those that are not done in a professional and tasteful manner. As a public official, the Notary should not resort to "hucksterism" in an effort to generate notarial business.

The *Code* takes a much stronger stance against misrepresentation and endorsements. Notaries are only empowered to perform specified acts. Misrepresenting those powers is a serious breach of one's professional obligation and, in some instances, may violate the law. (*See, e.g.*, OR. REV. STAT. § 194.162; and TEX. GOV'T CODE ANN. § 406.017(d).) Of particular concern is the fact that many foreign countries confer broader authority upon their Notaries than is given to Notaries in the United States. The *Code* makes clear that any attempt by a United States Notary to deceive non-United States citizens into believing the Notary can perform certain acts not authorized by state statute is unethical. (*See* Illustration for Standard I-D-2 and CAL. GOV'T CODE § 8219.5 (prohibiting deceptive non-English advertising of notarial services).)

Any improper use of the notarial office is wrong. The *Code* focuses on the "endorsement" question. It concludes that endorsements and testimonials are improper, and admonishes Notaries not to make them. This position has both statutory and regulatory support. (*See, e.g.*, UTAH CODE ANN. § 46-1-10; and WASH. ADMIN. CODE § 308-30-160.)

ARTICLE E: Ability and Availability to Serve

Standards I-E-1 and -2 reinforce the professional role of the Notary. The Illustrations are straightforward. A Notary whose health makes proper notarizations problematic is advised to resign the commission. A Notary who does not understand the technicalities of a specific notarial service is directed not to act. These are commonsense, reasonable restrictions that are beyond dispute.

Standard I-E-3 addresses "availability," but uses this term to mean "physical presence." A Notary who leaves the jurisdiction in which he or she is commissioned to serve as a Notary is obligated to resign the commission. This direction is in accord with a number of statutes that rule on this matter. (*See, e.g.*, OKLA. STAT. tit. 49, § 9; and IDAHO CODE § 51-115(2).)

GUIDING PRINCIPLE II

The Notary shall act as an impartial witness and not profit or gain from any document or transaction requiring a notarial act, apart from the fee allowed by statute.

<u>Standards of Professional and Ethical Practice</u>

Article A: Improper Gain

II-A-1: Actual or Potential Gain Improper

The Notary shall decline to notarize in any transaction that would result, directly or indirectly, in any actual or potential gain or advantage for the Notary, financial or otherwise, apart from the fee for performing a notarial act allowed by statute.

> **Illustration:** The Notary sells machinery and related maintenance contracts, which must be notarized. The Notary's receipt of a sales commission depends on the employer's receipt of a notarized contract signed by the customer. After convincing a customer to purchase a contract, the Notary then often quickly notarizes the customer's signature out of fear that the person's mind will change, even though there usually are other employees available who could notarize.

> *The Ethical Imperative:* The Notary decides not to notarize while profiting financially from a transaction, letting an uninvolved person perform the required notarization. The roles of impartial witness and advocate are incompatible. Notaries should never take actions to deter signers from changing their minds; one of the major purposes of notarization is to ensure that signers are acting freely.

II-A-2: Commission or Fee Improper

The Notary shall not notarize for a client or customer who will pay the Notary a commission or fee for the resulting transaction, apart from the fee for performing a notarial act allowed by statute.

> **Illustration:** The Notary is an attorney preparing documents for an ailing client who will pay a fee for the task. Several of the documents require notarization. Since the attorney must go to the home of the bedridden client to secure the needed signatures, there will be no paralegal or secretary on hand to notarize the papers. The attorney considers the propriety of serving as Notary in this situation.

> *The Ethical Imperative:* The Notary decides not to notarize, lest it be falsely alleged that a financial interest in the documents resulted in undue influence or the overlooking of lack of mental capacity. Instead, the attorney arranges to have a truly impartial Notary visit the client's home to notarize the documents.

Article B: Improper Personal Interest

II-B-1: Notarization of Own Signature Improper

The Notary shall not notarize his or her own signature.

> **Illustration:** The Notary is about to sign an insurance affidavit of loss for a fire in the Notary's house. At the end of the document is a jurat with blank space for a Notary's

---

COMMENTARY

GENERAL

Guiding Principle II enunciates the Notary's primary role: being an impartial witness. The Principle is consistent with other official interpretations on this point. (*See, e.g., Notary Public Information*, 2nd ed., Wis. Sec. of State (1994), which reads, "A notary public is...to serve the public as an impartial witness ...") The Notary is first and foremost an impartial witness. It is the Notary's impartiality that lends credence to other parties' actions, whether it be signing a document or some other participation in a transaction. Importantly, the Principle does not suggest that a Notary guarantees the genuineness of the parties' intentions or future performances. The Notary only serves as a witness to other parties' present actions with respect to a document or transaction. (For an early judicial pronouncement supporting this proposition, *see Coffin v. Bruten*, 95 S.W. 462 (Ark. 1906).)

In order to ensure impartiality, the Principle mandates that a Notary not provide notarial services in any situation where the Notary would financially profit or otherwise benefit from the notarized document or transaction. In this respect the Principle mirrors the rule found in preferred legislation. (*See, e.g., Model Notary Act*, Section 3-102(2), which "disqualifies" a Notary from acting when any benefit, apart from the statutory fee, would be received. Several statutes provide similar restrictions. *See, e.g.,* W. VA. CODE § 29C-3-102.) The prohibition does not apply to fees allowed by statute for rendering notarial services.

ARTICLE A: Improper Gain

The Standards, through their Illustrations, demonstrate a variety of ways in which a Notary could improperly "gain" from providing a notarial service. The Standards make clear that the Notary should refrain from acting if a benefit would flow either directly or indirectly to the Notary. Thus, the Standards embrace the notion that a Notary should not act if a close relative rather than the Notary himself or herself will gain from the transaction. Furthermore, the Principle uses the word "gain" to supplement "profit" and contemplates that a Notary should refrain from acting if he or she would receive any advantage or benefit, including non-financial ones, from the transaction. The message is clear. The only way to ensure impartiality is to make sure the Notary would have no reason whatsoever to provide services, other than to fulfill his or her obligations as a public servant. By failing to follow this practice a Notary will unnecessarily create actual or perceived conflicts of interest and breaches of ethical conduct.

The Illustration for Standard II-A-1 provides a simple example of how a Notary could improperly profit from a notarized document. After highlighting the Notary's conflict of interest, the Illustration stresses the point that "[t]he roles of impartial witness and advocate are incompatible." Although the conflict in the Illustration appears straightforward, there nonetheless may be some authority for the Notary to act. (*See, e.g.,* 5 ILL. COMP. STAT. 312/6-104(a); and N.C. GEN. STAT. § 10A-9(c)(2).) Irrespective of any countervailing view, the *Code* adopts the position that ethical concerns dictate a Notary take all reasonable steps to avoid a conflict of interest, notwithstanding the fact that the action at issue may otherwise be legal.

Standard II-A-2 addresses a more direct conflict of interest. The Illustration presents a situation in which the Notary will actually receive a fee for acting in a capacity other than a Notary in a transaction that requires the Notary to render notarial services. The gravamen of the problem is that there is a great likelihood the Notary will be more interested in seeing the transaction completed than in following proper notarial procedure. This is so because the notarial fee will be insignificant as compared to the

▼

signature and seal. The Notary ponders whether the insurance company will mind or even notice if the affiant and the Notary are the same person.

The Ethical Imperative: The Notary finds another person to notarize the signature. There is no greater breach of the Notary's requisite role as impartial witness than "notarizing" one's own signature. Indeed, the very concept of "notarizing for oneself" is as much a contradiction in terms as "marrying oneself" or "pardoning oneself."

II-B-2: Notarization of Cosignature Improper

The Notary shall not notarize a signature on a document that the Notary has cosigned.

Illustration: The Notary and the Notary's business partner need to have their signatures notarized on a document. Aware that notarizing one's own signature is improper, the Notary ponders whether to notarize the partner's signature.

The Ethical Imperative: The Notary does not notarize the partner's signature because, as a cosigner, the Notary has an obvious personal interest in the document that is incompatible with a requisite impartial role. The two partners arrange to have another Notary notarize the two signatures.

II-B-3: Notarization of Document Naming Notary Improper

The Notary shall not notarize a document that bears the name of the Notary or of a close relative, as defined below in Standard II-B-5.

Illustration: The Notary is asked by a friend to be the named agent on a document giving the Notary authority to make health care decisions for the friend in case of severe illness. The friend then asks the Notary to notarize this same document.

The Ethical Imperative: The Notary declines to notarize because, being named in the document as the individual

who is thereby given certain life-and-death decision-making powers, the Notary has an obvious personal interest in it that is incompatible with a requisite impartial role.

II-B-4: Notarization of Personal Document Improper

The Notary shall not notarize a document that will affect or involve the Notary's personal affairs.

Illustration: The Notary is informed by the Notary's roommate that the roommate will receive the gift of a condominium from a grandmother. Promising that the Notary may live in one of the bedrooms rent-free, the roommate asks the Notary to visit the grandmother to notarize her signature on the gift-deed.

The Ethical Imperative: The Notary declines to notarize because the Notary will personally benefit from the transaction. Such a beneficial financial impact on one's personal affairs is incompatible with the Notary's requisite impartial role. The roommates arrange to have an uninvolved Notary visit the grandmother.

II-B-5: Notarization for Close Relative Improper

The Notary shall decline to notarize the signature of a close relative or family member, particularly a spouse, parent, grandparent, sibling, son, daughter or grandchild of the Notary, or a stepchild, stepsibling, stepparent, stepgrandparent or stepgrandchild of the Notary.

Illustration: The Notary is asked by the Notary's father to notarize a document that specifies desired medical treatment in the event the father becomes unable to make such decisions. The Notary is not mentioned in the document.

The Ethical Imperative: The Notary declines to notarize and asks the father to have a Notary who is unrelated and truly disinterested notarize the document. It will thereby be rendered less open to challenge and the charge that undue influence was exerted on the signer by a family member.

---

remuneration to be had in the Notary's other capacity. The conflict perhaps most visibly arises with attorney-Notaries, but real estate brokers and other Notaries who serve clients also can become involved as dual-capacity actors in transactions.

The basis for the position taken in the *Code* is the recognition that it is difficult to retain impartiality when one has an interest in the transaction. The *Code* does not suggest that being a dual-capacity actor *ipso facto* breaches a duty. The *Code* is concerned with the risk that it will happen. The fear is that the Notary's other interest in the transaction may move the Notary to be less rigorous in following required notarial procedures, such as applying the requisite proof of identity standard. This, in turn, can lead to an increased number of legal challenges to notarized transactions — a particularly unfortunate consequence given that one of the benefits of a proper notarization is to validate a transaction in a way designed to minimize future disputes.

The "conflict" issue is perhaps most controversial in the case of attorney-Notaries. Many attorney-Notaries will notarize a client's documents for transactions in which the attorney represents the client. The conflict is readily apparent. Since, most probably, the attorney's fee will exceed the statutory Notary fee, there is a greater financial incentive for the attorney to see the transaction completed, than there is to comply strictly with proper notarial procedures. This is not to say that the mere presence of a conflict will result in "bad" notarizations. Actually, to the contrary, it is quite likely that the attorney will know the client better than would another Notary. Thus, one of the principal duties of a Notary, proving identity, is probably better accomplished by the attorney-Notary for a client, than by a Notary to whom the client is unknown. But the *Code* is not overly concerned with the Notary's personal knowledge of the client's identity. Presumably every Notary would take the necessary steps to verify the signer's identity. The greater issue is whether the attorney-Notary's financial incentive will result in a transaction that does not best serve the client and those who rely upon the notarization itself. The *Code* only views the situation in the context of the Notary-client relationship. Questions concerning the attorney-client relationship are governed by the appropriate rules of attorney ethics.

There is statutory authority for both attorneys and others to notarize documents for their clients. (*See, e.g.,* Cal. Gov't Code 8224; and Kan. Stat. Ann. § 53-109(c).) Nonetheless, the *Code* seeks to impose an ethical mandate that will eliminate the risks inherent in conflict situations. The ultimate goal is not to penalize the dual-capacity actor, but to better serve the public by guaranteeing more reliable transactions that are less susceptible to legal challenge.

ARTICLE B: Improper Personal Interest

Standards II-B-1 through -5, and the Illustrations thereto, are designed to reinforce the view that impartiality is compromised when the Notary has a personal interest in the transaction to be notarized. The Standards cover a wide range of potential conflicts, running the gamut from the obvious (Standard II-B-1 and -2: notarizing one's own name as either sole or cosigner) to the less evident (Standard II-B-4: notarizing a document that may touch upon the Notary's personal affairs even though the Notary is neither a signer of nor a party named in the document). Each Standard has statutory support. (*See, generally,* Conn. Gen. Stat. § 3-94g; Idaho Code § 51-108(2) through -(4); and Va. Code Ann. § 47-1.30.)

Article C: Avoiding Appearance of Partiality

II-C-1: Compromise of Impartiality

The Notary shall decline to notarize in any transaction that would impugn, compromise or call into question the Notary's impartiality or propriety, or has the potential for doing so.

> **Illustration:** The Notary is asked by the godmother of the Notary's children to notarize a document that will create a trust fund to benefit the children. The godmother will endow the trust with her own funds. The Notary is not mentioned in the document.
>
> *The Ethical Imperative:* The Notary declines to notarize, since impartiality and undue influence may otherwise become issues in a transaction that will greatly benefit the Notary's own children. The Notary asks the godmother to have an uninvolved person notarize the document.

Article D: Proper and Improper Influence

II-D-1: Avoidance of Influence in Lawful Transaction

The Notary shall not attempt to influence a person to sign or not sign, to act or not act, nor to proceed or not proceed in any lawful transaction requiring a notarial act that is to be performed by the Notary.

> **Illustration:** The Notary is asked by an acquaintance to notarize that person's signature on documents related to the purchase of a restaurant. Aware of the high failure rate of such businesses, the Notary considers whether to urge the acquaintance to reconsider the decision to purchase.
>
> *The Ethical Imperative:* The Notary notarizes the documents, if no improprieties are requested or detected. It is not the role of the impartial Notary to argue for or against a signer's participation in a lawful transaction.

II-D-2: Refusing Unlawful Transaction

The Notary shall refuse to participate and shall attempt to influence a person not to sign, not to act or not to proceed in any unlawful transaction requiring a notarial act that is to be performed by the Notary.

> **Illustration:** The Notary is asked by an acquaintance to notarize that person's signature on an affidavit for an immigration petition. The affidavit contains false statements that the Notary knows are fabrications by the signer.
>
> *The Ethical Imperative:* The Notary refuses to notarize and thereby abet the unlawful act of perjury. The Notary urges the acquaintance not to sign an untruthful affidavit.

Article E: Notarization for Employer

II-E-1: Notarization by Employee Proper

The Notary who is an employee shall be permitted to notarize for any officer, executive, supervisor, coworker, subordinate, client or customer of the employing organization, as long as the Notary will not gain a commission, bonus or other consideration as a result of the notarial act, other than the regular salary or hourly wage and the statutory notarial fee.

> **Illustration:** The Notary is employed in an office and every day notarizes the signature of a supervisor on dozens of documents. The Notary wonders whether it is proper to be notarizing for the person who supervises one's work and signs one's paycheck.
>
> *The Ethical Imperative:* As long as the "in-house" Notary receives no special compensation as a result of any notarization and is not asked to notarize improperly, that Notary may notarize company documents.

The *Code* also singles out two other questionable activities. Standard II-B-5 admonishes the Notary not to notarize the signature of a close relative. A similar prohibition can be found in the statutes of a number of jurisdictions. (*See, e.g.,* ME. REV. STAT. ANN. tit. 4, § 954-A; and FLA. STAT. ANN. § 117.05.) The Standard identifies a number of specific "close" relationships, but the preferred view is to treat the list as illustrative rather than inclusive, and consider any close relationship as being within the purview of the rule. Standard II-B-3 warns the Notary against notarizing a document that contains the name of either the Notary or any close relative of the Notary. (*Accord* 5 ILL. COMP. STAT. 312/6-104(b).) Both Standards are justified on the theory that the situations presented constitute a conflict that may compromise the Notary's ability to act impartially.

ARTICLE C: Avoiding Appearance of Partiality
Standard II-C-1 is in a sense a catch-all provision designed to preserve the integrity of the notarial act. It calls for the Notary to refrain from acting in any instance where to do so would raise the appearance of a conflict that could compromise the Notary's integrity. Like Caesar's wife, the Notary must be not only above reproach, but above the thought of reproach. (*Accord* CONN. GEN. STAT. § 3-94a(7)(B) (defining Notary misconduct to include any action "against public interest").)

ARTICLE D: Proper and Improper Influence
Standard II-D-1 presents the simple general rule that a Notary should not influence the person seeking the notarization. To do so clearly compromises the Notary's impartiality. (*Accord* UTAH CODE ANN. § 46-1-8(1).) Standard II-D-2 provides a proactive exception to the rule that posits a Notary may properly try to influence someone else from executing a proposed illegal transaction. The *Code* does not contemplate that the Notary will make determinations as to the legality or illegality of any specific transaction. The Standard is directed to obvious irregularities apparent on the face of the document to be notarized.

ARTICLE E: Notarization for Employer
Standard II-E-1 addresses the sometimes controversial issue of whether or not a Notary may render notarial services for the Notary's employer. Following the lead of the statutes that specifically permit this action (*see, e.g.,* IND. CODE § 33-16-2-7; and S.C. CODE ANN. § 26-1-120), the *Code* similarly condones such notarizations. However, the Standard supplies an important *caveat*. The notarization is unethical if the Notary receives additional special compensation for acting. (*Accord* W. VA. CODE § 29C-3-102.) Receipt of any additional payment over and above the Notary's normal salary and Notary fee constitute a conflict and potentially compromises the Notary's impartiality. Also, Notaries who are bank employees, stockholders, officers or directors are advised to review local law to determine those situations wherein they are prohibited from rendering notarial services for their employers or corporations. (*See* OR. REV. STAT. § 194.100(b); ARIZ. REV. STAT. ANN. §§ 41-32A and B; and GA. CODE ANN. § 45-17-12(b) (each authorizing Notaries to act provided they are not a party to the instrument to be notarized).)

GUIDING PRINCIPLE III

The Notary shall require the presence of each signer and oath-taker in order to carefully screen each for identity and willingness, and to observe that each appears aware of the significance of the transaction requiring a notarial act.

<u>Standards of Professional and Ethical Practice</u>

Article A: Physical Presence

III-A-1: Insisting That Signer Appear

The Notary shall insist that the signer and any witness identifying the signer be present before the Notary at the time of the notarization.

> **Illustration:** The Notary is telephoned by a client who has just signed and mailed several documents for the Notary to notarize without personal appearance. "You know my signature, so there shouldn't be any problem," the client says over the telephone.

> *The Ethical Imperative:* The Notary declines to perform a "telephone notarization" without the physical presence of the signer, since it would be a clear violation of the law, even though the Notary feels relatively certain about the identity, volition and awareness of the signer.

Article B: Screening for Identity and Willingness

III-B-1: Three Identification Methods

The Notary shall carefully identify each signer through either personal knowledge, at least one reliable identification document bearing a photograph, or the sworn word of a credible witness.

> **Illustration:** The Notary is approached by a friend and a stranger identified by the friend as a business associate. The friend requests notarization of the associate's signature on a document, but is not involved in the transaction. When the Notary asks the associate for identification, the friend becomes indignant that "you won't take my word as my bond."

> *The Ethical Imperative:* The Notary continues to insist either that the associate produce a reliable form of identification bearing a photograph or that the friend be formally sworn in as a credible witness vouching for the associate's identity.

III-B-2: Deterring Undue Influence

The Notary shall not notarize for any person if the Notary has a reasonable belief that can be articulated that the person is being bullied, threatened, intimidated or otherwise unduly influenced into acting against his or her will or interest.

> **Illustration:** The Notary is called to the hospital room of a patient to notarize that person's signature on several documents. The patient appears disinterested in the documents and expresses a desire to be allowed to sleep. Also present is the patient's spouse, who insists that the patient first attend to signing the documents. The spouse places a pen in the patient's hand and directs it to the signature space on one of the documents, but the patient makes no effort to sign.

COMMENTARY

GENERAL

Guiding Principle III prescribes appropriate conduct on a number of interrelated issues that, taken together, address the very essence of notarization. Some of the practices addressed are mandated by statute in most jurisdictions. Thus, the *Code* only serves to reinforce them. Other issues, particularly regarding the proper role, if any, the Notary should play in determining a signer's capacity, are more problematic. Since most notarial statute is silent on these issues, the *Code* takes a more proactive position with respect to them. Standards III-A-1 and III-B-1 principally restate the accepted practice necessary for a proper notarization. Standards III-B-2 and III-C-1 through -3 address the Notary's obligation to assess the capacity of the person for whom the notarization is performed. Whether or not a Notary is required to be concerned about "capacity" and the ramifications of imposing such a requirement have proven to be a controversial subject. The *Code* adopts a position that forces the Notary to take a thoughtful, professional approach to notarizations, and recognizes that a Notary may exercise some discretion with respect to whether or not the notarization should be performed. Standards III-D-1 through -7 offer the Notary guidance on how to properly handle notarizations that involve the use of witnesses confirming the identity of the person who signed the document to be notarized.

ARTICLE A: Physical Presence

The *Code* mandates that the Notary require the physical presence of a signer or any person serving in a witness capacity. The use of "shall" makes this a mandatory charge. The use of "insist" leaves no room for discretion. Physical presence is the only reliable way a Notary can verify the identity of the signer or witness. This verification is the essence of the notarial act itself, and is routinely required by statute. (*See, e.g.,* N.J. Rev. Stat. § 46:14-2.1(b); Tex. Civ. Prac. & Rem. Code Ann. § 121.004; and Mich. Comp. Laws § 565.264.) Failure to meet this directive is not only unethical, but probably unlawful as well. (*See, e.g.,* S.D. Codified Laws § 18-1-11; and N.C. Gen. Stat. § 10A-12(b).)

ARTICLE B: Screening for Identity and Willingness

Standard III-B-1 reminds the Notary that the identity of every signer must be carefully established. Indeed, some jurisdictions impose a higher standard of care for proving identity than for performing other notarial functions. (*See, e.g.,* Idaho Code § 51-111(1).) The applicable statute in every jurisdiction requires proper identification. Some statutes enumerate the different types of acceptable identification (*see, e.g.,* Cal. Civ. Code § 1185; and Fla. Stat. Ann. § 117.05(5)), others merely call for satisfactory evidence (*see, e.g.,* Ohio Rev. Code Ann. § 147.53; and Iowa Code § 9E.9.6). The Standard emphasizes that the Notary must properly follow the state-imposed rules. The key word is "properly." The Illustration makes clear that although a signer's identity can be proved by a credible witness, the witness must formally swear to the signer's identity. The act of establishing the identity of and swearing in the witness becomes the notarial act. As such, the Notary must perform the act in conformity with established rules of law. A person's identity cannot properly be established by the unsworn testimony of a witness, regardless of how highly regarded or well-known the witness is to the Notary.

The *Code* states that "reliable identification" is acceptable proof of identity. The *Code*, however, neither specifies nor attempts to define what is "reliable identification." Notaries are presumed to know what constitutes acceptable proof of identification under the law of their respective jurisdictions. For those Notaries who do not, the Standard implicitly directs them to ascertain what is required.

The Ethical Imperative: The Notary respects the patient's wish to sleep, promising to return later and to notarize if the patient appears alert and willing to sign the documents.

Article C: Screening for Awareness

III-C-1: Awareness Essential in Signer

The Notary shall not notarize for any person if the Notary has a reasonable belief that can be articulated that the person at the moment is not aware of the significance of the transaction requiring a notarial act.

> **Illustration:** The Notary is called to the home of an elderly person to notarize that individual's signature on several documents. The Notary is introduced to the would-be signer by the person's relative. Acting in a childlike manner, the elderly person appears disinterested in the documents. Though the relative urges the Notary to act, the Notary is unable to get a coherent response to simple questions regarding the notarial act (*e.g.*, "Is that your signature, and have you signed this document willingly?").

> *The Ethical Imperative:* The Notary does not notarize the documents, since the person's conduct indicates a strong likelihood that the individual is not at the moment capable of responsible action.

III-C-2: Coherent Communication Necessary

The Notary shall not notarize for any person unable to communicate coherently with the Notary at the time of notarization.

> **Illustration:** The Notary is called to a nursing home to notarize documents for a bedridden patient, whose friend is also present. The patient is awake and sitting up, with both documents signed and resting on a tray table. However, the patient's speech is slurred and the individual

is not coherently responsive to the Notary's greeting and questions. The friend urges the Notary to notarize.

> *The Ethical Imperative:* The Notary declines to notarize because, without clear and direct two-way communication with the signer, the Notary cannot be sure of the individual's awareness. The Notary must not rely on an "interpreter" who may have a motive for misrepresenting the signer's condition or intent.

III-C-3: Direct Communication Necessary

The Notary shall not notarize for any person with whom the Notary cannot directly communicate in the same language, regardless of the presence of a third-party interpreter or translator.

> **Illustration:** The Notary is approached by a client and a stranger who does not speak English, but offers a foreign passport as proof of identity. The client says the stranger wants to have a signature notarized on an English-language power of attorney authorizing the client to conduct business on the stranger's behalf. With no knowledge of the stranger's language, the Notary must rely on the client to communicate.

> *The Ethical Imperative:* The Notary declines to notarize for the stranger, since there can be no certainty of this individual's intent or awareness without direct communication. Further, the client has a clear interest in the transaction that compromises reliability as a truthful interpreter. The safest policy would be to direct the two to a Notary who speaks the stranger's language or to the nearest consulate of the stranger's country.

Article D: Qualification of Witnesses

III-D-1: Honesty, Capacity and Disinterest Essential

The Notary shall require any witness identifying a principal signer to be honest, mentally capable and

---

In those jurisdictions where a jurat does not require the Notary to verify the signer's identity, the Notary may legally proceed without doing so. (*See, e.g.,* Cal. Civ. Code § 1185, which stipulates identification requirements for acknowledgers but not for affiants.) However, good practice dictates that the Notary nonetheless screen *all* signers for identity. This deters fraud and provides important information for the Notary who maintains a notarial journal. (*See,* Standard VIII-A-2 and accompanying Commentary.)

Standard III-B-2 tackles a more difficult and, perhaps, controversial issue: deterring undue influence. Although recognized as a laudable goal, there are those who suggest that this activity is not within the purview of performing a notarial act. Today, notarial authority is exclusively a product of statute. Statutes usually do not specifically direct a Notary to ascertain whether or not a party to a notarization is subject to undue influence, but there are exceptions. (*See, e.g.,* Ga. Code Ann. § 45-17-8(b)(2) (providing a Notary is not "obligated" to act if he "feels" the person seeking the notarization "is being coerced").) Consequently, there is little direct authority for a Notary to refrain from acting if undue influence is suspected.

The *Code* adopts the position that the Notary, as a public official who performs a function relied upon by innocent third parties not privy to the notarization, should be proactive in executing his or her obligations. Consistent with the view that notarizations in general are designed to deter fraud, it logically follows that Notaries should strive to strengthen lawful documents so that they will not fall victim to challenge. While a Notary does not and cannot guarantee the efficacy of a document, users of that document ought to be able to rely on the fact the signature is what it purports to be. The *Code* favors the view that a signature not voluntarily provided is suspect.

The *Code* does not obligate the Notary to investigate all of the facts surrounding every transaction. Instead, it assumes the Notary will rely on personal observation to determine whether or not the signer is acting under his or her own free will. The Standard uses the terms "bullied, threatened and intimidated" for illustrative purposes only. The drafters recognize that from a legal perspective these terms imply acting under duress, and not undue influence. Although the two concepts are related, they are distinct. In not drawing the legal distinction, the *Code* sends the general message that the Notary should not participate in a transaction that on its face involves an unwilling signer, regardless of how that fact is manifested. The *Code* recognizes that there is no "bright line" test as to when a person has been deprived of his or her own free will. Each situation is special unto itself, and the Notary is left to use his or her best judgment as to whether or not to proceed with the requested notarization. The Standard serves to alert Notaries to the "undue influence" issue and admonishes them to avoid becoming involved in these situations.

ARTICLE C: Screening for Awareness

Standards III-C-1 and -2 wrestle with perhaps the thorniest issue confronting Notaries: signer awareness. This problem is distinguishable from the "willingness" issue of Standard III-B-2, although both standards address "capacity." The "willingness" problem arises when a person with full control of his or her mental faculties is being improperly persuaded or forced to act. The "awareness" problem involves only the signer, and focuses on whether or not the signer understands what he or she is doing.

Both in earlier drafts of the *Code* and in other texts, the "awareness" issue has been referred to as "signer competence." Although the same matter is being addressed, *i.e.,* the signer's ability to understand his or her acts, the *Code* adopts the view that testing for "awareness" is a more meaningful and reasonable function.

Proponents of a strict test for competence rest their position on the fact that the law allows no less. Although it is true that by definition an "acknowledgment" implicitly requires the Notary to determine the signer's competence (*see* Ariz. Rev. Stat. Ann. § 33-505; Ind. Code § 26-3-60; and *Poole v. Hyatt*, 689 A.2d 82 (Md. 1997)), not all notarizations are "acknowledgments." Indeed, many are not. (*See, e.g.,* Wash. Rev. Code § 42.44.090.100.) Nonetheless, this camp suggests that the very nature of every notarial act implies the unaffected by the transaction requiring a notarial act.

> **Illustration:** The Notary is asked by a former school classmate to swear that person in as a subscribing witness vouching for the signature of an absent "business associate" on a deed. Over the years, the Notary has developed a poor opinion of the classmate's integrity, having knowledge of a conviction for trafficking in stolen goods.

> *The Ethical Imperative:* The Notary declines to accept the former classmate as a reliable subscribing witness, urging this individual to have the absent business associate appear in person before a Notary.

III-D-2: Oath or Affirmation Necessary for Identifying Witness

The Notary shall administer an oath or affirmation to any witness identifying a principal signer in order to compel truthfulness.

> **Illustration:** The Notary is telephoned by a client who promises to stop by later in the day with a deed to be notarized. The client mentions that the deed requires one witness in addition to the Notary, and asks if a friend may witness the signature on the document before it is brought in.

> *The Professional Choice:* The Notary explains that the client may sign the deed and have the signature witnessed outside of the Notary's presence prior to appearing before the Notary to acknowledge the signature. The Notary also explains that it will not be necessary for the witness to appear and take an oath, since the Notary will positively identify the client based on personal knowledge of identity and not rely on the witness to make the identification.

III-D-3: Personal Knowledge of Identifying Witness Essential

The Notary shall personally know any individual serving as the sole witness identifying a principal signer in the Notary's presence, and the witness shall personally know the principal signer.

> **Illustration:** The Notary works in an office. An elderly stranger walks in and requests notarization of a document. However, the stranger no longer drives and cannot present a driver's license or other reliable ID card as identification. At that moment, a longtime coworker of the Notary enters and greets the stranger by name. The coworker has known the individual for years.

> *The Professional Choice:* The Notary notarizes the signature of the elderly stranger, who is identified through the vouching under oath of the coworker. The critical chain of personal knowledge exists: the Notary personally knows the identifying witness and the identifying witness personally knows the signer. State law may provide assistance in usefully defining "personal knowledge of identity."

III-D-4: Identifying Witness Must Be Unaffected

The Notary shall disqualify any person from serving as an identifying witness if that individual is named in or affected by the document signed by the principal.

> **Illustration:** The Notary is asked by a married couple to notarize their signatures on a document. The Notary personally knows one of the two as a former college classmate, but has never met the other, who does not drive nor have a driver's license or other photo ID. The couple suggests that the Notary swear in the classmate as a witness to identify the spouse.

> *The Professional Choice:* The Notary agrees to notarize the signature of the spouse who is personally known, but declines to notarize the signature of the unknown spouse, since identification would be based on the word of a

---

requirement to screen for competence. Notwithstanding this belief, if the signer merely seeks to have a document "witnessed," there is no authority requiring the Notary to determine the signer's competence. (*But see* FLA. STAT ANN. § 117.107(5) (requiring a Notary to refrain from acting if it appears the signatory is "mentally incapable of understanding the nature and effect of the document"); and GA. CODE ANN. § 45-17-8(b)(3) (giving the Notary the opportunity to decline to act if he has "compelling doubts" about whether the signer "knows the consequences of the transaction requiring the notarial act").) To self-impose a standard of determining signer competence could expose the Notary to legal liability if the Notary uses a perceived lack of competence as a basis for improperly refusing a notarization, and harm results.

The *Code* accepts the position that determining competence is problematic. Not only is it of dubious legal necessity, but it also may require abilities beyond the ken of many Notaries. Moreover, when "competency" is tested for legal matters such as a will or a contract, much more than a cursory examination is made. Attorneys have statutory and judicial guidance detailing how they should proceed on these matters. Moreover, the process can be quite time-consuming. Thus, even for those Notaries who would feel comfortable in performing such a review, the time involved for such a task is probably prohibitive.

The *Code* does not posit that the Notary should mindlessly proceed with any notarization upon request. Instead, it erects an "awareness" standard. Notaries are expected to judge for themselves whether the signer has the requisite awareness to proceed. Standard III-C-1 calls for the Notary reasonably to believe the signer to be "aware of the significance of the transaction requiring a notarial act." The Standard does not require the signer to understand detailed legal ramifications of the act, or to be able to recite from memory any part of the document. The key to the "awareness" standard is the signer's self-recognition that he or she is engaged in a transaction sufficiently significant to require proof of the signer's participation in it.

In meeting the "awareness" test, the signer need not divulge particulars of the document nor provide the Notary with an overview of the transaction. Such a requirement might violate confidentiality rules established in Guiding Principle IX of the *Code*. (*See* Standards IX-A-1 and B-2.) Instead, it is sufficient for a signer to indicate, for example, that the document is a will or a contract, although such specificity is not required. Indeed, a Notary ethically could proceed upon hearing the signer say he needs an important document notarized, if the signer's demeanor conveyed to the Notary that the signer understood the significance of the act. Recognizing that there is not just one exclusive method for determining "awareness," the *Code* does not offer any methodology on how a Notary should proceed, partially out of concern that the suggestions might become the only ones used. Such a result clearly would be contrary to the *Code's* position that determining "awareness" is not an exact science. Instead, the *Code* relies upon the Notary's ability to judge from the facts and circumstances presented whether or not the signer satisfies the "awareness" standard.

The Illustration for Standard III-C-1 presents a typical dilemma faced by many Notaries. The signer demonstrates a sufficient disorientation to raise a question in the Notary's mind as to whether the signer is aware of what is transpiring. The Notary asks some simple, yet straightforward questions to determine the signer's "willingness." If a signer cannot identify or acknowledge a signature as his or her own, the Notary should not proceed. If the signer responds that he or she did not sign the document willingly, the Notary must not proceed. In the latter situation, the Notary who proceeds not only acts unethically, but also may be considered a party to a fraud.

The essence of the *Code's* position is that while being commissioned as a Notary does not qualify one to determine legal competence, a Notary may nonetheless make a basic assessment as to whether or not the signer is willing and aware enough to proceed. The *Code* does not require the Notary to actually prove "awareness," but asks only that the Notary formulate a reasonable belief that the signer has "awareness." The issue will not arise in many notarizations. The *Code* seeks to provide guidance for those situations in which the signer's actions raise doubt in the Notary's mind as to whether the signer can proceed.

witness who is clearly involved in and affected by the transaction. The Notary suggests that the unknown spouse visit a Notary who personally knows that spouse, or rely on a disinterested credible acquaintance who personally knows a Notary to make the identification.

III-D-5: Personal Knowledge of Subscribing Witness Essential
The Notary shall personally know any individual offering to serve as a subscribing witness to identify a principal signer who is not in the Notary's presence.

> **Illustration:** The Notary is asked by a stranger to take a proof of execution for the signature of the stranger's absent spouse. The stranger explains that the spouse was suddenly called out of town on emergency business, but that the stranger saw the spouse sign the document.

> *The Professional Choice:* The Notary declines to allow the stranger to serve as a subscribing witness for a proof of execution because this individual is not personally known to·the Notary. Because proofs have a high potential for fraud, Notaries must know well any individual they trust to vouch for an absent signer's identity, volition and awareness.

III-D-6: Subscribing Witness Must Be Unaffected
The Notary shall disqualify any person from serving as a subscribing witness if that individual is named in or affected by the document signed by the absent principal.

> **Illustration:** The Notary is asked by a friend to perform

a proof of execution for the signature of the friend's parent on a health care power of attorney naming the friend as attorney in fact. The parent is described as too sick to appear before the Notary.

> *The Professional Choice:* The Notary declines to allow the friend to serve as a subscribing witness for a proof of execution because this individual is named in and affected by the document and the person's credibility as a reliable witness would be compromised.

III-D-7: Two Witnesses to Mark Must Be Disinterested
The Notary shall require that two individuals in addition to the Notary witness the affixation of a mark, and neither witness shall be named in or affected by the marked document.

> **Illustration:** The Notary is called to the bedside of a patient to notarize this person's signature on a power of attorney naming a spouse as attorney in fact. Ill and extremely weak, the patient is only able to affix an "X" rather than a normal signature. The spouse offers to sign as a witness to the mark.

> *The Professional Choice:* The Notary explains that two persons in addition to the Notary must witness the making of the mark. The Notary disqualifies the spouse as a witness, since this individual is both named in and affected by the document. Instead, the spouse finds two neighbors, both of whom present reliable ID cards, to witness the patient's mark.

Standard III-C-2 and -3 address a different aspect of the "awareness" issue, that of the signer being able to communicate effectively with the Notary. The Illustration for Standard III-C-2 cites a situation wherein the physical condition of the would-be signer raises doubts as to the signer's awareness of the transaction. Although the Illustration instructs the Notary not to proceed, it must not be mindlessly applied to all similar situations. Individuals with slurred speech or who cannot speak at all often may nonetheless effectively communicate their wishes in a variety of other ways. The result reached in the Illustration rests largely on the fact that the would-be signer could not respond effectively to the Notary's questions. Standard III-C-3 takes the communication problem a step further by admonishing Notaries not to perform notarizations through an interpreter, even though several states allow translators to explain the nature and effect of an English-language document to a non-English-speaking signer. (*See, e.g.,* FLA. STAT. ANN. § 117.107(6).) Drafters of the *Code* considered the inherent risk of fraud to be too great when the Notary relies on the words of a third party who may have a motive for dissembling. There are other ways for persons who speak a foreign language not understood by the Notary to obtain notarizations, including taking advantage of consular services. Advising the client to take one of those options is the ethical path to pursue.

ARTICLE D: Qualification of Witnesses
Standards III-D-1 through -7 offer advice on the proper use of witnesses in notarization. Although not mandatory, taken together the Standards create a protocol of good practice.
Standard III-D-1 states the three minimum requirements for a witness: honesty, mental capacity and disinterest. The Notary will have to draw upon his or her personal knowledge of the witness to assess these qualifications. As to "disinterest," the Notary will have to ascertain this fact at the time of notarization. Standard III-D-4 addresses this issue more directly. Any witness with a direct interest in the document to be notarized must be disqualified. (*Accord* CAL. CIV. CODE § 1185(c)(1)(E).) Standard III-D-6 provides the same rule for subscribing witnesses. (For guidance as to what may constitute an improper personal interest, *see* Guiding Principle II, Article B.)
Standards III-D-3 and -5 set out the foundation for the Notary's knowledge of the witness' identity. The former relates to identifying witnesses in general, the latter to subscribing witnesses. In both instances the Notary must have personal knowledge of the witness' identity. Standard III-D-3 indicates that state laws may usefully define "personal knowledge of identity" (*see, e.g.,* ARIZ. REV. STAT. ANN. § 41-311 (defining personal knowledge of identity as "familiarity with an individual resulting from interactions with that person over a sufficient time to eliminate reasonable doubt that the individual has the identity claimed")). Notaries are advised to review the relevant law in their respective jurisdictions on this matter.
Standard III-D-2 requires that an identifying witness be put under oath, an action dictated by many statutes. (*See, e.g.,* FLA. STAT. ANN. § 117.05(5)(b).) This simple procedure is designed to provide the assurance needed to verify the unknown signer's identity. It is an essential link in the notarial process needed to deter fraud.
Standard III-D-7 addresses the use of marks as signatures. This situation can arise when the signer is physically incapable of writing his or her own signature, or does not know how to write the signature. In either event, a mark (*e.g.,* "X") can constitute a valid signature, as long as proof is provided of the mark's authenticity. The Standard suggests that the Notary always use at least two disinterested witnesses when notarizing a document signed with a mark, a requirement imposed by many state laws. Use of two witnesses in addition to the Notary will help guarantee the validity of the document should it ever be challenged. As with any other witness, the Standard alerts the Notary of the need to make the witnesses prove their identities. Note that since the witnesses are not serving to verify the identity of the signer, they need not be personally known to the Notary nor put under oath.

GUIDING PRINCIPLE IV

The Notary shall not execute a false or incomplete certificate, nor be involved with any document or transaction that is false, deceptive or fraudulent.

Standards of Professional and Ethical Practice

Article A: Certificate Mandatory

IV-A-1: Notarial Wording Required

The Notary shall not notarize any document unless it bears jurat, acknowledgment or other notarial "certificate" wording that specifies what the Notary is attesting.

> **Illustration:** The Notary is asked by a stranger to "certify" an engineering drawing to protect an invention. When the Notary appears perplexed by the request, the stranger says, "Just stamp, date and sign it — that's all I need."

> *The Ethical Imperative:* The Notary declines to "notarize" any document that does not bear notarial certificate language. Merely "stamping, dating and signing" is insufficient because there is no wording to indicate exactly what the Notary's seal and signature are certifying.

Article B: Fraudulent Certificate

IV-B-1: False Statement Improper

The Notary shall not knowingly issue a certificate containing information that is false, deceptive, inaccurate or incomplete.

> **Illustration:** The Notary is asked by a friend to notarize a deed bearing the signatures of the friend and an absent spouse, who "is out of town on business for several days." The acknowledgment form has been prepared beforehand and states that both friend and spouse "personally appeared" before the Notary. The friend explains that the document must be quickly notarized and recorded before the spouse returns because of an escrow deadline.

> *The Ethical Imperative:* The Notary declines to notarize using the prepared notarial certificate, since it falsely states that the spouse was in the Notary's presence. However, the Notary offers to notarize the signature of the friend alone if permitted to cross out the spouse's name and modify the notarial certificate to reflect that only the friend appeared.

IV-B-2: False Date Improper

The Notary shall not knowingly issue a certificate for a notarial act that indicates a date other than the actual date on which the notarial act was performed.

> **Illustration:** The Notary is asked by a friend to notarize several documents related to charitable contributions. All of the notarial certificates have been prepared for the Notary, who notices that the jurat on one of the documents bears a date in the previous year. When the Notary points this out, the friend explains that a significant financial loss will be suffered unless a contribution is backdated to fall on or before the previous December 31. The friend asks the Notary to "just do a small favor and overlook the minor discrepancy regarding the date."

> *The Ethical Imperative:* The Notary declines to notarize using a certificate with a false date, since it untruthfully states that the notarization was performed on a day on which the friend had not actually appeared.

COMMENTARY

GENERAL

The Principle presents quite simply the basic premise that a Notary, both as a public officer and someone others depend upon for impartiality and honesty, shall not engage in improper activities. Doing so will detract from the public trust and confidence necessary in order for notarial acts to be accorded respect. Despite its simplicity, the Principle addresses some situations that do not lend themselves to easy resolution. In each of these, the *Code* takes the position that the Notary must refrain from acting because the possibility of actual or perceived impropriety is too great.

ARTICLE A: Certificate Mandatory

Standard IV-A-1 addresses whether a Notary should notarize a document that does not have a notarial certificate. Notarial certificates routinely are required by statute. (*See, e.g.,* KAN. STAT. ANN. § 53-505; and WASH. REV. CODE § 42.44.090.) The Standard concludes that a Notary should not notarize without a certificate because it would then be uncertain exactly what service the Notary provided. The Standard does not preclude a Notary from adding a certificate to the document, but the Notary as a ministerial official should not be the authority who determines the correct type of certificate to be added. (*See, generally,* Guiding Principle VI and Standards thereto addressing "unauthorized advice" issues.)

ARTICLE B: Fraudulent Certificate

Standards IV-B-1 and -2 are based upon the directive found in the *Model Notary Act*, Section 3-104. The Illustrations in these Standards provide clear examples of invitations to the Notary to perform unethical acts. The Standards are unwavering in the position that, regardless of the relationship between the Notary and the person requesting notarial services, the Notary should never notarize a document inconsistent with its certificate nor intentionally misdate the notarization. The Standards are consistent with the view taken in many jurisdictions that prohibit such activities. (*See, e.g.,* GA. CODE ANN. § 45-17-8(d).)

ARTICLE C: Certificate Completion and Attachment

Standard IV-C-1 addresses a matter of good practice. It is not unusual for a Notary to be asked to notarize a document that has a preprinted certificate or one that does not have ample space for a certificate and seal. Notaries should inspect preprinted certificates to ensure they properly state the type of notarial service the Notary is providing. The certificate should also be reviewed for errors or omissions. A Notary should not surrender his or her accountability for proper document certification to the document preparer. Doing so ultimately could result in the notarization being challenged.

▼

Article C: Certificate Completion and Attachment

IV-C-1: Completion by Notary Essential

The Notary shall personally prepare or verify all information and insertions on a notarial certificate, and allow no other person to affix the Notary's official signature and seal.

> **Illustration:** The Notary is asked by a stranger to notarize that person's signature on a document. The Notary notices, however, that the document's notarial certificate wording has been filled in beforehand with an incorrect out-of-state venue.

> *The Professional Choice:* Before completing the certificate, the Notary corrects its venue by lining through the inappropriate state and county, then right above printing the state and county in which the notarization is actually being performed. After initialing the venue changes, the Notary completes the certificate.

IV-C-2: Secure Attachment by Notary Essential

The Notary shall take steps in attaching a "loose" notarial certificate to a document that will deter its fraudulent removal and reattachment to an unintended document.

> **Illustration:** The Notary is asked by a stranger to notarize that person's signature on a document that was prepared in another state. However, the document bears preprinted acknowledgment certificate wording that is unacceptable in the Notary's state because it does not detail how the signer was identified. The Notary explains to the stranger that a "loose" certificate bearing acceptable wording will have to be attached. The Notary then completes, signs and seals the certificate, stapling it to the left margin of the document's signature page.

> *The Professional Choice:* To make fraudulent reattachment of the certificate difficult, the Notary writes a brief description of the document on the certificate (*e.g.,* "This

certificate is attached to a grant deed dated . . . for property in . . ."). In addition, the Notary embosses the certificate and signature pages together with a seal bearing the Notary's name, writing, "Attached document bears this embossment," on the certificate as well.

IV-C-3: Completion or Attachment by Another Improper

The Notary shall not deliver a signed notarial certificate to another person and trust that person to complete or attach that certificate to a document outside of the Notary's presence.

> **Illustration:** The Notary receives a telephone call from a person for whom eight days earlier the Notary had notarized a deed. Calling from out of state, this individual reports that the Notary neglected to affix a seal imprint on the deed's acknowledgment certificate and that the missing seal has prevented the document from being recorded, thereby "putting an important deal on hold." The caller claims that the Notary's mistake has delayed and possibly endangered a land transaction involving multiple parties and hundreds of thousands of dollars in escrow. The caller asks the Notary to complete and overnight-mail another certificate to replace the defective one. "Since we're being held up by your mistake, you have an obligation to help us get this deal back on track as soon as possible," the caller tells the Notary.

> *The Ethical Imperative:* The Notary declines to complete and mail a new acknowledgment certificate, not trusting an unseen person to attach it to the appropriate document. However, the Notary offers to correct the original certificate by adding the missing seal imprint, if the deed is returned.

Article D: Potentially Fraudulent Documents

IV-D-1: Incomplete Documents Improper

The Notary shall refuse to notarize any document whose text is blank or incomplete.

Similarly, Notaries must take extra care when executing "loose" certificates. Standard IV-C-2 offers the good practice procedure of securely fastening the certificate to the appropriate document. Failure to do so could result in an unscrupulous party transferring the certificate to another document. Standard IV-C-3 addresses the Notary's delivery of an unattached, completed "loose" certificate. As the Illustration demonstrates, this situation can arise when a Notary is asked to correct his or her prior notarization error. The *Code* adopts the position that it is unethical for the Notary to comply with any such request to forward a loose completed certificate. Although this is often an easy and practical remedy to the problem, it is an invitation to trouble. Once sent, the Notary has no control over the use of the certificate, and may end up being a party to a fraud. Although critics may suggest that strict adherence to this Standard will be difficult and may sometimes produce a hardship for the erring Notary, the drafters feel the position is justified because the risk of impropriety attendant to the delivery of a "loose" certificate is just too great. The *Code* only speaks to ethical considerations. On a practical note, the Notary may consider offering to pay for all delivery and incidental costs created by the error.

ARTICLE D: Potentially Fraudulent Documents

Standards IV-D-1 and -2 address situations that raise practical concerns. The first suggests that a Notary not notarize any document that has blanks or is otherwise incomplete. Although some jurisdictions specifically require this by statute (*see, e.g.,* FLA. STAT. ANN. § 117.107(3)), others do not. There is no hard and fast rule that a Notary must read a document before notarizing the signature on it. Indeed, there are those who believe that maintaining confidentially argues against such an intrusion. Nonetheless, the *Code* adopts the position that both the signer and society are better served by having a completed document notarized, and advises Notaries to act accordingly. The second Standard urges Notaries to certify only original signatures. Although there may not be a statutory proscription against notarizing facsimile signatures, such an action may lead to difficulties because in some instances the facsimile may not be accepted as a lawful signature. Consequently, the *Code* adopts the position against notarizing facsimile signatures as a protection for the client.

ARTICLE E: Fraudulent Notarization or Transaction

Standards IV-E-1 through -3 impose ethical obligations upon Notaries to deter fraud. Standard IV-E-1 mandates that the Notary not perform notarizations that are in any way improper, and obligates the Notary to adhere to Principles of the *Code.* Standard IV-E-2 further stipulates that the Notary not perform a notarization if the Notary knows or has a reasonable suspicion that either the transaction or document itself is illegal or otherwise improper. (*Accord* GA. CODE ANN. § 45-17-8(d).) Drafters of the Standard do not contemplate that a Notary be required to make a detailed investigation every time he or she is asked to perform a notarial act. Instead, they anticipate a commonsense approach whereby either irregularities apparent on the face of the document or circumstances attendant to the transaction would raise a "red flag" for a reasonable person that something improper is afoot. The central message is that, as a public official, a Notary should neither be a part of nor abet an improper act. Finally, Standard IV-E-3 requires the Notary to report knowledge of Notary-related illegalities to the appropriate authority. The *Code's* position is consistent with the Notary's role as a fraud-deterrent public official and member of a profession. (*See* Standard X-C-1 and accompanying Commentary.)

Illustration: The Notary is asked by a stranger to notarize that person's signature on a document containing blank spaces. "That information isn't available right now and I want to get the notarization out of the way," the stranger says. "It shouldn't make any difference, since you're just certifying my signature, not the terms in the document."

The Professional Choice: The Notary refuses to proceed as asked, explaining to the stranger that the document will be less subject to legal challenge if the signer knows all its terms at the time of notarization.

IV-D-2: Facsimile Signature Improper

The Notary shall refuse to notarize any signature not affixed by hand in pen and ink, unless the law expressly allows otherwise.

Illustration: The Notary works in an office and notarizes several dozen documents every day for an executive. One day, the executive presents a stack of documents for notarization that, instead of being signed by pen, have been stamped with an inked facsimile signature. "I've decided to start using the stamp to save time," the executive tells the Notary.

The Professional Choice: The Notary asks the executive to affix an *actual* signature on the documents in pen and ink, explaining that the stamped facsimile may not be accepted as a lawful signature.

Article E: Fraudulent Notarization or Transaction

IV-E-1: Improper Notarization

The Notary shall refuse to perform any notarial act that is illegal, dishonest, deceptive, false, improper or in violation of The Ethical Imperatives of this *Notary Public Code of Professional Responsibility.*

Illustration: The Notary is asked by a client to notarize a document bearing the client's own signature and that of a stranger whom the client introduces as a spouse. The stranger has no documentary identification, claiming to have left it in a car several blocks away. The client grows indignant when the Notary expresses concern about the stranger's lack of IDs and suggests that the person return to the car to get them. The client threatens to do business elsewhere if the Notary does not "trust me enough to do me a small favor."

The Ethical Imperative: The Notary refuses to notarize unless the stranger returns with proper identification, because an introduction by a clearly interested party does not suffice as a reliable identification. It would be illegal and deceptive for the Notary to certify the stranger as personally known or positively identified when this is not actually the case.

IV-E-2: Improper Transaction

The Notary shall refuse to perform any notarial act in connection with a document or transaction that the Notary knows, or has a reasonable suspicion that can be articulated, is illegal, dishonest, deceptive, false or improper.

Illustration: The Notary is asked by an acquaintance to notarize that person's signature on an "affidavit of citizenship" to facilitate travel in a foreign country. The affidavit contains statements that the Notary knows are false.

The Ethical Imperative: The Notary refuses to notarize, explaining to the acquaintance that, having knowledge that statements in the affidavit are false, the Notary has an obligation as a public official not to abet a deception.

IV-E-3: Reporting Illegality

The Notary shall report to appropriate law enforcement or disciplinary authorities any illegality requested, required, proposed or performed that involves a notarial act by the Notary or by any other Notary.

Illustration: The Notary is asked by a stranger to notarize that person's signature on a property deed. The stranger presents a Social Security card and a birth certificate as identification. When the Notary explains that these are inadequate proofs of identity and that a governmentally issued photo-bearing ID such as a driver's license must be presented, the stranger says, "I've lost my driver's license. Will five hundred dollars be enough to expedite this notarization?"

The Ethical Imperative: The Notary refuses to notarize because of the inadequate documentation of identity. Having a strong suspicion that the stranger is an impostor, the Notary reports the encounter to the forgery division of the local police department, providing whatever information the police require.

GUIDING PRINCIPLE V

The Notary shall give precedence to the rules of law over the dictates or expectations of any person or entity.

<u>Standards of Professional and Ethical Practice</u>

Article A: Precedence of Law

V-A-1: Conflict with Dictate or Expectation

The Notary shall obey and give precedence to any pertinent law, regulation or official directive, or any of The Ethical Imperatives of this *Notary Public Code of Professional Responsibility*, when they conflict with the dictates or expectations of an employer, supervisor, client, customer, coworker, associate, partner, friend, relative or any other person or entity.

> **Illustration:** The Notary notarizes daily for executives in a company headquarters. State law requires the Notary to maintain a journal of all notarial acts, including the signature of each document signer. As a convenience to the busy executives, a supervisor directs the Notary to secure the signature of each in the front of the Notary's journal and to have that suffice as the required signature for any future notarial act. The supervisor explains that this will take up less of the executives' time.

> *The Ethical Imperative:* The Notary declines, explaining to the supervisor that state law requires a journal signature from each document signer at the time of notarization; doing so provides physical evidence that the signer actually appeared before the Notary and willingly engaged in the transaction. The Notary further explains that such strict adherence to procedure will render each document

less subject to legal challenge, and that failure to comply may cause revocation of the Notary's commission.

V-A-2: Waiving Personal Appearance Improper

The Notary shall not waive the requirement that each signer personally appear before the Notary at the time of notarization at the direction or request of an employer, supervisor, client, customer, coworker, associate, partner, friend, relative or any other person or entity.

> **Illustration:** The Notary is asked by a supervisor to notarize several documents that have been signed and handed to the supervisor by the firm's president, who "will be in important meetings all day and won't have time to be interrupted." All documents bear acknowledgment certificates stating that the signer "personally appeared" before the Notary. The supervisor explains that the Notary may rely on familiarity with the president's signature, having notarized for this executive "hundreds of times before." The supervisor promises that the president will sign the Notary's journal as soon as time allows.

> *The Ethical Imperative:* The Notary refuses to notarize unless the executive is present, as the acknowledgment certificates clearly stipulate and as the law clearly requires. The Notary suggests that the supervisor consider whether proofs of execution might be acceptable substitutes for the acknowledgments, with the supervisor serving as a subscribing witness and declaring under oath that the signatures were acknowledged in the supervisor's presence and are genuine; such proofs, however, would

COMMENTARY

GENERAL

The Principle states a universally applicable rule. It is included in the *Code* primarily to reinforce the absolute obligation imposed upon Notaries to obey all applicable laws. Despite the Principle's seemingly unassailable nature, the Standards highlight situations wherein parties may have to be reminded of this basic rule.

ARTICLE A: Precedence of Law

The three standards in this Article each address a serious problem that often occurs. The situations presented are often particularly difficult for the employee-Notary. In each instance the Notary is asked to disregard the law by waiving the requirement either to make a journal entry, to be in the presence of the signer, or to be shown identification documents. Such requests typically are made by a close friend, relative or employer, believing that the Notary should do as asked because of the personal or professional relationship. The *Code* takes as strong a position as possible against the Notary honoring such requests. Under no circumstances should a Notary ever disregard an applicable law with respect to notarial acts. Aside from ethical concerns, potential criminal sanctions await the Notary who does. (*See, generally,* W.Va. Code § 29C-6-201 and -202; S.D. Codified Laws § 18-1-11; and N.M. Stat. Ann. § 14-12-18.)

The drafters appreciate that many employers believe their employee-Notaries owe a special obligation to the employer, and this justifies the Notary disregarding the rules. This can be especially troublesome for the Notary when the employer suggests that by not honoring the request, the Notary is showing a lack of trust of or disrespect for the employer. This can put the Notary in an unpleasant situation, one which the Notary may feel puts his or her job in jeopardy. Nonetheless, the *Code* insists that the Notary not violate the law or breach ethical dictates. The Notary is better served to surrender the commission than to perpetrate an illegal act. Indeed, the employer would be wise to encourage the Notary to follow the letter of the law, and institute policies to ensure the same; otherwise, any misdeed of the Notary may be attributed to the employer and result in liability to injured parties. (*See* 5 Ill. Comp. Stat. 312/7-102; Idaho Code § 51-118; and Va. Code Ann. § 47.1-27. *Accord Islen-Jefferson Fin. Co. v. United Calif. Bank,* 549 P.2d 142 (Cal.1976); and *Transamerica Ins. Co. v. Valley Nat'l Bank,* 462 P.2d 814 (Ariz. Ct. App. 1969).)

ARTICLE B: Commission of Employee

Standard V-B-1 provides guidance to the employee-Notary upon leaving employment. The Standard states the rule that the commission belongs to the individual Notary, and not to the Notary's employer, even if the employer paid for the commission. A Notary commission is not delegable. Consequently, the decision to resign a commission or surrender a commission certificate is solely that of the individual Notary. (*See* Cal. Gov't Code § 8207.)

The *Code* only recites the legal rule and provides The Ethical Imperative. It does not address private arrangements that may have existed between the parties. Thus, if the employer and employee had agreed as part of the employment engagement that the commission would be resigned upon the Notary's termination of employment, a cause of action may lie against the Notary who does not resign the commission. The employment contract can only give rise to damages for the employer, but it cannot force necessitate replacing the acknowledgment forms.

V-A-3: Informal Introduction Improper

The Notary shall not base the identification of any signer on the word of an employer, supervisor, client, customer, coworker, associate, partner, friend, relative or any other person unless the latter is formally sworn in as a credible witness and is not personally a party or beneficiary of the transaction.

> **Illustration:** The Notary is asked by a supervisor to notarize the signature of a client who will be visiting later in the day to sign a contract. The client is a stranger to the Notary. The supervisor directs the Notary to be "as unobtrusive as possible." When the Notary asks what being unobtrusive means, the supervisor says, "It means don't bother the client by asking for ID cards."

> *The Ethical Imperative:* The Notary informs the supervisor that state law requires "satisfactory evidence of identity" for any document signer not personally known. Though the law does not define "satisfactory evidence of identity," it is the Notary's policy to accept only a reliable ID bearing a photograph, or the sworn word of a personally known credible witness who is not involved in the transaction, in lieu of personal knowledge. Knowing the visiting client

and not being personally involved in the transaction, the supervisor offers to be sworn in as a credible witness.

Article B: Commission of Employee

V-B-1: Notary Retains Commission

The Notary shall not be required by an employer to surrender or resign the commission upon termination of employment, even if the employer paid for the commission.

> **Illustration:** The Notary informs an employer of the intent to leave in two weeks for another job. The employer says that office policy will require the Notary to hand over the commission certificate and cancel the bond, because the Notary was commissioned and bonded at the company's expense.

> *The Ethical Imperative:* The Notary declines to surrender the commission certificate or resign the commission. Regardless of who paid for the commission, it belongs solely to the Notary, not the employer, and any decision to resign belongs solely to the Notary. In addition, the Notary's surety bond may not unilaterally be cancelled by the Notary or an employer; it must remain in place for the full commission term to protect the public against misconduct by the Notary.

---

the Notary to resign the commission. Granting and regulating a Notary commission is a state power. It cannot be controlled by agreements between private parties. (*But see* Or. Rev. Stat. § 194.152 (providing that the Notary journal shall be delivered to the employer upon the Notary employee's termination of employment); and *compare* Cal. Gov't Code § 8206(d) (ruling that the notarial records of a Notary are the Notary's exclusive property and must not be delivered to the employer upon the Notary-employee's termination of employment).)

GUIDING PRINCIPLE VI

The Notary shall act as a ministerial officer and not provide unauthorized advice or services.

<u>Standards of Professional and Ethical Practice</u>

Article A: Prescribing Notarial Act

VI-A-1: Selecting Certificate Improper

The Notary who is not an attorney, or a professional duly trained or certified in a pertinent field, shall not determine or prescribe the particular type of notarial act or notarial certificate required in a given transaction.

> **Illustration:** The Notary is asked by a stranger to notarize a letter giving the stranger's friend permission to authorize medical treatment for a child. When the Notary asks the type of notarization needed — jurat or acknowledgment — the stranger says, "You decide for me. I have no idea."

> *The Ethical Imperative:* The Notary shows the language of a standard jurat and a standard acknowledgment certificate, then asks the stranger to decide which is appropriate. If the stranger cannot decide, the Notary must ask this individual to contact either the person or agency directing that the letter be notarized, or the medical facility where the letter would be presented, for further instructions.

Article B: Prescribing or Preparing Document

VI-B-1: Selecting Document Improper

The Notary who is not an attorney, or a professional duly trained or certified in a pertinent field, shall not determine or prescribe the particular type of document required in a given transaction.

> **Illustration:** The Notary is asked by a stranger for assistance in obtaining documentary proof that the stranger is a U.S. citizen. Planning to start a trip to a neighboring country the next day and with no time to get a U.S. passport, the stranger was told by a travel agent that any Notary could provide the proof of U.S. citizenship that foreign authorities will need to see. The stranger asks the Notary to supply whatever is needed.

> *The Ethical Imperative:* The Notary directs the stranger to telephone a consulate of the neighboring nation for definitive information on the paperwork needed to visit that nation.

VI-B-2: Preparing Document Improper

The Notary who is not an attorney, or a professional duly trained or certified in a pertinent field, shall not prepare a document for another person or provide advice on how to fill out, draft or complete a document.

> **Illustration:** The Notary is asked by a stranger to provide a "notarized affidavit of citizenship" that will allow the stranger to visit a neighboring country. An airline had informed the stranger that any Notary may prepare such a document.

> *The Ethical Imperative:* The Notary informs the stranger that a nonattorney is not authorized to prepare documents

---

COMMENTARY

GENERAL

Although Notaries are public officials, the *Code* recognizes that they possess limited, albeit important, powers. Notwithstanding the significant effect a notarization can have on a document or transaction, a Notary's powers are ministerial in nature. The United States Supreme Court has stated this to be the case. (*See Bernal v. Fainter*, 467 U.S. 216 (1984).) The *Code* adopts that view and in this Principle places ethical restraints on attempts to use the Notary office in any other manner. The *Code* limits the Notary only in his or her capacity as a Notary. Consistent with applicable law, Notaries who are licensed or otherwise authorized to provide services to the public are not prohibited from doing so. (*See* S.C. Code Ann. § 26-1-110.) The thrust of the Principle is to reinforce the view that Notaries not mislead the public with respect to notarial authority. (*See, generally,* Idaho Code § 51-112(c) and -(d) (identifying as sanctionable misconduct activities that lead members of the public to believe the Notary is cloaked with authority that, in fact, does not exist). *Accord* 5 Ill. Comp. Stat. 312/7-109; and Ga. Code Ann. § 54-17-8.2.)

ARTICLE A: Prescribing Notarial Act

Standard VI-A-1 admonishes a Notary from providing advice about the type of notarial certificate needed for a given document. It is, however, permissible to show the client a variety of different notarial certificates, and have the client determine or find out which one to adopt. In such circumstances the Notary should not select the certificate for the client, nor even suggest which one would be more appropriate. (*But see* Or. Rev. Stat. § 194.162(1) (permitting a Notary to select from the statutorily approved certificates).) A Notary who is an attorney or qualified as an expert in a pertinent field could select the notarial certificate, but only pursuant to the authority of being an attorney or otherwise qualified. The position adopted by the *Code* is consistent with the statutory rule in numerous jurisdictions. (*See, e.g.,* N.M. Stat. Ann. § 14-12-13(3); and Mo. Rev. Stat. § 486.385(6).)

ARTICLE B: Prescribing or Preparing Document

Standards VI-B-1 and -2 expand the prohibition of Standard VI-A-1 to selecting or suggesting the type of the document the client should use, and preparing or completing any document presented by the client. Again, the *Code* is setting the standard that a Notary has limited powers that do not include offering advice in matters apart from the proper performance of a notarial act. The Standards provide the same exception found in Standard VI-A-I for attorneys and other qualified individuals.

ARTICLE C: Providing Unauthorized Advice

Standard VI-C-1 ethically restrains Notaries from offering any unauthorized advice. The proscription is intended to be interpreted broadly and apply to all Notaries other than attorneys and those otherwise duly qualified to provide advice on the specific matter in question. (*Accord* W. Va. Code § 29C-7-201 (providing injunctive relief against a non-attorney Notary who renders services that constitute the unauthorized practice of law).)

for other persons. The Notary asks the stranger to compose the document after finding out what it must contain. Once the document is in its final form, the Notary will be able to witness the stranger's signature, administer an oath and execute a jurat certificate, as required for any affidavit.

Article C: Providing Unauthorized Advice

VI-C-1: Legal Counseling Improper

The Notary who is not an attorney, or a professional duly trained or certified in a pertinent field, shall not provide advice on how to act or proceed in a given legal matter that may or may not involve a notarial act.

> **Illustration:** The Notary is asked by a friend, "Do you know anything about wills?" The friend then expresses a desire to make sure that a relative will receive all the friend's property in the event of death. The friend asks, "Can I just write out what I want and then have you notarize it?"

> _The Ethical Imperative:_ As a nonattorney, the Notary declines to offer legal advice about the preparation of a last will and testament, urging the friend to seek the advice of an attorney.

Article D: Providing Unauthorized Services

VI-D-1: Certifying Vital Record or Recordable Document Improper

The Notary shall not certify the accuracy and completeness of a copy if the original is a photocopy, a vital record or a recordable document, nor certify any hand-rendered reproduction.

> **Illustration:** The Notary is asked by a stranger "to certify a copy of my birth certificate." The stranger needs a birth certificate for foreign travel but does not want to risk losing the "original."

The Ethical Imperative: The Notary declines to certify a copy of a birth certificate, because it is a vital record that only a custodian of vital statistics may properly certify; a Notary's "certification" of a birth, death or other vital record may lend credence to a counterfeit or tampered document. Very likely, the "original" presented by the stranger is itself a certified copy and, for a modest fee, the stranger may obtain another such copy from the bureau of vital statistics in the locality of birth.

VI-D-2: Certifying Photograph Improper

The Notary shall not certify the accuracy or authenticity of a photograph.

> **Illustration:** The Notary is asked by a stranger to notarize that person's signature on a document bearing text, jurat language and a photograph of the stranger at the end. The stranger directs the Notary to affix the seal partially over the photograph.

> _The Professional Choice:_ The Notary complies with the stranger's instruction. In notarizing a document with text, a signature and some form of jurat or acknowledgment certificate, the Notary may affix the seal partially over an attached photograph. The document's text may declare the accuracy or authenticity of the photograph, but the Notary's certificate may not.

VI-D-3: Certifying Translation Improper

The Notary shall not certify the accuracy or completeness of a translation.

> **Illustration:** The Notary is asked by a stranger to "certify" a translation of that person's foreign birth certificate for an immigration petition.

> _The Ethical Imperative:_ The Notary declines to perform such a certification, because Notaries in the United States are not authorized to certify the accuracy of translations, though they may notarize the signature of a translator on a translator's declaration.

ARTICLE D: Providing Unauthorized Services

Standards VI-D-1 through -3 identify specific activities that can raise problems for Notaries.

Standard VI-D-1 instructs the Notary not to certify the accuracy and completeness of copies of certain documents. The ethical restraint is justified on the ground that in some instances the Notary either is not authorized to perform the act (_e.g.,_ only a custodian of vital records can certify the records) or that performing the act would produce an unreliable reproduction (_e.g.,_ a handwritten copy).

Standard VI-D-2 indicates that it is not good practice to certify the accuracy or authenticity of a photograph. The Illustration recognizes, however, that in some instances, such as applications for medical licensing, photographs may be attached to documents on which an applicant's signature may properly be notarized.

Standard VI-D-3 provides an ethical restraint on the practice of certifying the accuracy or completeness of a translation. The certification of translations is not an authorized notarial power for the ministerial Notary of the United States. (For examples of procedures for dealing with would-be signers who neither speak nor understand English, _see_ IND. CODE § 33-16-2-2; and FLA. STAT. ANN. § 117.107(6).)

GUIDING PRINCIPLE VII

The Notary shall affix a seal on every notarized document and not allow this universally recognized symbol of office to be used by another or in an endorsement or promotion.

<u>Standards of Professional and Ethical Practice</u>

Article A: Affixation of Seal

VII-A-1: Seal Important on Every Document

The Notary shall affix a legible imprint or impression of an official seal on every document notarized.

> **Illustration:** The Notary resides in a state that does not require Notaries to affix seals of office on notarized documents; however, using a seal is not prohibited and many Notaries do opt to affix a seal. The Notary ponders whether use of a seal justifies the expense.

> *The Professional Choice:* Even though state law does not require a seal, the Notary opts to obtain and use one, believing it imparts a sense of ceremony and official completion to the act of notarizing that most document signers seem to expect and appreciate. The Notary also knows that a well-placed seal impression can deter forgers and eliminate potential recording problems when a document is sent out of state to a jurisdiction where Notaries use seals. The Notary decides that the minor expense of purchasing a seal is far outweighed by its advantages.

VII-A-2: Manual Affixation of Seal Necessary

The Notary shall manually affix every impression of the official seal, unless electronic affixation is expressly permitted by law, in which case the Notary shall maintain exclusive control over the means of such affixation.

> **Illustration:** The Notary considers whether it might be handy to "scan" the inked impression of the Notary seal and store it in a computer. That way, each notarial certificate may be printed out with a Notary seal already neatly and legibly affixed. Law in the Notary's state is silent about electronic affixation of seals.

> *The Professional Choice:* Since state law does not expressly authorize electronic affixation of Notary seals, the Notary continues to affix the seal manually at the time of each notarization, keeping it under lock and key when not in use. The Notary realizes that putting an image of an official seal in a computer compounds the seal security problem. Persons with access to the computer would be able to print out the seal on unauthorized documents, or copy it for use on other computers.

VII-A-3: Preprinted Seal Disallowed

The Notary shall not affix nor allow the official seal to be affixed or preprinted on any certificate or document prior to the time of notarization.

> **Illustration:** The Notary is asked by a supervisor for an impression of the Notary's seal so that it may be reprinted on multiple copies of certain standard office forms. "That way, we don't have to worry about smeared or illegible seal impressions," the supervisor says. The Notary is told that the resulting copies will be under the Notary's strict control.

COMMENTARY

GENERAL

Principle VII furnishes advice and guidance on the proper use and handling of the notarial seal. The *Code* recognizes the seal as an important symbol of office, and requires that it not be used in a fraudulent or deceitful manner or in any way that could bring disrespect to the Notary profession.

ARTICLE A: Affixation of Seal

Standards VII-A-1 and -2 prescribe the proper use of the notarial seal. Although some jurisdictions do not require the use of a notarial seal (*see, e.g.,* N.J. Rev. Stat. § 52:7-19; S.C. Code Ann. § 26-1-60; Iowa Code § 9E.6(3); and Me. Rev. Stat. Ann. tit. 4, § 951), most do (*see, e.g.,* Ark. Code Ann. § 21-14-107; Haw. Rev. Stat. § 456-3; and Mont. Code Ann. § 1-5-416). Standard VII-A-1 offers the view that use of a seal represents the preferred practice. The seal not only imparts a psychological significance to the notarization, but also helps deter fraud when properly affixed to a document. Standard VII-A-2 disapproves the electronic storing and use of one's seal because of the attendant security risks. Seals should be affixed manually to each document notarized. (*Accord* Tex. Gov't Code § 406.013(c); and 5 Ill. Comp. Stat. 312/3-102.)

Standard VII-A-3 states it is unethical for a Notary to affix the notarial seal prior to the time of notarization. (*Accord* 5 Ill. Comp. Stat. 312/3-102 (stating the seal shall be affixed at the *time of notarization*) [emphasis supplied].) If a Notary affixes the seal to an unsigned document, there are no safeguards to protect against a subsequent forgery. The dictates against notarizing blank certificates (*see* Standards IV-C-1 and -3) apply equally to affixing one's seal to an unsigned document. Such an act is tantamount to the Notary relinquishing personal control of the seal, and invites false notarizations.

ARTICLE B: Control of Seal

The seal is the exclusive property of the Notary (*see* Mo. Rev. Stat. § 486.285.3; and Wash. Rev. Code § 42.44.090(4)), and as such is the Notary's responsibility (*see* N.C. Gen. Stat. § 10A-11). Consequently, Standard VII-B-1 advises Notaries to safeguard their notarial seals. Failure to do so can result in fraudulent notarizations. Lost or stolen seals should be reported to the appropriate authority. (*Accord* Ga. Code Ann. § 45-17-14; and W. Va. Code § 29C-4-203.) Also, worn or damaged seals should be replaced to eliminate potential challenges. (*See* N.C. Gen. Stat. § 10A-11.)

Standard VII-B-2 states the rule that it is unethical for a Notary to allow another person to use his or her notarial seal. This prohibition even applies to a situation wherein one Notary allows another duly commissioned Notary of the same state to use the former's seal. The notarial seal can be used only by the Notary to whom it was issued. (*Accord* Wash. Rev. Stat. § 42.44.090(4); and Mo. Rev. Stat. § 486.285.3.) Indeed, mere possession of a Notary seal by unauthorized persons can constitute a criminal act. (*See* Fla. Stat. Ann. § 117.05(9); Mo. Rev. Stat. § 486.380; Wash. Rev. Code § 42.44.050; and W.Va. Code Ann. § 29C-6-204.) Also, it is unethical for two or more duly licensed Notaries to share a seal.

Standard VII-B-3 addresses a serious concern over improper use of the Notary seal after it is affixed to a document. The seal should only be used to complete a notarial certificate. It should never be used for commercial, advertisement, solicitation or testimonial purposes by the Notary or anyone else. (*See, generally,* Standard I-D-3

The Ethical Imperative: The Notary refuses to allow the official seal to be preprinted on any document, because it would effectively mean surrendering control of the seal.

Article B: Control of Seal

VII-B-1: Safeguarding When Not in Use

The Notary shall safeguard the official seal to prevent its misuse by others when it is out of the Notary's sight.

> **Illustration:** The Notary maintains a desk in a large and busy office with nearly 30 other desks nearby. The Notary finds it convenient to keep the official seal and journal at this desk.

> _The Professional Choice:_ The Notary always keeps the seal and journal in a locked drawer when not in use. The key is safeguarded on the Notary's person.

VII-B-2: Use or Possession by Another Improper

The Notary shall not allow the official seal to be used or possessed by another person.

> **Illustration:** The Notary is asked by a coworker for permission to "borrow" the Notary's seal and sign the Notary's name until the coworker's commission is renewed. Having failed to keep track of the commission expiration date, the coworker tearfully claims that not being able to notarize may result in dismissal from the job.

> _The Ethical Imperative:_ Understanding that Notaries are commissioned to deter fraud and not to abet it, the Notary refuses to let another person use the official seal and title to perform deceptive notarizations that will amount to criminal acts on the part of both individuals. To help out, the Notary offers to notarize for any person referred by the coworker.

VII-B-3: Reproduction in Advertisement Improper

The Notary shall not allow others to use or reproduce the Notary's seal in a commercial advertisement, solicitation or testimonial.

> **Illustration:** The Notary is asked by a stranger to notarize an affidavit. After signing the document in the Notary's presence, the stranger instructs the Notary to "be extra neat" and take special care in affixing the seal because "we intend to duplicate the affidavit by the thousands in advertisements" for a new product.

> _The Ethical Imperative:_ The Notary declines to notarize, not wanting the official signature, seal, certificate and title "Notary" reproduced in a commercial solicitation that may mislead some people into believing that the product is governmentally sanctioned or approved. A Notary need not investigate every transaction to ensure that a particular notarial certificate will not be reproduced, but the Notary should decline to notarize when having knowledge that the Notary's name or the words "Notary" or "notarized" will appear in a promotion.

Article C: Disposal of Seal

VII-C-1: Surrendering Seal to Employer Improper

The Notary shall not surrender the seal to an employer or supervisor upon termination of employment, even if the employer paid for the seal.

> **Illustration:** The Notary gives an employer two weeks' notice before leaving for a new job. The employer responds that the Notary must surrender the seal before departing, since the employer paid for it.

> _The Ethical Imperative:_ The Notary informs the supervisor that the seal will not be surrendered, since it is the personalized symbol and certifying tool of the notarial office and its use by anyone but the Notary would be unlawful.

VII-C-2: Destruction or Defacement Necessary

To prevent its misuse by others, the Notary shall destroy or deface the official seal when the term of office it denotes ends or is cut short by revocation or resignation, provided the law does not prescribe another disposition.

> **Illustration:** The Notary moves to another state for a new job.

> _The Professional Choice:_ Before moving, the Notary sends a letter of resignation to the state Notary-regulating office by certified mail, indicating a date of resignation. On that date, the Notary defaces the seal so that it may not be misused.

---

and accompanying Commentary.) The Notary can control his or her own use of the seal, and here personal accountability is not a problem. But the Notary cannot control how the seal image is used once the document to which it is affixed returns to the client's possession. The client could then quite easily use the seal image for improper purposes. The _Code_ requires the Notary to refrain from notarizing a document that the Notary knows will result in the seal impression being used to certify or impart credibility to anything but the performance of a notarial act.. The Notary acts unethically only if he or she knows or has reason to know that the seal image will be misused, but nonetheless proceeds with the notarization. A Notary cannot be accountable for matters beyond his or her control, but in any event is advised to be alert to potential misuse of the seal and guard against the situation as best as possible.

ARTICLE C: Disposal of Seal

Standards VII-C-1 and -2 address issues concerning the proper disposal of the Notary seal. Just as the Notary commission cannot be delegated to another (_see_ Standard V-B-1 and accompanying Commentary), neither can the Notary seal. In a sense, the seal is a part of the office and cannot be separated from it. Consequently, Standard VII-C-1 provides that a Notary cannot surrender the seal to his or her employer upon termination of employment even when the employer paid for the Notary's commission, seal and supplies. (This accords the rule for resigning one's commission, _see_ Standard V-B-1 and accompanying Commentary. _And see_ Mo. Rev. Stat. § 486.285.3; and Wash. Rev. Code § 42.44.090(4).) Additionally, Standard VII-C-2 suggests that when the Notary's commission either expires or is resigned, the Notary should take steps to ensure that the seal is not misused by others. The Standard indicates that either destroying or defacing the seal may be appropriate, but advises the Notary to look to controlling local law for any legally required steps to be taken with respect to the seal in such situations. Some jurisdictions require the Notary, or the Notary's personal representative, to tender the seal to the appropriate authority after the Notary's commission expires without renewal, is resigned, is revoked or ends with the Notary's death. (_See, e.g.,_ Ga. Code Ann. §§ 45-17-16 through -18; Haw. Rev. Stat. § 456-3; W. Va. Code §§ 29C-4-401 through -404; and Ohio Rev. Code. Ann. § 147.04.)

GUIDING PRINCIPLE VIII

The Notary shall record every notarial act in a bound journal or other secure recording device, and safeguard it as an important public record.

Standards of Professional and Ethical Practice

Article A: Record of Notarial Acts

VIII-A-1: Entering Every Official Act Critical

The Notary shall maintain a complete, sequential record of every notarial act performed by the Notary in a bound journal or other secure recording device allowed by law.

> **Illustration:** The Notary resides in a state where keeping a record of notarial acts is not required by law. The Notary ponders whether to document each notarization in a recordbook.

> *The Professional Choice:* Even though state law does not mandate record keeping, the Notary opts to maintain a journal in the belief that all responsible and businesslike public servants should keep a record of their official activities. In addition, the journal will prove invaluable as protective evidence of the Notary's use of reasonable care in the event of a lawsuit.

VIII-A-2: Essential Components of Entry

For every notarial act performed, the corresponding entry in the Notary's journal shall contain, at least: the date, time and type of the notarial act; the date and description of the document or transaction; the name, address and signature of each person whose signature was notarized or who served as a witness; a description of the evidence used to identify any signer who is not personally known; and the fee charged for the notarial act.

> **Illustration:** The Notary is asked by a stranger to notarize "some sensitive personal papers." The stranger presents only the signature pages of the documents. "They relate to a very messy and painful divorce," the stranger tells the Notary, "and there's no need for anyone but myself, my ex-spouse and our lawyers to know the details." The stranger keeps the text of all the documents hidden from the Notary.

> *The Professional Choice:* The Notary refuses to notarize unless handed all pages of each document. "I have no intention of reading or divulging information from your documents," the Notary tells the stranger, "but I do have a need to scan them for certain data to record in my journal, including each document's title and number of pages." The Notary further explains that the act of notarization that will protect the stranger's rights in the divorce necessarily requires surrendering to the public record certain minimally descriptive information about the transaction; it is part of the small cost of protection assured by the notarial act.

VIII-A-3: Entry Contemporaneous with Act

A complete record of any notarial act performed by the Notary shall be entered in the journal at the actual time of the notarial act, not before and not after.

> **Illustration:** The Notary arrives at the home of a client to

---

COMMENTARY

GENERAL

Guiding Principle VIII addresses the proper use of and control over Notary journals. Some jurisdictions require Notaries to maintain journals (*see, e.g.*, ALA. CODE § 36-207; CAL. GOV'T CODE § 8206; and 57 PA. CODE § 16(a)), but most do not. The *Code* favors the use of journals in all jurisdictions, including those wherein they are not required. This position is grounded in the belief that a Notary's maintenance of a journal serves the public interest. The journal not only provides a reliable record of notarized documents that can be referred to when questions arise in the future, but also helps deter fraud by requiring the Notary to obtain important information incident to the notarization that impostors may not be able to produce. The Standards offer professional guidance on how Notaries should maintain their journals to maximize their effectiveness and prevent their misuse.

ARTICLE A: Record of Notarial Acts

Standard VIII-A-1 presents the basic tenet that a Notary should maintain a journal, regardless of whether or not state law requires it. The Illustration offers the supporting rationale for this position. Standard VIII-A-3 establishes the good practice that all journal entries be made contemporaneously with the notarization.

Standard VIII-A-2 specifies the essential elements of a proper journal entry. Although it takes a cue from the *Model Notary Act*, Sections 4-102(a)(1) through (6), the *Code* does not adopt all of the *Model Act* journal requirements. For example, the *Code* does not call for the Notary to record the place of notarization if it is different from the Notary's place of business. (*See Model Notary Act*, Section 4-102(7).) The Standard offers the essential elements needed for a useful entry. Notwithstanding the *Code's* suggestion to the contrary, some jurisdictions have minimal journal requirements. (*See* ALA. CODE § 36-20-7 (requiring only that the Notary "keep a fair register of all his official acts"); and 57 PA. CODE 161 (not requiring addresses of parties, names of witnesses, nor evidence used to prove identities). More notably, *see* OR. REV. STAT. § 194.152(1) and OHIO REV. CODE ANN. § 147.04, mandating that only commercial note protests need be recorded in the journal.) Other jurisdictions have journal requirements that more closely mirror those suggested by the *Code*. (*See, e.g.*, CAL. GOV'T CODE § 8206(2)(A) through (F); TEX. GOV'T CODE ANN. § 406.014 (a)(1) through (9); and ARIZ. REV. STAT. ANN. § 41-319.A(1) through (6).) In any event, the Notary must record all items required by the controlling statute. It is worth noting that, unless specifically stated to the contrary, the statutes enunciate only the minimum entry requirements. Thus, the *Code* can be read as an advisory for Notaries to expand upon the journal entry elements prescribed by the controlling statute.

As to the journal entries themselves, most of this information is easily obtainable and presents no problems for the Notary. In calling for the description of the document or transaction, the *Code* does not contemplate that the Notary must make a detailed inspection of the document or investigation of the transaction. Nor is it anticipated that the Notary have legal, real estate or any other professional training in order to be able to make the journal entry. The entry requirement is satisfied simply by referring to the title of the document or identifying in general terms the physical nature of the paper or acts that are the subject of the notarization.

The Illustration to Standard VIII-A-2 responds to the difficult task of balancing proper journal entries with client confidentiality. Clients may seek to prevent the Notary from reading the contents of the documents to be notarized. A commonly held view by the public at large is that a Notary only "notarizes" the client's signature, and that it notarize documents but forgot to bring the journal of notarial acts along. The client urges the Notary to proceed with the notarization anyway, and promises to stop by the Notary's office later to sign the journal.

The Professional Choice: Declining to notarize without the journal, the Notary leaves to retrieve it and returns shortly to the client's home. The Notary realizes the importance of securing a journal signature and ID description at the time of the notarization rather than later, when a change of mind by the signer might cause the notarization to be falsely challenged.

Article B: Public Inspection

VIII-B-1: Limiting Access to Journal

The Notary shall show or provide a copy of any entry in the journal of notarial acts to any person identified by the Notary who presents a written and signed request specifying the month and year, the document type, and the name of the signer(s) for the respective notarization.

> **Illustration:** The Notary is approached by a stranger who claims to be an attorney representing a person for whom the Notary had notarized a document several months earlier. The stranger says the document is now at issue in a lawsuit, and asks to look at the journal of notarial acts.

> *The Professional Choice:* As a public official and servant, the Notary understands that private citizens may have a legitimate need to verify facts related to a particular notarization by looking at the journal. The Notary asks the stranger to present identification, as well as a written, signed request stating the month and year of the

notarization, the name of the person whose signature was notarized, and the type of document. The Notary explains that the stranger may only see the entries specified in writing, to respect the privacy of other signers and discourage opportunistic "fishing expeditions."

VIII-B-2: Control of Record Essential

To prevent loss, theft or tampering, the Notary shall safeguard and maintain control over the journal of notarial acts, and not surrender it to any person who does not present a subpoena or other lawful written authorization.

> **Illustration:** The Notary is asked by an acquaintance to see a particular entry in the journal of notarial acts, through presentation of a written, signed request. After viewing the entry, the acquaintance asks to make a photocopy. When the Notary responds that there is no photocopier available on the premises, the acquaintance asks, "May I take the journal to the copy shop around the corner and come right back?"

> *The Professional Choice:* The Notary declines, explaining, "It's my policy never to surrender control of the journal of notarial acts except when presented with a subpoena." As a courtesy, the Notary offers to make a copy of the journal entry that evening, if the acquaintance will return the next day.

Article C: Disposal of Journal

VIII-C-1: Surrender to Employer Improper

The Notary shall not surrender the journal to an employer upon termination of employment, even if the employer paid for the journal, unless law expressly authorizes.

---

is only necessary for the Notary to observe the client sign the document. Of course, this is not completely accurate. Some notarizations, such as acknowledgments and proofs, require more and necessitate that the Notary look at the documents to be notarized. Additionally, Standard IV-D-1 advises Notaries not to notarize documents that contain blanks or are otherwise incomplete. This practice helps deter fraud. In order to meet these obligations and to make an accurate journal entry, the Notary must have access to all of the pages of the document. (*See, also,* Standard IX-A-1 and accompanying Commentary.)

The *Code* does not require or even suggest that the Notary actually read each word or every page. The Notary's principal objective is to determine if the document contains blank sections or obvious omissions, and to glean enough information to record an accurate description of the document in the journal of notarial acts. This goal can be achieved by carefully looking at the pages without actually reading the text. The *Code* takes the position that it is possible both to allow the client confidentiality and help prevent fraud.

ARTICLE B: Public Inspection

Public access to the Notary journal is a critical issue that has stirred much debate. The problem can be analyzed by answering two sequential questions. The first question asks whether or not individual members of the public can gain access to the journal. If answered in the affirmative, the second question asks how that access should be allowed.

Standard VIII-B-1 takes the position that a Notary should allow members of the public access to the journal provided the request sufficiently identifies the document, its signer and the date it was notarized. The Standard seeks to require that the Notary be given enough information to locate the journal entry with reasonable ease, while simultaneously putting sufficient restraints on the parties seeking the information to prevent "fishing expeditions." Additionally, there are confidentiality concerns. (*See* ARIZ. REV. STAT. ANN. 41-319A, specifically providing that "[r]ecords of notarial acts that violate the attorney client privilege are not public record," even though the balance of notarial journal entries are. Consequently, those acts are not subject to journal inspection. *See* ARIZ. REV. STAT. ANN. 41-319D.)

Special issues not addressed directly by the Standard may arise for employee-Notaries whose commissions are paid for by their employers. In these instances the employee-Notary may have special contractual obligations to or be performing notarizations exclusively for the employer. In these situations it may be appropriate to allow the employer access to the journal, but only for the purpose of checking notarizations executed for the benefit of the employer. Although this view has statutory support (*see, e.g.,* CAL. GOV'T CODE § 8206(d)), it puts the onus on the Notary to develop procedures that will assure the confidentiality for non-employer clients.

The restriction suggested by the Standard should only be applied if there are no applicable contradictory statutes or administrative rules. Some jurisdictions consider the Notary journal to be a public document open to unrestricted public use. (*See, e.g.,* ALA. CODE § 36-20-7; and 57 PA. CODE § 161(b).) Notaries in these jurisdictions must obey the governing rules and make their journals accessible to the public as prescribed by law. (*Compare* TEX. GOV'T CODE ANN. § 406.014(c) (requiring the Notary, upon payment of fee, to supply a certified copy of any journal entry) *with* CAL. GOV'T CODE § 8206(c) (requiring the Notary to reproduce copy of an entry only upon receipt of clearly identifying information).)

Another camp concludes that if the applicable jurisdiction does not require the Notary to maintain a journal, then the Notary's journal is a private, personal record. The main purpose of keeping the journal in such cases, they argue, is for the Notary's personal use and protection. By having a record of the documents notarized and what identification was required, the Notary will be better able to defend against liability suits or present testimony as needed. In order to preserve client confidentiality, unauthorized access to the journal must be denied. This may be particularly important for journals that record personal information from driver's licenses or other forms of identification that can be used by unscrupulous parties to gain access to bank accounts or other private property. Since artful computer hackers can easily use such information for improper purposes, taking extra care to maintain certain critical information as confidential may be the order of the day.

Whereas the *Code* drafters do not gainsay there are risks inherent in making the journal accessible to the public, they adopted the position that a Notary can provide access without unduly compromising confidentiality. The Standard offers a prudent procedure which when followed should sufficiently limit the risk of serious confidentiality breaches. In any event, the Standard makes clear that the journal, whether a public record or not, is always subject to inspection pursuant to court or other enforceable order.

Illustration: The Notary gives notice of intent to leave for a new job in two weeks. The Notary's supervisor says that the firm will require the official journal of notarial acts to be left behind, since "it contains important information for our business records."

The Professional Choice: The Notary refuses to surrender the journal to the employer. The journal is the official record of a particular notarial officer; it must be kept in the custody of that officer, who will be solely accountable for its accuracy and its availability as evidence for the public benefit. However, the Notary is not prohibited from providing the firm with copies of all entries made in connection with its business.

VIII-C-2: Storage of Record

In the absence of official rules for disposal of the journal of notarial acts, the former Notary shall store and safeguard each journal at least 10 years from the date of the last entry in the journal.

Illustration: The Notary reports for work at a new job to find that there are a more than sufficient number of Notaries on staff to handle the office's business. With the commission about to expire, the Notary decides not to renew and to "retire" as a Notary.

The Professional Choice: On the day after commission expiration, the Notary stores the journal of notarial acts in the locked fireproof cabinet used to store all of the Notary's important personal documents. The Notary attaches a note on the cover that the journal must not be discarded or destroyed prior to a particular date, 10 years from the last entry in the journal. Notaries in states where statutory limits on civil lawsuits extend beyond 10 years may opt to preserve the journal as potential evidence as long as they feel it prudent.

(*Accord* Mo. Rev. Stat. § 486.270.)

Once it is established that there is a right to inspect the Notary journal, the second question concerning the development of workable rules for permitting access must be answered. The Standard seeks to set a reasonable procedure that does not unduly impact clients who are not the subject of the inquiry. When the journal is considered a public record, unless state law provides otherwise, there may not be any mechanism available to prevent unreasonable requests. (*See, e.g.,* Ariz. Rev. Stat. Ann. § 41-319D; and Tex. Gov't Code Ann. § 406.014(c).) Searching the journal for numerous, inadequately defined requests may place an undue burden on the Notary's time. Consequently, the better approach is not to allow indiscriminate searches, but to require a specific, well-defined, written request. (*See* Cal. Gov't Code § 8206(c); and Ariz. Rev. Stat. Ann. § 41-319D.) Moreover, some Notaries may elect not to allow public inspection of and access to the journal itself, but instead only supply a photostatic copy of the appropriate entry line from the journal. (*See* Ala. Code § 36-20-7.)

Standard VIII-B-2 suggests that the Notary never relinquish control of the journal (*accord* Cal. Gov't Code § 8206(d) (stating the journal is the Notary's exclusive property); and 57 Pa. Code § 161(b) (insulating the journal from seizure and attachment)), except pursuant to court order or other legal authorization. In those jurisdictions where the journal is a public record, the Notary is an official custodian and should ascertain what additional requirements, if any, are imposed because of this fact. The Notary also should safeguard the journal from theft or loss, such as by keeping it in a locked drawer or file cabinet. (*Accord* Mo. Rev. Stat. § 486.305 (requiring Notary to immediately notify the secretary of the state if the journal is lost or stolen).) For other issues regarding control of the journal, *see,* Standard IX-B-3 and accompanying Commentary.

ARTICLE C: Disposal of Journal

Standard VIII-C-1 suggests that it is improper for an employee to surrender the Notary journal to his or her employer upon terminating employment, even if the employer paid for the Notary commission, journal and other supplies. (*Accord* Me. Rev. Stat. Ann. tit. 4, § 955-B; *but see* Or. Rev. Stat. § 194.152(3) (allowing employer to retain journal of Notary-employee).) The Illustration elaborates on this point by noting that the Notary is the custodial officer of the journal, and as such has full responsibility for it. (*Accord* Cal. Gov't Code § 8206(d) (stating the journal is the exclusive property of the Notary).) The Notary should only surrender the journal to appropriate, legally recognized authorities. A Notary seeking to surrender a Notary journal should investigate the applicable law of his or her jurisdiction, and then act according to its directives. Although the *Code* does not specifically address the point, the Notary journal must be surrendered if the law requires when the Notary's commission is resigned, surrendered, revoked or terminated by the Notary's death. (*Accord* Ala. Code § 36-20-8 (delivery of journal to probate judge); and Ariz. Rev. Stat. Ann. § 41-317.A (delivery of journal to county recorder).)

Standard VIII-C-2 advises the Notary to ascertain and abide by local law rules with respect to completed journals, *i.e.,* journals for which there is no room for additional entries. The Standard suggests that in the absence of such rules, the Notary properly store and safeguard a completed journal. Given the confidential nature of some of the entries, it seems appropriate to require the Notary to continue to honor the rights of past clients. The Standard suggests keeping the journal for at least 10 years after the last entry. (*See* Cal. Gov't Code § 8209(c): "After 10 years from the date of deposit with the county clerk, if no request for or reference to such records has been made, they may be destroyed upon order of court.") The time period was selected with an eye toward the use of the journal in possible future lawsuits. It was believed most lawsuits would be stale, or past the applicable statute of limitations, after 10 years. Although some statutes of limitations reach 20 years (notably those relating to real estate adverse possession claims), the *Code* adopts a shorter time period. Since this is not an ethical imperative, the Notary is free to retain the journal for as long as he or she feels is necessary. In Arizona, after a journal is delivered to a county recorder, the recorder is only required to retain the journal for five years. (*See* Ariz. Rev. Stat. § 41-317B.) In California, the holding period after relinquishing a journal is 10 years. (*See* Cal. Gov't Code § 8209(c).) Once the Notary's commission expires, is surrendered or terminates with the Notary's death, appropriate disposition of the journal must be made. (*See* Standard VIII-C-1 and accompanying Commentary.) Failure to do so could result in penalties. (*See* Ariz. Rev. Stat. Ann. § 41-317.A (fine of between $50 and $500); Ala. Code § 36-20-9 (fine not less than $100); and Cal. Gov't Code § 8209(a) (a misdemeanor).)

GUIDING PRINCIPLE IX

The Notary shall respect the privacy of each signer and not divulge or use personal or proprietary information disclosed during execution of a notarial act for other than an official purpose.

<u>Standards of Professional and Ethical Practice</u>

Article A: Needless Intrusions

IX-A-1: Scrutinizing of Text

The Notary shall scrutinize the non-notarial text of a document for two purposes only: to ascertain if it appears complete and to extract data for recording in the journal of notarial acts.

> **Illustration:** The Notary is asked by a man and woman to notarize their prenuptial agreement. After they identify themselves and hand over the document, the couple is distracted for several minutes in making a telephone call. Alone with the document, the Notary is tempted to closely read its provisions.

> *The Ethical Imperative:* The Notary intrudes no further than to scan the document for blank spaces and missing pages, and to glean certain bits of data to record in the journal, including the document's title, date and number of pages. The Notary realizes that reading the document would be an invasion of the couple's privacy and a breach of public trust.

IX-A-2: Extracting or Copying Unnecessary Information

The Notary shall not needlessly extract or copy information from the text of a notarized document or from other documents possessed by its signer.

> **Illustration:** The Notary observes that a coworker Notary always makes and keeps a copy of each document notarized and of each ID card presented. The coworker explains, "It's protection for me in case I'm sued."

> *The Professional Choice:* The Notary points out to the coworker that this policy constitutes an unwarranted invasion of each signer's privacy, and risks the possibility of theft or loss of a copy and unauthorized dissemination of sensitive personal information. The Notary explains that a detailed journal entry for each notarial act that includes a description of any ID card presented and a signature will serve the same protective purpose in the event of a lawsuit.

Article B: Unauthorized Use of Information

IX-B-1: Revealing Document Particulars Improper

The Notary shall not divulge information about the circumstances of a notarial act to any person who does not have clear lawful authority and a need to know.

> **Illustration:** The Notary is notarizing mortgage papers for a stranger when a close friend walks in. After the signer has left, the friend asks, "That person just bought the house down the street from me. Did you happen to notice the selling price?"

> *The Ethical Imperative:* Though by chance noting the price on one of the documents just notarized, the Notary declines

---

COMMENTARY

GENERAL

In keeping with the notion that a Notary is a public official whose duties may provide access to a client's personal matters, the *Code* stresses the importance of respecting the privacy rights of those who are served. To this end, the *Code* exhorts the Notary to act professionally when dealing with clients, especially when sensitive matters are involved, and to be diligent in protecting the confidentiality of private information.

ARTICLE A: Needless Intrusions

A Notary is obligated to determine whether or not a document is complete before performing the requested notarization with respect to it. (*See* Guiding Principle IV, Article D and accompanying Commentary.) A Notary who maintains a journal will record information that is obtained from the document. (*See* Standard VIII-A-2 and accompanying Commentary.) Standard IX-A-1 ethically restricts the Notary's purview of information in a client's document to these two purposes. In a sense, the Standard establishes and seeks to enforce a "limited-access" rule. Although the Standard directs a Notary to scrutinize a document for these purposes, the use of "scrutinize" is not intended to authorize the Notary to closely read the document for the purpose of learning its contents or particulars. The drafters debated with whether to use "scrutinize" or "scan" and opted for the former. This choice was made principally because they felt "scan" would result in Notaries either merely glancing at documents or performing cursory checks that could not determine the completeness of the document. In weighing the risks of the overly zealous Notary who would interpret "scrutinize" as a license to intrude upon the client's privacy against that of the lazy Notary who would interpret "scan" to necessitate little more than a cavalier flip through the pages, the drafters determined it was preferable to err on the side of deterring fraud and protecting those who rely on notarizations. Notaries are strongly admonished, however, to follow the dictates of the Standard closely. There is no call for a Notary to examine a document beyond checking for blank spaces and obtaining necessary descriptive journal information. (*Accord* GA. CODE ANN. § 45-17-8(f).) Furthermore, as to the latter objective, the Notary's actions should be consistent with the mandates established in correlative Standards. (*See* Standards VIII-A-1 through -3 and accompanying Commentary.)

Consistent with the justification for a limited-access rule, Standard IX-A-2 offers guidance on how best to meet its spirit. The Standard specifically advises against "needless" extraction from or copying of a client's document. Regrettably, "needless" is not defined, and thus it is left up to the discretion of each Notary to determine its meaning. The conclusion to be drawn from the Illustration is that making copies for the Notary's personal files as a protection in the event of a possible future lawsuit is not appropriate. Properly maintaining a detailed journal will provide ample protection and not be as intrusive on the client's confidentiality. Moreover, although the Illustration does not address the matter, a Notary who retains personal copies of all notarized documents would have ethical obligations to safeguard those papers against theft or unauthorized reading. Over the years the Notary might accumulate a substantial library of documents which could cause serious security and space concerns.

ARTICLE B: Unauthorized Use of Information

Standards IX-B-1 through -3 are designed to alert Notaries to their obligation not to use any information obtained from a notarization in an unauthorized manner. Failure to observe these dictates is unprofessional and constitutes a breach of public trust. The drafters contemplate that the Standards will be interpreted liberally, and to inform the friend about any particulars in the documents. The Notary would regard such a revelation as an invasion of the stranger's privacy and a breach of public trust.

IX-B-2: Personal Use of Information Improper

The Notary shall not use for personal gain any information extracted from the text of a document that he or she has notarized.

> **Illustration:** Notarizing a heavy volume of documents for walk-in customers every day, the Notary is approached by the agent of a company that prepares and files homestead documents for homeowners. The agent offers to pay the Notary a finder's fee for providing the names and addresses of new home purchasers from the many deeds notarized daily.

> *The Ethical Imperative:* The Notary declines the offer, refusing to profit personally from use of information extracted from the text of notarized documents.

IX-B-3: Random Journal Perusal Improper

Except for the access allowed by Standard VIII-B-1, the Notary shall not allow perusal of the journal of notarial acts by any person who does not present a subpoena or other evidence of official authorization.

> **Illustration:** The Notary is approached by a stranger who presents identification and a written request to see a particular entry in the Notary's journal pertaining to the notarization of a deceased spouse's signature on a deed. The signed request is specific about the date of notarization and the type of document. The Notary finds the requested journal entry, but, before showing it, covers other entries on the same page. After studying the information, the stranger asks to look at other entries in the journal, fearing that the deceased spouse "may have been involved in other scams to cheat me out of property."

> *The Ethical Imperative:* The Notary declines to show the stranger any other journal entries unless the person is equally specific about these recorded notarial acts. The Notary is sensitive about all signers' privacy and will not reveal their transactions to anyone who cannot be specific or present a subpoena or other evidence of official authorization.

that to the extent a question arises concerning disclosure or personal use of information, the Notary should err on the side of caution and refrain from compromising the client's privacy unless required to do so by order of law.

Standard IX-B-1 posits the simple rule that a Notary must not disclose information concerning notarial acts performed. Although the Standard specifically proscribes disclosure regarding "circumstances" of the notarization, the Illustration points out that information obtained from the a reading of the document itself cannot be disclosed. Thus, the drafters intended the word "circumstances" to be given a broad interpretation. Consistent with this view, a Notary must not disclose the type, nature, purpose or contents of the document, as well as the client's demeanor, time of day, who, if anyone, appeared with the client, or any other fact attendant to the notarization.

Strict application of the above Standard is imperative. Since a Notary is prohibited from reading a tendered document for content (see Standard IX-A-1 and accompanying Commentary), a Notary should not know about detailed facts in the document. Having this information itself could constitute a breach of ethics. Disclosing it would only compound the misdeed. Sometimes, however, a Notary will inadvertently obtain confidential information while performing the notarization. (See Standard IX-A-1 and accompanying Commentary allowing the Notary to ascertain the completeness of the document and obtain material needed to complete journal entries.) The inadvertently-gained information must not be disclosed. It is private information obtained by a public official incident to performing an official act and generally not available for the public at large unless otherwise prescribed by rule or law. (For limited disclosure based on access to journal entries, see Standard VIII-B-1 and accompanying Commentary.) As a practical matter, disclosure of inadvertently-gained information will not only make the Notary answerable for the improper disclosure, but also will force the Notary to sufficiently explain the circumstances under which the information was obtained. This will be necessary so as to avoid the additional charge of violating the ethical obligation not to breach the client's privacy rights or the public trust by reading documents for improper purposes.

Standard IX-B-1 places an additional restriction on the Notary before he or she discloses information to otherwise authorized persons based upon their "need to know" the requested information. The additional requirement is not intended to give the Notary discretion to determine who has a legitimate "need to know." Instead, it was designed to protect the Notary by prescribing disclosure only to authorized officials when acting in their official capacities. This protects the public from unwarranted privacy intrusions by individuals cloaked with authority, but not pursuing legitimate interests.

Standard IX-B-2 makes clear that a Notary cannot use information contained in a document he or she has notarized for personal gain, benefit or advantage. Although not explicitly stated, the same proscription applies to any information that the Notary obtained incident to his or her official role as a Notary. The restriction, however, is limited to information directly related to the notarization. Thus, if during casual conversation while the Notary was signing the certificate the client offered investment advice, the advice would not be considered information gained incident to the notarization. The Standard is designed to prevent the misuse of information obtained solely by dint of the Notary's public official status.

Standard IX-B-3 seeks to balance the rights of the general public to gain access to information in a Notary's journal against the privacy rights of those individuals whose dealings are recorded in the journal. The Standard operates from the position as set out in Standard VIII-B-1 that the public, upon making a proper specific request, has limited access to journal information. Standard IX-B-3 directs the Notary not to allow an otherwise unauthorized person unlimited access to the entire journal. Furthermore, when a person produces a satisfactory request to inspect an journal entry, the Notary has the duty to ensure that only that specific journal entry is inspected. The balance of the journal entries should be protected from an unwarranted search. (For a complete discussion of permitting access to Notary journals, see Standards VIII-B-1 and accompanying Commentary.)

GUIDING PRINCIPLE X

The Notary shall seek instruction on notarization, and keep current on the laws, practices and requirements of the notarial office.

<u>Standards of Professional and Ethical Practice</u>

Article A: Seeking Knowledge

X-A-1: Studying Official Literature Essential

The Notary shall study all official pamphlets, handbooks, manuals and other literature pertaining to the performance of notarial acts in the Notary's jurisdiction.

> **Illustration:** An employee is asked by a supervisor to become a Notary. The supervisor provides a telephone number to call to request commission application materials. The employee soon receives an application form, an instruction sheet and a slim brochure titled "Notary Handbook."

> *The Professional Choice:* The would-be Notary completes and returns the application form. While waiting for the new commission, the employee studies the "Notary Handbook."

X-A-2: Studying Laws and Regulations Essential

The Notary shall study all laws, regulations and official directives that pertain to the performance of notarial acts in the Notary's jurisdiction.

> **Illustration:** After receiving a commission in the mail, the first-time Notary follows instructions to file an oath of office and purchases a seal. However, the Notary still feels inadequately prepared to perform official acts, since the "Notary Handbook" offers just a minimal description of notarial duties, with no specific instructions or practical guidelines.

> *The Professional Choice:* The new Notary obtains copies of the statute sections cited in the "Handbook." The Notary carefully studies these laws and keeps them handy at work.

X-A-3: Supplemental Guidance Often Necessary

In order to achieve a solid understanding of the basic principles and practices of notarization, the Notary shall be proactive in seeking out expert guidance and in supplementing any official training or materials with those provided by respected educational institutions and professional organizations.

> **Illustration:** The newly commissioned Notary has studied the state's Notary laws and "Notary Handbook," but finds they offer no practical procedures and guidelines for performing notarial duties. The Notary still lacks confidence about how to notarize.

> *The Professional Choice:* The new Notary finds a helpful, experienced Notary, who tells the beginner to call if any questions arise while performing a notarization. The experienced Notary also lends the new Notary several publications from professional organizations for Notaries.

X-A-4: Continuing Education Essential

The Notary shall keep current on new laws and regulations and on any other developments that affect the performance of notarial acts in the Notary's jurisdiction.

> **Illustration:** The Notary is asked to notarize a document by a stranger who presents a "green card" as proof of identity. When the Notary explains that such a card is not on the statutory list of acceptable IDs, the stranger claims to have no other IDs. However, another Notary advises that a recent change to the state's Notary code now allows use of green cards to identify signers, and shows an announcement of the law change in a periodical from a professional organization for Notaries.

> *The Professional Choice:* The Notary completes the notarization, resolving to subscribe to the publication in order to keep abreast of new laws affecting notarial duties.

Article B: Dispensing Knowledge

X-B-1: Providing Expertise to Others

COMMENTARY

GENERAL

Drafters of the *Code*, as evidenced by its title, consider the Notary a professional, albeit within a narrow field — an individual trained and trusted to execute duties imposed by law. The *Code* drafters also anticipate that the conscientious and professional Notary will abide by its Guiding Principles, Standards, Ethical Imperatives and Professional Choices where these are not inconsistent with applicable law. To further foster the status of the Notary as a professional, the *Code* enunciates aspirational educational and personal goals consistent with those set for other professionals. The *Code* recognizes that professionalism is not a status to be achieved and then neglected, but instead results from an on-going process of self-development and commitment to excellence.

ARTICLE A: Seeking Knowledge

Standards X-A-1 through -4 lay the educational foundation one would expect from a professional. The Notary should study all relevant material to ensure that he or she is fully knowledgeable in notarial matters. The public has a right to expect that the Notary will be able to properly perform any lawful notarization requested and provide any needed directions relative to such acts. Generally, incident to their initial appointment, Notaries are required to either state or swear they have read and are familiar with the applicable notarial laws. (*See, e.g.,* 5 ILL. COMP. STAT. 312/2-104; W.VA. CODE § 29C-2-204; and FLA. STAT. ANN. § 117.01(3).) Some jurisdictions require the person to pass an examination prior to appointment as a Notary (*see, e.g.,* OR. REV. STAT. 194.022), or take a notarial training course (*see* N.C. GEN. STAT. § 10A-4(b)(3)). The Standards further

The Notary shall freely provide notarial expertise to less experienced Notaries and step forward to offer needed corrective advice on the proper performance of notarial acts.

> **Illustration:** The Notary observes that another Notary in the same office consistently fails to ask document signers to present identification.

> *The Ethical Imperative:* The Notary approaches the coworker and tactfully explains the disservice to the public and the potential personal liability of failing to identify strangers.

Article C: Maintaining Standards

X-C-1: Reporting Misconduct

The Notary shall report to the commissioning authority violations of the statutes, regulations and directives governing the conduct of Notaries.

> **Illustration:** The Notary observes that another Notary in the same office consistently fails to ask document signers to present identification. After the coworker ignores repeated tactful warnings about the danger of this policy, the Notary reports the misconduct to their supervisor. However, even after a word from the supervisor, the colleague remains cavalier and careless about notarial duties. "I don't care," the coworker tells the Notary, "If they fire me, they fire me."

> *The Ethical Imperative:* Worried that the coworker's carelessness will be exploited to facilitate frauds, the Notary sends a letter to the state Notary-commissioning authority, detailing the colleague's habitual misconduct.

---

exhort Notaries, as professionals, to continue their educations, and keep abreast of changes and recent development relative to Notary law and practices. (*Accord* Idaho Code § 51-120 (furnishing each applicant with a Notary handbook); Me. Rev. Stat. Ann. tit. 5, § 82-A (requiring the Secretary of State to send informational publications to Notaries seeking to have their commissions renewed); and Tex. Gov't Code Ann. 406.008 (sample certificate forms sent to Notaries).) Some states require that handbooks be published and made available to Notaries. (*See, e.g.,* Va. Code Ann. § 47.1-11.)

ARTICLE B: Dispensing Knowledge

Standard X-B-1 suggests that as a member of a professional group, the Notary is obligated to share his or her expertise with less experienced Notaries. As a professional, the Notary must realize that he or she has a responsibility to the group as a whole. Helping other members better serves the public and develops the *espirit de corps* shared by professionals.

ARTICLE C: Maintaining Standards

Standard X-C-1 speaks to the importance of maintaining standards within the profession. A profession cannot exist without standards. Standards that are not enforced are meaningless. The only way for a profession to earn its deserved recognition is for its members to enforce fair and reasonable standards. Regrettably, it is not enough for a member to learn and abide by the Standards; he or she must be willing to protect the integrity of the group by reporting violations when discovered. Only by honest self-policing can Notaries elevate themselves to the status of professionals.

THE DRAFTING COMMISSION OF THE
NOTARY PUBLIC CODE OF PROFESSIONAL RESPONSIBILITY

Allen J. Beermann
Nebraska Secretary of State, 1971 - 1995

Catherine M. Brennan
Attorney at Law/Notary Public, Maryland

Denise A. Brewer
Notary Public, Oklahoma

Michael L. Closen
Professor, The John Marshall Law School
Illinois

Charles N. Faerber
Vice President, National Notary Association

Fran Fish
Notary Public Coordinator, Utah

Marian E. (Mimi) Griffiths
Director, Public Services Department
Arizona Secretary of State's Office

John T. Henderson, Jr.
Deputy Chief Counsel, Department of State
Commonwealth of Pennsylvania

Lonna R. Hooks
New Jersey Secretary of State, 1994 - 1998

Deborah K. Kearney
Deputy General Counsel
Florida Governor's Office

Ronnie J. Le Boeuf
Notary Public, Louisiana

James E. Lee
President, Old Republic Surety Company
Wisconsin

Dennis McCraven
Manager, Document Recording
Los Angeles County Registrar-Recorder/Clerk
California

Tracey R. Minnick
Notary Public, California

Malcolm L. Morris
Professor, College of Law
Northern Illinois University

Linda Perkins
Notary Public
State Bar of Arizona

William G. Peterson
Member, South Dakota House of Representatives
Assistant Vice President, Western Surety Company

Elizabeth J. Scheffee
Attorney at Law/Member, Board of Governors
Maine State Bar Association

Roberta H. (Bobbi) Shorthouse
Notary Public/Paralegal, Connecticut

Nancy P. Spyke
Assistant Professor, The Law School
Duquesne University
Pennsylvania

Deborah M. Thaw
Executive Director, National Notary Association

Milton G. Valera
President, National Notary Association

Carol S. Westwood
Notary Public, Arizona

Michael G. Wright
Notary Public, Florida

Special acknowledgment is extended to Professor Malcolm L. Morris, College of Law, Northern Illinois University, who served as Reporter for the Commentary; Professor Michael L. Closen, The John Marshall Law School, and Assistant Professor Nancy P. Spyke, School of Law, Duquesne University, for their invaluable critique of the Commentary; and Michael S. Baum, Chairman of the American Bar Association's Information Security Committee and EDI/IT Division, for his review and comments on the *Code's* final draft.

APPENDIX 2

State Notary Officials and Key Law Provisions

ALABAMA

Office of Notary Official:

Office of Secretary of State
State Capitol, Room S-105
P.O. Box 5616
Montgomery, AL 36103-5616

State Capitol, Room S-105
600 Dexter Ave.
Montgomery, AL 36104

1-334-242-7205

Key Notary Provisions:

Commission Term: 4 Years
Jurisdiction: State or County
Bond: $10,000
Seal: Embosser
(Unnecessary on
Acknowledgments)
Journal: Required

ALASKA

Office of Notary Official:

Office of Lieutenant Governor
Notary Public Office
240 Main St., Suite 301
Juneau, AK 99801

1-907-465-3509

Key Notary Provisions:

Commission Term: 4 Years
Jurisdiction: Statewide
Bond: $1,000
Seal: Inked Stamp or Embosser
Journal: Recommended
Fee Schedule: Required

AMERICAN SAMOA

Office of Notary Official:

American Samoa Government

Secretary of American Samoa

Office of Governor

Executive Office Bldg., Utulei

Pago Pago, American Samoa 96799

1-684-633-4116

Key Notary Provisions:

Commission Term: 1 Year

Jurisdiction: Manu'a and Tutuila

Bond: Not Required

Seal: Inked Stamp or Embosser

Journal: Not Required

ARIZONA

Office of Notary Official:

Office of Secretary of State

Business Services Division

Notary Department

1700 W. Washington, 7th Floor

Phoenix, AZ 85007-2888

1-602-542-4758

Key Notary Provisions:

Commission Term: 4 Years

Jurisdiction: Statewide

Bond: $5,000

Seal: Inked Stamp

Journal: Required

Fee Schedule: Required

ARKANSAS

Office of Notary Official:

Office of Secretary of State

Business & Commercial Services

1401 W. Capitol Ave., Ste. 250

Little Rock, AR 72201-1094

1-501-682-3409

1-888-233-0325

Key Notary Provisions:

Commission Term: 10 Years

Jurisdiction: Statewide

Bond: $7,500

Seal: Inked Stamp or Embosser

Journal: Recommended

CALIFORNIA

Office of Notary Official:

Office of Secretary of State

Business Programs Division

Notary Public & Special Filings Section

P.O. Box 942877 (1500 11th St., 2nd Flr.)

Sacramento, CA 94277–0001

1-916-653-3595

Key Notary Provisions:

Commission Term: 4 Years

Jurisdiction: Statewide

Bond: $15,000

Seal: Inked Stamp or Embosser*

Journal: Required

Fee Schedule: Required for Notaries who advertise in a foreign language

*Seal impression must be photographically reproducible.

COLORADO

Office of Notary Official:

Office of Secretary of State

Division of Licensing

Notary Desk

1700 Broadway, Suite 300

Denver, CO 80290

1-303-894-2200 Ext. 6405

Key Notary Provisions:

Commission Term: 4 Years

Jurisdiction: Statewide

Bond: Not Required

Seal: Inked Stamp or Embosser

Journal: Required only for documents affecting title to real property

CONNECTICUT

Office of Notary Official:

Office of Secretary of State

Legislation & Elections Admin. Division

Notary Public Unit

30 Trinity Street

Hartford, CT 06106

1-860-509-6100

Key Notary Provisions:

Commission Term: 5 Years

Jurisdiction: Statewide

Bond: Not Required

Seal: Recommended

Journal: Recommended

DELAWARE

Office of Notary Official:

Office of Secretary of State

Notary Division

401 Federal Street, Suite 3

Dover, DE 19901

1-302-739-4111

Key Notary Provisions:

Commission Term: 2 or 4 Years

Jurisdiction: Statewide

Bond: Not Required

Seal: Inked Stamp or Embosser

Journal: Not Required

DISTRICT OF COLUMBIA

Office of Notary Official:

Office of Secretary of

District of Columbia

Notary Commissions &

Authentications Section

441 4th Street, NW, Suite 810-S

Washington, DC 20001

1-202-727-3117

Key Notary Provisions:

Commission Term: 5 Years

Jurisdiction: District of Columbia

Bond: $2,000

Seal: Embosser

Journal: Required

FLORIDA

Offices of Notary Officials:

Department of State
Division of Corporations
Notary Commissions
P.O. Box 6327
Tallahassee, FL 32314

1-850-245-6975

Executive Office of the Governor
Notary Section
Room 209, The Capitol
Tallahassee, FL 32399-0001

1-850-922-6400

Key Notary Provisions:

Commission Term:	4 Years
Jurisdiction:	Statewide
Bond:	$7,500
Seal:	Inked Stamp
Journal:	Recommended

GEORGIA

Office of Notary Official:

Georgia Superior Court Clerks'
    Cooperative Authority
Notary Public Division
1875 Century Blvd., Suite 100
Atlanta, GA 30345

1-404-327-6023

Key Notary Provisions:

Commission Term:	4 Years
Jurisdiction:	Statewide
Bond:	Not Required
Seal:	Inked Stamp or Embosser
Journal:	Not Required
Fee Schedule:	Required for Notaries who advertise their notarial services

GUAM

Office of Notary Official:

Office of the Attorney General
Administration Division
287 West O'Brien Drive
    Hagatna, GU 96910

1-671-475-3324

Key Notary Provisions:

Commission Term:	4 Years
Jurisdiction:	Guam
Bond:	$1,000
Seal:	Inked Stamp & Embosser
Journal:	Required
Fee Schedule:	Required

HAWAII

Office of Notary Official:

Department of Attorney General
Notary Public Office
425 Queen Street
Honolulu, HI 96813
1-808-586-1216

Key Notary Provisions:

Commission Term:	4 Years
Jurisdiction:	Statewide
Bond:	$1,000
Seal: Inked Stamp or Embosser	
Journal:	Required

IDAHO

Office of Notary Official:

Office of Secretary of State
Notary Department
450 N. 4th St.
P.O. Box 83720
Boise, ID 83720-0080

1-208-332-2810

Key Notary Provisions:

Commission Term:	6 Years
Jurisdiction:	Statewide and outside the state for certain documents
Bond:	$10,000
Seal:	Inked Stamp
Journal:	Recommended

ILLINOIS

Office of Notary Official:

Office of Secretary of State
Index Department
Notary Public Division
111 East Monroe Street
Springfield, IL 62756

1-217-782-7017

Key Notary Provisions:

Commission Term:	4 Years
Jurisdiction:	Statewide
Bond:	$5,000
Seal:	Inked Stamp
Journal:	Not Required
Fee Schedule:	Required to post with non-English Ads

INDIANA

Office of Notary Official:

Office of Secretary of State
Notary Department
State House, Room 201
200 W. Washington Street
Indianapolis, IN 46204

1-317-232-6542

Key Notary Provisions:

Commission Term:	8 Years
Jurisdiction:	Statewide
Bond:	$5,000
Seal: Inked Stamp or Embosser	
Journal:	Not Required

IOWA

Office of Notary Official:

Office of Secretary of State

Notary Division

Lucas Building, 1st Floor

321 East 12th Street

Des Moines, IA 50319

1-515-281-5204

Key Notary Provisions:

Commission Term:	3 Years
Jurisdiction:	Statewide
Bond:	Not Required
Seal:	Not Required
Journal:	Recommended

KANSAS

Office of Notary Official:

Office of Secretary of State

Notary Clerk

Memorial Hall, 1st Floor

120 S.W. 10th Avenue

Topeka, KS 66612-1594

1-785-296-2239

Key Notary Provisions:

Commission Term:	4 Years
Jurisdiction:	Statewide
Bond:	$7,500
Seal:	Inked Stamp of Embosser
Journal:	Not Required

KENTUCKY

Office of Notary Official:

Office of Secretary of State

Notary Branch

700 Capital Avenue, Suite 86

148 Capitol Building, P.O. Box 821

Frankfort, KY 40602-0821

1-502-564-2848

Key Notary Provisions:

Commission Term:	4 Years
Jurisdiction:	Statewide/Countywide
Bond:	Varies by County
Seal:	Not Required
Journal:	Recommended
	(Required for Protests)

LOUISIANA

Office of Notary Official:

Office of Secretary of State

Notary Division

P.O. Box 94125

Baton Rouge, LA 70804-9125

1-225-922-0507

Key Notary Provisions:

Commission Term:	Lifetime
Jurisdiction:	Parishwide/
	Attorneys Statewide
Bond:	$10,000/Attorneys Exempt
Seal:	Not Required
Journal:	Required in Orleans Parish

MAINE

Office of Notary Official:

Department of Secretary of State
Bureau of Corporations, Elections
   and Commissions
Notary Public Section
101 State House Station
Augusta, ME 04333-0101

1-207-624-7752

Key Notary Provisions:

Commission Term:	7 Years
Jurisdiction:	Statewide
Bond:	Not Required
Seal:	Not Required
Journal:	Recommended
	(Required for Marriages)

MARYLAND

Office of Notary Official:

Office of Secretary of State
Notary Division
State House
Annapolis, MD 21401

1-410-260-3860

Key Notary Provisions:

Commission Term:	4 Years
Jurisdiction:	Statewide
Bond:	Not Required
Seal:	Inked Stamp or Embosser
Journal:	Required

MASSACHUSETTS

Offices of Notary Officials:

Office of Secretary of Commonwealth
Public Records Division
Commissions Section
One Ashburton Place, Room 1719
Boston, MA 02108

1-617-727-2836

Key Notary Provisions:

Commission Term:	7 Years
Jurisdiction:	Statewide
Bond:	Not Required
Seal:	Inked Stamp or Embosser
Journal:	Required/
	Attorneys Exempt

MICHIGAN

Office of Notary Official:

Department of State
Office of the Great Seal
7064 Crowner Drive
Lansing, MI 48918-1750

1-888-767-6424

Key Notary Provisions:

Commission Term:	6 to 7 Years
Jurisdiction:	Statewide
Bond:	$10,000
Seal:	Not Required
Journal:	Recommended
Fee Schedule:	Required or
	Notary must advise signer
	before performing the act

▼

MINNESOTA

Office of Notary Official:

Office of Secretary of State
Retirement Systems Bldg.
60 Empire Drive, Suite 100
St. Paul, MN 55103

1-651-296-2803
1-877-551-6767

Key Notary Provisions:

Commission Term:	5 Years or Less*
Jurisdiction:	Statewide
Bond:	Not Required
Seal:	Inked Stamp
Journal:	Recommended

*All commissions expire Jan. 31, 2005, and at 5-year intervals thereafter.

MISSISSIPPI

Office of Notary Official:

Office of Secretary of State
Notary Division
P.O. Box 136, 700 North Street
Jackson, MS 39205-0136

1-601-359-1615
1-800-256-3494

Key Notary Provisions:

Commission Term:	4 Years
Jurisdiction:	Statewide
Bond:	$5,000
Seal:	Inked Stamp
Journal:	Required

MISSOURI

Office of Notary Official:

Office of Secretary of State
Commissions Division
James C. Kirkpatrick State Info. Ctr.
P.O. Box 784
Jefferson City, MO 65102-0784

1-573-751-2783

Key Notary Provisions:

Commission Term:	4 Years
Jurisdiction:	Statewide
Bond:	$10,000
Seal:	Inked Stamp or Embosser
Journal:	Required

MONTANA

Office of Notary Official:

Office of Secretary of State
Notary Section
P.O. Box 202801
State Capitol Bldg., Rm. 260
Helena, MT 59620-2801

1-406-444-5379

Key Notary Provisions:

Commission Term:	4 Years
Jurisdiction:	Statewide
Bond:	$10,000
Seal:	Inked Stamp or Embosser
Journal:	Recommended

NEBRASKA

Office of Notary Official:

Office of Secretary of State

Business Services Division (Notary)

State Capitol, Room 1301

1445 "K" St., P.O. Box 95104

Lincoln, NE 68509

1-402-471-2558

Key Notary Provisions:

Commission Term:	4 Years
Jurisdiction:	Statewide
Bond:	$15,000
Seal:	Inked Stamp
Journal:	Recommended

NEVADA

Office of Notary Official:

Office of Secretary of State

Notary Division

101 N. Carson Street, Suite 3

Carson City, NV 89701

1-775-684-5708

Key Notary Provisions:

Commission Term:	4 Years
Jurisdiction:	Statewide
Bond	$10,000
Seal:	Inked Stamp
Journal:	Required
Fee Schedule:	Required

NEW HAMPSHIRE

Office of Notary Official:

Office of Secretary of State

State House, Room 204

107 North Main Street

Concord, NH 03301

1-603-271-3242

Key Notary Provisions:

Commission Term:	5 Years
Jurisdiction:	Statewide
Bond:	Not Required
Seal:	Inked Stamp or Embosser (Acknowledgments only)
Journal:	Recommended

NEW JERSEY

Office of Notary Official:

Department of Treasury

Division of Revenue

Notary Public Unit

P.O. Box 452

Trenton, NJ 08646

1-609-292-9292

Key Notary Provisions:

Commission Term:	5 Years
Jurisdiction:	Statewide
Bond:	Not Required
Seal:	Not Required
Journal:	Recommended

▼

NEW MEXICO

Office of Notary Official:

Office of Secretary of State
Operations Division
State Capitol North Annex
325 Don Gaspar, Suite 300
Santa Fe, NM 87503

1-505-827-3600
1-800-477-3632

Key Notary Provisions:

Commission Term: 4 Years
Jurisdiction: Statewide
Bond: $10,000
Seal: Inked Stamp or Embosser
Journal: Recommended
      (Required for Protests)

NEW YORK

Office of Notary Official:

Department of State
Division of Licensing Services
Alfred E. Smith Building
80 South Swan St., 10th Flr.
P.O. Box 22001
Albany, NY 12201-2001

1-518-474-4429

Key Notary Provisions:

Commission Term: 4 Years
Jurisdiction: Statewide
Bond: Not Required
Seal: Not Required
Journal: Not Required

NORTH CAROLINA

Office of Notary Official:

Department of Secretary of State
Notary Public Section
Electronic Notary Public Section
P.O. Box 29626
Raleigh, NC 27626-0626

1-919-807-2219

Key Notary Provisions:

Commission Term: 5 Years
Jurisdiction: Statewide
Bond: Not Required
Seal: Inked Stamp or Embosser
Journal: Recommended
Fee Schedule: Required to
      charge for notarial services

NORTH DAKOTA

Office of Notary Official:

Office of Secretary of State
Administration and Licensing
600 E. Boulevard Avenue, Dept. 108
Bismarck, ND 58505-0500

1-701-328-2901

Key Notary Provisions:

Commission Term: 6 Years
Jurisdiction: Statewide
Bond: $7,500
Seal: Inked Stamp
Journal: Recommended
      (Required for Protests)

NORTHERN MARIANAS

Office of Notary Official:

Commonwealth of Northern
   Mariana Islands
Office of Attorney General
2nd Floor, Admin. Bldg., Box 10007
Capitol Hill
Saipan, MP 96950-8907

1-670-664-2341

Key Notary Provisions:

Commission Term:	2 Years
Jurisdiction:	Commonwealth
Bond:	$1,000
Seal: Inked Stamp or Embosser	
Journal:	Required
Fee Schedule:	Required

OHIO

Office of Notary Official:

Office of Secretary of State
Notary Commission Clerk
180 E. Broad St., 15th Flr.
P.O. Box 1658
Columbus, OH 43216-1658

1-614-644-4559

Key Notary Provisions:

Commission Term:	5 Years
Jurisdiction:	Statewide
Bond:	Not Required
Seal: Inked Stamp or Embosser	
Journal:	Required

OKLAHOMA

Office of Notary Official:

Office of Secretary of State
Notary Public Department
2300 N. Lincoln, Room 101
Oklahoma City, OK 73105-4897

1-405-521-2516

Key Notary Provisions:

Commission Term:	4 Years
Jurisdiction:	Statewide
Bond:	$1,000
Seal: Inked Stamp or Embosser	
Journal:	Recommended

OREGON

Office of Notary Official:

Office of Secretary of State
Corporation Division
Notary Public Section
255 Capitol Street, N.E., Suite 151
Salem, OR 97310-1327

1-503-986-2593

Key Notary Provisions:

Commission Term:	4 Years
Jurisdiction:	Statewide
Bond:	Not Required
Seal:	Inked Stamp
Journal:	Required
Fee Schedule:	Required

PENNSYLVANIA

Office of Notary Official:

Department of State

Bureau of Commissions, Elections
  and Legislation

Notary Division

210 North Office Building

Harrisburg, PA 17120-0029

1-717-787-5280

Key Notary Provisions:

Commission Term:	4 Years
Jurisdiction:	Statewide
Bond:	$10,000
Seal:	Inked Stamp
Journal:	Required
Fee Schedule:	Required

PUERTO RICO

Office of Notary Official:

Supreme Court of Puerto Rico

Office of Notarial Inspection

Judicial Center, 3rd Floor

Munoz Rivera Ave.

P.O. Box 190860

San Juan, PR 00919-0860

1-787-751-7780

Key Notary Provisions:

Commission Term:	Indefinite
Jurisdiction:	Commonwealth
Bond:	$15,000
Seal:	Inked Stamp or Embosser
Journal:	Not Required
("Protocol" Maintained Instead)	

RHODE ISLAND

Office of Notary Official:

Office of Secretary of State

Notary Public Section

148 W. River St.

Providence, RI 02904-2615

1-401-222-1487

Key Notary Provisions:

Commission Term:	4 Years
Jurisdiction:	Statewide
Bond:	Not Required
Seal:	Recommended
Journal:	Not Required

SOUTH CAROLINA

Office of Notary Official:

Office of Secretary of State

Notary Division

P.O. Box 11350

Columbia, SC 29211

1-803-734-2119

1-803-734-2512

Key Notary Provisions:

Commission Term:	10 Years
Jurisdiction:	Statewide
Bond:	Not Required
Seal:	Inked Seal or Embosser (not required if Notary's official title affixed instead)
Journal:	Not Required

SOUTH DAKOTA

Office of Notary Official:

Office of Secretary of State
Notary Administrator
State Capitol, Suite #204
500 East Capitol Ave.
Pierre, SD 57501

1-605-773-3537

Key Notary Provisions:

Commission Term:	6 Years
Jurisdiction:	Statewide
Bond:	$5,000
Seal:	Inked Stamp or Embosser
Journal:	Recommended

TENNESSEE

Office of Notary Official:

Department of State
Division of Business Services
Notary Commissions Unit
312 Eighth Avenue North
William R. Snodgrass Tower, 6th Floor
Nashville, TN 37243

1-615-741-3699

Key Notary Provisions:

Commission Term:	4 Years
Jurisdiction:	Statewide
Bond:	$10,000
Seal:	Inked Stamp
Journal:	Required

TEXAS

Office of Notary Official:

Office of Secretary of State
Statutory Documents Section
Notary Public Unit
P.O. Box 13375
Austin, TX 78711-3375

1-512-463-5705

Key Notary Provisions:

Commission Term:	4 Years
Jurisdiction:	Statewide
Bond:	$10,000
Seal:	Inked Stamp or Embosser*
Journal:	Required
Fee Schedule:	Required

*Seal impression must be
photographically reproducible.

UTAH

Office of Notary Official:

Office of Lieutenant Governor
Notary Public and Authentication Office
Utah State Capitol
P.O. Box 142325
Salt Lake City, UT 84114-2325

1-801-538-1041

Key Notary Provisions:

Commission Term:	4 Years
Jurisdiction:	Statewide
Bond:	$5,000
Seal:	Inked Stamp
Journal:	Recommended
Fee Schedule:	Required

▼

VERMONT

Office of Notary Official:	**Key Notary Provisions:**	
Office of Secretary of State	Commission Term:	4 Years
Vermont State Archives	Jurisdiction:	Statewide
26 Terrace Street	Bond:	Not Required
Montpelier, VT 05609-1101	Seal:	Not Required
	Journal:	Recommended
1-802-828-2308		

VIRGINIA

Office of Notary Official:	**Key Notary Provisions:**	
Office of Secretary of Commonwealth	Commission Term:	4 Years
Notary Public Division	Jurisdiction:	Statewide/
P.O. Box 1795		Worldwide*
Richmond, VA 23218-1795	Bond:	Not Required
	Seal: Inked Stamp or Embosser	
1-804-786-2441	Journal: Required for electronic	
		notarizations

*Virginia Notaries have worldwide jurisdiction
for documents that will be filed in Virginia.

VIRGIN ISLANDS

Office of Notary Official:	**Key Notary Provisions:**	
Office of the Lieutenant Governor	Commission Term:	4 Years
Admin. & Business Management Div.	Jurisdiction:	Virgin Islands
18 Kongens Gade	Bond:	$5,000 or
Charlotte Amalie		$10,000 in Property
St. Thomas, VI 00802	Seal:	Embosser
	Journal:	Required
1-340-774-2991		

WASHINGTON

Office of Notary Official:	**Key Notary Provisions:**	
Department of Licensing	Commission Term:	4 Years
Business and Professions Division	Jurisdiction:	Statewide
Notaries Public Unit	Bond:	$10,000
P.O. Box 9027	Seal: Inked Stamp or Embosser	
405 Black Lake Blvd., SW	Journal:	Recommended
Olympia, WA 98507-9027	Fee Schedule:	Required
1-360-664-1550		

WEST VIRGINIA

Office of Notary Official:

Office of Secretary of State
Notary Administrator
State Capitol, Building 1, Suite 157-K
1900 Kanawha Boulevard, East
Charleston, WV 25305-0770

1-304-558-6000

Key Notary Provisions:

Commission Term:	10 Years
Jurisdiction:	Statewide
Bond:	Not Required
Seal:	Inked Stamp
Journal:	Required

WISCONSIN

Office of Notary Official:

Office of Secretary of State
Notary Records Section
P.O. Box 7848
Madison, WI 53707-7848
(30 West Mifflin, 10th Floor
Madison, WI 53702)

1-608-266-5594

Key Notary Provisions:

Commission Term:	4 Years
Jurisdiction:	Statewide
Bond:	$500
Seal:	Inked Stamp or Embosser
Journal:	Recommended

WYOMING

Office of Notary Official:

Office of Secretary of State
Notary Division
State Capitol Building
200 West 24th Street
Cheyenne, WY 82002-0020

1-307-777-7311

Key Notary Provisions:

Commission Term:	4 Years
Jurisdiction:	Statewide
Bond:	$500
Seal:	Inked Stamp or Embosser
Journal:	Recommended

▼

APPENDIX 3

Apostilles and the Hague Convention

A single *apostille* normally is the only certificate needed to authenticate notarial seals on documents exchanged between the following nations. Procedures for obtaining *apostilles* vary from state to state. Contact either the respective state Notary-regulating office (see Appendix 2, page 363) or consult a reference such as the *U.S. Notary Reference Manual* (National Notary Association) for instructions.

HAGUE CONVENTION NATIONS

The following nations are parties to the *Hague Convention Abolishing the Requirement of Legalization (Authentication) for Foreign Public Documents* of October 5, 1961. For updates to this list, contact the U.S. Department of State at:

> U.S. Department of State
> Office of Authentications
> 518 23rd St., N.W.
> State Annex 1
> Washington, DC 20520
> (202) 647-5002

▼

Albania	Dominica[10]	Macao[4]	San Marino[10]
Andorra[10]	Ecuador	Macedonia[2]	Serbia and
Antigua and	El Salvador[10]	Malawi[10]	Montenegro[2]
Barbuda[10]	Estonia	Malta	Seychelles[10]
Argentina[1]	Fiji[10]	Marshall	Slovakia
Armenia[10]	Finland	Islands[10]	Slovenia[2]
Australia	France[3]	Mauritius[10]	South Africa
Austria	Georgia	Mexico	Spain
Azerbaijan	Germany	Moldava	Suriname
Bahamas[10]	Greece	Monaco	Swaziland[10]
Barbados[10]	Grenada[10]	Namibia[10]	Sweden
Belarus	Honduras[10]	Netherlands[6]	Switzerland
Belgium	Hungary	New Zealand	Tonga[10]
Belize[10]	Iceland	Niue[10]	Trinidad and
Bosnia-	India	Norway	Tobago[10]
Herzegovina[2]	Ireland	Panama	Turkey
Botswana[10]	Israel	Poland	Ukraine
Brunei	Italy	Portugal[7]	United Kingdom
Darussalam[10]	Japan	Romania	of Great
Bulgaria	Kazakhstan[10]	Russian	Britain and
China, People's	Korea, Republic	Federation	Northern
Republic of	of	Saint Kitts and	Ireland[8]
Colombia[10]	Latvia	Nevis[10]	United States of
Cook Islands	Lesotho[10]	Saint Lucia[10]	America[9]
Croatia[2]	Liberia[5]	Saint Vincent	Venezuela
Cyprus	Liechtenstein[10]	and the	
Czech Republic	Lithuania	Grenadines[10]	
Denmark	Luxembourg	Samoa[10]	

1. Excludes recognition of extension of the Convention by the United Kingdom to the Malvinas (Falkland Islands), South Georgia, South Sandwich Islands and the Argentine Antarctic Sector.

2. The former Yugoslavia was a party to the Convention. Only the breakaway nations of Bosnia-Herzegovina, Croatia, Macedonia, Serbia and Montenegro and Slovenia have confirmed that the Convention still applies.

3. Including *Comoros Islands, Djibouti*, French Guyana, French Polynesia, Guadeloupe, Martinique, New Caledonia, Reunion, St. Pierre and Miquelon, and Wallis and Futuna. (Names appearing in regular type denote territories; *italic type denotes now-independent nations that have not affirmed participation in the Convention.*)

4. Retained status as Hague nation after control was returned to China on July 1, 1997 (Hong Kong) and December 20, 1999 (Macao).

5. Convention does not apply between Liberia and the U.S. Liberia is a nonmember of the Convention which is a contracting state or has signed to the Convention.

6. Extended to all Aruba, Curacao and Netherlands Antilles.

7. Extended to Angola, Mozambique and all overseas territories.

8. United Kingdom of Great Britain and Northern Ireland is extended to Anguilla, Bermuda, British Antarctica Territory, British Virgin Islands, Cayman Islands, Falkland Islands, Gibraltar, Guyana, Guernsey, Isle of Man Jersey, *Kiribati*, Montserrat, St. Helena, Solomon Islands, Turks and Caicos Islands, *Tuvalu, Vanuatu* and *Zimbabwe*. (Names appearing in regular type denote territories; *italic type denotes now-independent nations that have not affirmed participation in the Convention.*)

9. Includes American Samoa, District of Columbia, Guam, Northern Mariana Islands, Puerto Rico and U.S. Virgin Islands.

10. Nonmember of the Convention which is a contracting state or has signed to the Convention. ■

APPENDIX 4

Answers for Chapter Test Questions

CHAPTER 1

1. (c) 2. (d) 3. (c) 4. (d) 5. (d) 6. (c) 7. (c) 8. Impartiality means the Notary has no motive for failing to detect an impropriety.

CHAPTER 2

1. (b) 2. (d) 3. (a) 4. (d) 5. (d) 6. (a) 7. (b) 8. (a) 9. Selecting the type of notarial act is a legal decision that is beyond the scope of the Notary's expertise. For a Notary to do so might be considered the unauthorized practice of law.

CHAPTER 3

1. (c) 2. (d) 3. (a) 4. (a) 5. (b) 6. (c) 7. (d) 8. (a) 9. (c) 10. Personal appearance means that the signer and the Notary are face to face, in the same room at the time of the notarization.

CHAPTER 4

1. (c) 2. (c) 3. (c) 4. (c) 5. (a) 6. (d) 7. (b) 8. A birth certificate contains neither a current photograph, signature or physical description of the

signer, and anyone may easily obtain another individual's birth certificate at a bureau of vital statistics.

CHAPTER 5

1. (c) 2. (b) 3. (b) 4. (d) 5. (a) 6. (d) 7. (a) 8. The best way to determine awareness is to draw the signer into a conversation and judge whether the signer can communicate understandably.

CHAPTER 6

1. (a) 2. (d) 3. (b) 4. (c) 5. (a) 6. (d) 7. (d) 8. (a) 9. (c) 10. (d) 11. The journal entry should be completed before the certificate to assure that vital information is recorded before the signer leaves. 12. Journal entry below:

	Month/Day/Year/Time of Notarization	Kind or Type of Notarization	Document Date (Month/Day/Year)	Document Kind or Type	Name and Address of Signer	
1	(Today's month, day and year) 3:15 p.m.	Acknowledgment	(Yesterday's month, day and year)	Grant Deed	Harold P. Garvey 4321 Elm Street Your City, Your State, Your Zip	☐ Pers ☐ ID/ ☐ C ☐ Pe

Identification of Signer	Additional Information	Notary Fee	Signature of Signer	Right Thumbprint of Signer	
☒ Personally Known by the Notary ☐ ID Cards — Describe each card below ☐ Credible Witness(es) — Include signature of each witness		no charge	x Harold P. Garvey (signature)	(Mr. Garvey's thumbprint)	1
☐ Personally Known by the Notary					

CHAPTER 7

1. (b) 2. (d) 3. (c) 4. (a) 5. (d) 6. (b) 7. (a) 8. (b), (d), (c) 9. (b), (c) 10. (a), (d) 11. Certificate below:

State of _____ Your State _____)

) SS.

County of _____ Your County _____)

On this __Today__ day of ____This Month____, __This Year__, before me, _____ Your Name _____, the undersigned Notary, personally appeared _____ Grace C. Winslow _____, ~~personally known to me (or~~ proved to me on the basis of satisfactory evidence) to be the person(X) whose name(X) is/~~X~~e subscribed to the within instrument and acknowledged that ~~X~~/she/~~X~~ey freely executed it.

Witness my hand and official seal.

_____ Your Signature, Notary Public _____   L.S.   (Notary Seal
(Signature and Quality of Officer)   Impression)

12. Certificate below:

State of _____ Your State _____)
) SS.
County of _____ Your County _____)

Subscribed and ~~sworn to (or~~ affirmed) before me on this _Today_ day of ___ This Month ___, _This Year_, by _____ Robert T. Simons _____.

_____ Your Signature, Notary Public _____   L.S.   (Notary Seal
(Signature and Title of Official)   Impression)

CHAPTER 8

1. (b) 2. (b) 3. (a) 4. (b) 5. (d) 6. (a) 7. (c) 8. (d) 9. A certificate from another state may be used only if it substantially complies with the certificate wording specified by the Notary's state's law. 10. An acknowledgment certifies that: 1) The signer personally appeared before the Notary, 2) The signer was positively identified by the Notary, 3) The signer acknowledged the signature as his or hers. 11. Journal entry below:

	Month/Day/Year/Time of Notarization	Kind or Type of Notarization	Document Date (Month/Day/Year)	Document Kind or Type	Name and Address of Signer	
1	(Today's month, day and year) (time of day)	Acknowledgment	(Yesterday's month, day and year)	Power of Attorney	Michelle C. Wong 4525 State Street Your City, Your State, Your Zip	☐ Pers ☐ ID ☐ C ☐ Pe

Identification of Signer	Additional Information	Notary Fee	Signature of Signer	Right Thumbprint of Signer	
☒ Personally Known by the Notary ☐ ID Cards — Describe each card below ☐ Credible Witness(es) — Include signature of each witness		$2.00	x Michelle C. Wong (signature)	(Ms. Wong's thumbprint)	1
☐ Personally Known by the Notary					

12. Certificate below:

State of _____ Your state _____)

) SS.

County of _____ Your county _____)

On this _Today_ day of __This Month___, _This Year_, before me,

_____ Your Name _____, the undersigned Notary, personally

appeared _____ Michelle C. Wong _____, personally known to me ~~(or~~

~~proved to me on the basis of satisfactory evidence)~~ to be the

person(~~s~~) whose name(~~s~~) is/~~are~~ subscribed to the within instrument

and acknowledged that ~~he~~/she/~~they~~ freely executed it.

Witness my hand and official seal.

_____ Your signature, Notary Public _____   L.S.   (Notary Seal
(Signature and Quality of Officer)   Impression)

CHAPTER 9

1. (a) 2. (b) 3. (d) 4. (c) 5. (b) 6. (a) 7. (a) 8. (b) 9. (c) 10. There is no
attorney in fact jurat certificate because one person may not take an
oath or affirmation on behalf of another; the oath or affirmation
required by a jurat is a personal commitment of conscience that
signers may only make for themselves. 11. Journal entry appears on
following page:

▼

Month/Day/Year/Time of Notarization	Kind or Type of Notarization	Document Date (Month/Day/Year)	Document Kind or Type	Name and Address of Signer	□ Pers □ ID/ □ C
(Today's month, day and year) (time of day)	Jurat	(Today's month, day and year)	Affidavit of Residency	William R. Cochrane 122- 2nd Street Your City, Your State, Your Zip	
					□ Pe

Identification of Signer	Additional Information	Notary Fee	Signature of Signer	Right Thumbprint of Signer	
□ Personally Known by the Notary ☒ ID Cards — Describe each card below □ Credible Witness(es) — Include signature of each witness (Your State) Driver's License #N39105503 exp. May 3, 2005 □ Personally Known by the Notary		$2.00	x William R. Cochrane (signature)	(Mr. Cochrane's thumbprint)	1

12. Certificate below:

State of _____ Your State _____)

_____) SS.

County of _____ Your county _____)

_____ William R. Cochrane _____ (name of affiant), having been duly sworn (affirmed) before me, makes this his/~~her~~ affidavit and states that, to the best of his/~~her~~ knowledge and belief…(affiant's statement continues)….

__ William R. Cochrane (signature) __ (signature of affiant)

Subscribed and sworn to ~~(or affirmed)~~ before me by _____ William R. Cochrane _____ this __Today__ day of __This Month___, This Year.

_____ Your signature, Notary Public _____   L.S. (Notary Seal Impression)
(Signature and Quality of Officer)

CHAPTER 10

1. (b) 2. (d) 3. (c) 4. (b) 5. (b) 6. (d) 7. (a) 8. (c) 9. When asked to

certify copies of a deed, the Notary should refuse, explaining that the county recorder is the proper and lawful certifier of copies of deeds and other recordable documents. 10. A duplicate of a certified copy kept by the Notary as part of a notarial record can provide evidence that a certified copy has later been altered, and it may prove useful if the certified copy and its original are lost. 11. Journal entry below:

	Month/Day/Year/Time of Notarization	Kind or Type of Notarization	Document Date (Month/Day/Year)	Document Kind or Type	Name and Address of Signer	
1	(Today's month, day and year) (time of day)	copy certification	september 29, 1996	Last Will and Testament	Anna Lisa Bradshaw 400 McArthur Blvd, #303 Your city, Your state, Your zip	☐ Pers ☐ ID ☐ C ☐ Pe

Identification of Signer	Additional Information	Notary Fee	Signature of Signer	Right Thumbprint of Signer	
☒ Personally Known by the Notary ☐ ID Cards — Describe each card below ☐ Credible Witness(es) — Include signature of each witness		no charge	x Anna Lisa Bradshaw (signature)	(Ms. Bradshaw's thumbprint)	1
☐ Personally Known by the Notary					

12. Certificate below:

State of _____ Your state _____)

) SS.

County of _____ Your county _____)

On this __Today__ day of ___This Month___, __This Year__ I certify that the attached or preceding document of __3__ (number of pages) pages is a true, exact and unaltered photocopy of the

___Last Will and Testament___ (name or description of original document) presented to me by _____Anna Lisa Bradshaw_____ (name of original document's custodian), and that, to the best of my knowledge, the original document is neither a public record nor a publicly recordable instrument.

_____Your signature, Notary Public_____   L.S.   (Notary seal Impression)

(Signature and Title of Officer)

CHAPTER 11

1. (b) 2. (c) 3. (a) 4. (d) 5. (c) 6. An ideal subscribing witness is honest and personally unaffected by (impartial to) the transaction at hand. 7. Journal entry below:

	Month/Day/Year/Time of Notarization	Kind or Type of Notarization	Document Date (Month/Day/Year)	Document Kind or Type	Name and Address of Signer	
1	(Today's month, day and year) (time of day)	Proof of Execution by Subscribing Witness	(Month, Day and year one week ago)	sales agreement	Gayle M. Kramer 4982 Euclid Street Your City, Your State, Your Zip	☐ Pers ☐ ID ☐ ☐ ☐ Pe

Identification of Signer	Additional Information	Notary Fee	Signature of Signer	Right Thumbprint of Signer	
☒ Personally Known by the Notary ☐ ID Cards — Describe each card below ☐ Credible Witness(es) — Include signature of each witness	Principal signer is Donna E. Nunez (out of the country on business)	no charge	x Gayle M. Kramer (signature)	(Ms. Kramer's thumbprint)	1
☐ Personally Known by the Notary					

8. Certificate below:

State of _____ Your State _____)

) SS.

County of _____ Your County _____)

On this ‾Today‾ day of ___This Month___, ‾This Year‾, before me, the undersigned, a Notary Public for the state, personally appeared

_____ Gayle M. Kramer _____ (name of subscribing witness) personally known to me ~~(or proved to me on the oath of~~

~~_____ [name of personally known individual identifying subscribing witness])~~ to be the person whose name is subscribed to the within instrument, as a witness thereto, who, being by me duly sworn, deposes and says that ~~he~~/she was present and saw _____ Donna E. Nunez _____ (name of principal), the same person described in and whose name is subscribed to the within and annexed instrument in ~~his~~/her authorized capacity(~~ies~~) as a party thereto, execute the same, and that said affiant subscribed ~~his~~/her

▼

name to the within instrument as a witness at the request of

_____ Donna E. Nunez _____ (name of principal).

_____ Your signature, Notary Public _____   L.S.   (Notary Seal

(Signature of Notary)   Impression)

CHAPTER 12

1. (d) 2. (c) 3. (a) 4. (c)

CHAPTER 13

1. (d) 2. (c) 3. (b) 4. (d) 5. If the Notary cannot read and write the document's language, he or she could have difficulty 1) understanding how to proceed (determining the type of notarial act), 2) gleaning accurate data for the journal entry, and 3) completing the certificate correctly. 6. Alternatives to notarizing a document written in a language the Notary cannot understand are 1) referring the signer to a bilingual Notary, 2) notarizing an English translation, 3) referring the signer to a foreign consulate. 7. Journal entry below:

Month/Day/Year/Time of Notarization	Kind or Type of Notarization	Document Date (Month/Day/Year)	Document Kind or Type	Name and Address of Signer	
(Today's month, day and year) (time of day)	Jurat	(Today's month, day and year)	Translator's Declaration	Juan A. Martinez 8883 Hamilton Avenue Your city, Your state, Your zip	☐ Pers ☐ ID/ ☐ CC

Identification of Signer	Additional Information	Notary Fee	Signature of Signer	Right Thumbprint of Signer	
☒ Personally Known by the Notary ☐ ID Cards — Describe each card below ☐ Credible Witness(es) — Include signature of each witness	English Translation of Jose Ruiz Rodriguez's Guatemalan Birth Certificate	no charge	x Juan A. Martinez (signature)	(Mr. Martinez's thumbprint)	1

8. Certificate below:

Translator's Declaration

I declare that I made the attached English-language translation of the Guatemalan birth certificate of Jose Ruiz Rodriguez, which was in the

Spanish language, and that to the best of my knowledge and belief it is an accurate and complete translation of its source document.

___Juan A. Martinez (signature)___ (signature of affiant)

State of _____Your state_____)

) SS.

County of _____Your county_____)

Subscribed and sworn ~~(affirmed)~~ before me this _Today_ day of ___This Month___, _This Year_ by _____Juan A. Martinez_____.

___Your signature, Notary Public___   L.S. (Notary seal
(Signature of Notary)   Impression)

CHAPTER 14

1. (b) 2. (d) 3. (c) 4. (b) 5. (a) 6. (c) 7. Journal entry below:

	Month/Day/Year/Time of Notarization	Kind or Type of Notarization	Document Date (Month/Day/Year)	Document Kind or Type	Name and Address of Signer	
1	(Today's month, day and year) (time of day)	Acknowledgment	(Today's month, day and year)	Power of Attorney	Marcel I. Benoit 4723 Santa Rosa Street Your city, Your state, Your zip	□ Per □ ID □ Cred
2						□ Pers □ ID □ Co ... □ Per

	Identification of Signer	Additional Information	Notary Fee	Signature of Signer	Right Thumbprint of Signer	
1	☒ Personally Known by the Notary □ ID Cards — Describe each card below □ Credible Witness(es) — Include signature of each witness	Witness to signature By Mark: Morris R. Taylor (family friend) 128 Elm St, Your city, state + zip	no charge	x X Marcel I. Benoit Christy A. Burns / Morris R. Taylor (signatures)	(Mr. Benoit's thumbprint)	1
2	□ Personally Known by the Notary □ ID Cards — Describe each card below □ Credible Witness(es) — Include signature of each witness	Witness to signature By Mark: Christy A. Burns (hospital employee) 721 8th St, Your city, state + zip		x		2
	□ Personally Known by the Notary					

CHAPTER 15

1. (a) 2. (d) 3. (b) 4. (c) 5. (a) 6. (b)

CHAPTER 16

1. (c) 2. (a) 3. (c) 4. (d) 5. (b) 6. (a) 7. (b) 8. (a) 9. (d) 10. Notaries should not notarize wills without instructions and a certificate provided because the signers may otherwise look to the Notary for advice and direction.

CHAPTER 17

1. (c) 2. (b) 3. (d) 4. (b) 5. (d) 6. (a) 7. Four discrepancies that commonly cause document rejection are 1) an improper seal impression (missing, illegible, overprinted or expired), 2) an improper or missing signature by the Notary or document signer, 3) an improper notarial certificate and 4) improper corrections or markings on the document or the notarial certificate. 8. The three steps in correcting a document or notarial certificate are 1) line through the incorrect wording, 2) print or type correct wording above the lined out wording and 3) initial and date the correction.

CHAPTER 18

1. (d) 2. (a) 3. (b) 4. (a) 5. (c)

CHAPTER 19

1. (a) 2. (b) 3. (c) 4. (c) 5. (b) 6. (d) 7. False statements in notarial certificates are most often about 1) the signer's personal appearance before the Notary, 2) the signer's identity and 3) the date of the notarization. 8. To prevent the unauthorized practice of law, Notaries should not 1) choose notarial wording, 2) prepare documents and 3) give advice. 9. Notarial misconduct may be punished by 1) administrative penalties, 2) criminal penalties or 3) civil penalties (civil lawsuits). 10. The most common act of negligence by Notaries is not properly identifying document signers.

CHAPTER 20

1. (c) 2. (d) 3. (b) 4. (c) 5. (a) 6. (a) 7. The two major differences between a bond and E&O insurance are 1) the bond is often required

by law, but E&O insurance is not, and 2) with a bond the Notary must repay funds paid out on his or her behalf, but E&O insurance requires no repayment. 8. In using reasonable care, the three duties requiring particular attention are 1) requiring personal appearance, 2) identifying the signer and 3) keeping a notarial journal record.

CHAPTER 21

1. (a) 2. (c) 3. (b) 4. (b) 5. (d) 6. (a) 7. (c) 8. (d) 9. The two sides of undue influence are 1) a Notary or third party improperly influencing an individual to sign or not to sign a document or 2) a signer or other party influencing a Notary to forsake required procedures in performing a notarial act.

CHAPTER 22

1. (b) 2. (c) 3. (a) 4. (d) 5. (a) 6. (c) 7. (b) 8. (d)

CHAPTER 23

1. (b) 2. (a) 3. (b) 4. (c) 5. (c) 6. (d) 7. (d) 8. Laws seldom address 1) notarizing for family members, 2) notarizing corporate documents as an officer of the corporation and 3) notarizing as an agent receiving a commission.

CHAPTER 24

1. (d) 2. (a) 3. (d) 4. (b) 5. (a) 6. (c) 7. Laws that regulate advertising by Notaries serve to 1) prevent misrepresentation of the powers of a Notary and 2) prevent commercial endorsements by Notaries.

APPENDIX 5

The Notary's Quick Reference

1. Require Every Signer to Personally Appear

The signer must appear in person before the Notary on the date and in the county stated in the notarial certificate.

Personal appearance means the signer is in the Notary's physical presence — face to face in the same room. A telephone call is not acceptable as personal appearance.

2. Make a Careful Identification

The Notary should identify every document signer through either personal knowledge, the word of a credible witness under oath or through reliable identification documents (ID cards).

When relying on identification documents (ID cards), the Notary must examine them closely to detect alteration, counterfeiting or evidence that they are issued to an impostor.

Notaries should not rely on a type of identification document with which they are not familiar, unless it is checked against a reliable reference guide such as the *U.S. Identification Manual* or the *I.D. Checking Guide*.

3. Be Certain the Signer is Aware and Comprehending

A conscientious and careful Notary will be certain not only of the signer's identity and willingness to sign but also will make a layperson's judgment about the signer's ability to understand the document. This ability to understand is called awareness. It is in the Notary's best interest to determine awareness.

A document signer who cannot respond intelligibly in a simple conversation with the Notary should not be considered aware enough to sign at that moment. If in doubt, the Notary can ask the signer if he or she understands the document and can explain its purpose. Or, if in a medical environment, the signer's doctor can be consulted for a professional opinion.

4. Check the Signature

The Notary must make sure that the document signer's signature on the document and name appearing on the identification presented correspond.

To check for possible forgery, the Notary should compare the signature that the person leaves in the journal of notarial acts against the signatures on the document and on the IDs. Also, it should be noted whether the signer appears to be laboring over the journal signature, a possible indication of forgery in progress.

In certain circumstances, it may be acceptable for a signer to sign with an abbreviated form of his or her name (John D. Smith instead of John David Smith, for example), as long as the individual is signing with less than and not more than what is on the identification document.

5. Look for Blank Spaces

Documents with blank spaces have a great potential for fraudulent misuse. A borrower, for example, might sign an incomplete promissory note, trusting the lender to fill it out, and then later find that the lender has written in an amount in excess of what was actually borrowed.

If the blanks are inapplicable and intended to be left unfilled, the signer should be asked to line through each space (using ink), or to write in "not applicable" or "N/A."

6. Scan the Document

Notaries are not required to read the documents they notarize. However, they should note certain important particulars about a document, such as its title, for recording purposes in the journal of notarial acts. Notaries must be sure to count and record the number of pages, as this can show whether pages are later fraudulently added or removed.

7. Check the Document's Date

For acknowledgments, the date of signing on the document must either precede or be the same as the date of the notarization but not follow it. For a jurat, the document signing date and the notarization date must be the same.

A document dated to follow the date on its notarial certificate risks rejection by a recorder, who may question how the document could have been notarized before it was signed.

8. Keep a Journal of Notarial Acts

A journal is highly recommended for all Notaries. If a notarized document is lost or altered, or if certain facts about the transaction are later challenged, the Notary's journal becomes valuable evidence. It can protect the rights of all parties to a transaction and help Notaries defend themselves against false accusations.

The Notary should include all the pertinent details of the notarization in the journal, such as the date and type of notarization, the date and type of document, the signature, printed name and address of the signer, how this person was identified and notarial fees charged, if any. Any other pertinent data, such as the capacity the signer is claiming, also may be entered.

9. Complete the Journal Entry First

The Notary should complete the journal entry entirely before filling out the notarial certificate. This prevents a signer from leaving before the important public record of the notarization is made in the journal.

▼

10. Make Sure the Document Has Notarial Wording

If a notarial certificate does not come with the document, the Notary must ask the document signer what type of notarization is required. The Notary then may type the appropriate notarial wording on the document or attach a preprinted, loose certificate.

If the signer does not know what type of notarization is required, he or she should contact the document's issuing agency, receiving agency or an attorney to determine this. This decision is never the Notary's to make unless the Notary is also an attorney.

11. Be Attentive to Details

When filling out the certificate, the Notary needs to make sure the venue correctly identifies the place of notarization. If the venue is preprinted and incorrect, the Notary must line through the incorrect state and/or county, write in the proper site of the notarization and initial and date the change.

Also, the Notary must pay attention to spaces on the notarial certificate that indicate the number and gender of the document signers, as well as how they were identified — for example, leave the plural "(s)" untouched or cross it out, as appropriate.

12. Affix Your Signature and Seal Properly

Notaries should sign exactly the same name appearing on their commissioning papers. And they must never forget to affix a legally required seal, a common reason for rejection by a recorder.

The seal should be placed as close to the Notary's signature as possible without overprinting it. To prevent illegibility, a Notary seal should not be affixed over wording, particularly over a signature.

13. Protect Loose Certificates

If the Notary has to attach a notarial certificate, it must be securely stapled to the left margin of the document. Notaries can protect against the removal of such loose certificates by embossing them together with the documents and writing the particulars of the document to which the certificate is attached in one of the certificate's margins. For example, the notation, "This certificate is attached to a 15-page partnership agreement between Stephen Franks and Linda Becker, signed July 14, 2005," would deter fraudulent removal and reattachment of a loose certificate.

14. Do Not Give Advice

Every state prohibits nonattorneys from practicing law. Notaries never should prepare or complete documents for others or give advice on any matter relating to a document unless they are attorneys or professionals certified or licensed in a relevant area of expertise. The nonattorney Notary never chooses the type of certificate or notarization a document needs, since this decision can have important legal ramifications. The Notary could be held liable for any damages resulting from an incorrectly chosen certificate or notarization. ■

Glossary

A

Acknowledge: To recognize as one's own. In the notarial act called an acknowledgment, the document signer recognizes before a Notary that a signature on a document is his or her own and indicates it was made voluntarily.

Acknowledgment: Notarial act in which a Notary certifies having positively identified a document signer who personally appeared before the Notary and admitted having signed the document freely.

A.D.: Abbreviation of the Latin term *Anno Domini*, meaning "in the year of our Lord."

Administer: To give formally, as in "giving" an oath or affirmation.

Administrative Penalty: Punishment imposed by authorities who regulate Notaries, in the form of revocation, suspension or denial of a notarial commission and, in some states, fines or mandatory education.

Advertisement: Paid public announcement intended to sell a product, service or idea.

Affiant: Signer of an affidavit.

Affidavit: Written statement signed before a Notary or other authorized official by a person who swears or affirms to the Notary that the statement is true.

Affidavit of Citizenship: Written statement that may be notarized in which the signer declares that he or she is a U.S. citizen, as sometimes required for travel without a passport in Mexico and Caribbean nations.

Affirm: To make an affirmation; to make a solemn promise on one's own personal honor with no reference to a Supreme Being.

Affirmant, Affirmation-Taker: One who makes an affirmation.

Affirmation: Spoken, solemn promise on one's personal honor, with no reference to a Supreme Being, that is made before a Notary in relation to a jurat or other notarial act, or as a notarial act in its own right.

Age of Majority: Age at which persons can exercise all normal legal rights — varying from 18 to 21 years, depending on state law. Also called legal age.

Agent's Commission: Fee for performing as a representative or advocate on behalf of another person.

AKA: Abbreviation for "also known as"; otherwise named.

All-Purpose Acknowledgment Certificate: Acknowledgment certificate wording that is adaptable to any signer's representative capacity.

Also Known As: Otherwise named; AKA.

Alteration: Method of creating a false identification document by tampering with a valid ID.

Annexed: Attached or accompanying.

Appointment: Written authorization to perform notarial acts that is issued by a state's governor, secretary of state or other empowering official. Called a commission in some states and jurisdictions.

Apostille: Authenticating certificate required by Hague Convention that replaces a traditional chain of certificates.

Attorney in Fact: Person who has authority to sign for another.

Authentication: Process of proving the genuineness of the signature and seal of a Notary or other official, usually through attachment of a certificate of authority.

Authority: Legal empowerment to sign for another person, organization or legal entity, as in the case of an attorney in fact, trustee, corporate officer, partner and others.

Awareness: Being able to understand a document's significance.

B

Beneficial Interest: Advantage.

Bilingual: Able to read, write and speak two languages.

Bond, Notary: Written guarantee that money up to a limit will be paid by a surety to a person financially damaged by a Notary's misconduct in the event the Notary fails to do so.

Bound Pages: Pages that are securely fastened together to deter their unauthorized removal or replacement.

C

Capacity: Specific role of a representative signer — attorney in fact, trustee, corporate officer, partner or other — when signing for another person, organization or legal entity.

Carbon Copy: Reproduction of a document produced by carbon paper.

Certificate, Notarial: Wording completed, signed and sealed by a Notary that states the particulars of a notarization and appears at the end of a signed document or on a paper attached to it.

Certificate of Authority: Paper stating that the signature and seal on an attached document belong to a legitimate Notary or other official.

Certificate of Capacity: Certificate of authority.

Certificate of Naturalization or Certificate of Citizenship: Documents authenticating the granting of U.S. citizenship that are issued by the U.S. Citizenship and Immigration Services.

Certificate of Prothonotary: Certificate of authority issued by a prothonotary — the equivalent of a county clerk in some states.

Certified Copy: Document certified by an official, such as a Notary, to be an accurate reproduction of an original.

Chain Certification: Traditional authentication procedure that requires sequential attachment of certificates of authority, each validating the genuineness of the preceding one.

Chain of Personal Knowledge: Knowledge of identity linking the Notary with the signer through a credible identifying witness to establish the signer's identity. The Notary personally knows and can identify the credible witness, and the credible witness personally knows and can identify the document signer.

Chronological: In the sequence of occurrence.

Civil Lawsuit: Legal action taken by a private person, corporation or other legal entity to recover losses caused by a Notary's alleged misconduct.

Civil Penalty: Payment of funds by a Notary resulting from a lawsuit to recover financial losses that were claimed to have been caused by the Notary's misconduct.

Combined Acknowledgment Certificate: Acknowledgment certificate wording indicating a person signed in two or more representative capacities.

Commission: To authorize to perform notarial acts; written authorization to perform notarial acts that is issued by a state's governor, secretary of state or other empowering official. Called an appointment in some states and jurisdictions.

Commission Revocation: Voiding the notarial powers of a Notary.

Commission Suspension: Voiding the notarial powers of a Notary for a set period of time.

Conformed Copy: Reproduction of an original document whose unreproduced parts are filled in on the copy by hand.

Conservator: Guardian; person with the lawful power and duty to manage the affairs of another individual.

Conspiracy: Association of persons to commit a crime; unlawful plot.

Consulate: The office of an official, called a consul, appointed by his or her home country to reside in a foreign nation and care for the interests of that government's citizens through notarization, authentication of documents and other functions.

Copy Certification: Notarial act in which a Notary certifies that a copy of a document is a true and accurate reproduction of the original.

Copy Certification by Document Custodian: Alternative to a Notary-certified copy. The custodian of a document signs a declaration that a copy of that document is identical to the original; the Notary, using a jurat, then notarizes the custodian's signature on this declaration.

Corporate Officer: Agent appointed to conduct business for a corporation.

Corporation: Legal entity with many of the rights of an individual that may own property and sign contracts through its officers and agents.

Counterfeit: False document made from scratch in imitation of an authentic one.

County Auditor: County Recorder, in some states.

County Clerk: Official whose duties may include keeping a file of the bonds and signed oaths of office of Notaries, issuing certificates of authority for those Notaries, and accepting custody of journals surrendered by those Notaries upon retirement. See also "prothonotary."

County Recorder: Official who registers deeds and certain other documents in the public record.

Court Reporter: Person whose training in stenography qualifies him or her to transcribe spoken words into such form as a deposition. Also sometimes called a shorthand reporter.

Credible Identifying Witness: Believable person who identifies a document signer to the Notary after taking an oath or affirmation. The credible identifying witness must personally know the document signer and should also be personally known by the Notary.

Credible Witness: Credible identifying witness.

Crime: Law violation that is punishable, in the case of a misdemeanor, by a fine and/or confinement in a jail, or, in the case of a felony, usually by confinement in a penitentiary.

Custodian or Document Custodian: Keeper of a document.

Custodian-Certified Copy: Document verified to be an accurate reproduction of an original by the original's permanent custodian.

D

Date of Document: Date of signing, or, in the case of multiple signers, of the most recent or final signing.

Declaration of Intention to Become a Citizen: Document issued by the U.S. Citizenship and Immigration Services that is used in the process of becoming a U.S. citizen.

Deed: Document transferring ownership of property and requiring notarization.

Defendant: Person accused of causing damages and from whom compensation is sought in a lawsuit.

Deponent: Person who, under oath or affirmation, gives oral testimony that is transcribed for use in a legal proceeding.

Deposition: Written statement used in a lawsuit that is transcribed from words spoken by a person (deponent) under oath or affirmation and that is usually signed by this person.

Depose: To make a deposition; to testify under oath or affirmation orally or in writing.

Disability: Physical, intellectual or legal condition that renders one incapable of performing certain functions such as writing, communicating and handling one's own affairs.

Discretion: Freedom to act or judge on one's own, aware and heedful of the consequences.

Dishonor: Refusal to pay the sum of money promised or requested.

Disqualifying Interest: Advantage or potential advantage resulting in ineligibility to perform a notarial act.

Document Custodian: Permanent keeper of an original document.

E

Emancipated Minor: Person under the age of majority who has been freed from the control and responsibility of his or her parents.

Embosser Seal: Press-like device that imprints a raised image into a paper surface to form a notarial seal.

Endorsement: Public expression of approval.

Errors and Omissions Insurance: Contract between a Notary and an indemnity company whereby, in the event of a lawsuit against the Notary resulting from certain acts in performing a notarization, the company absorbs the Notary's costs and financial liabilities up to an agreed limit.

Ethics: Principles of good conduct; moral values.

F

False Certificate: Notarial wording that contains incorrect information.

Flag: Jargon term for certificate of authority.

Foregoing: Preceding.

Forgery: False signature, writing, document or other creation made to imitate a genuine thing; the act of making such a false creation.

Fraud: Deception aimed at causing a person unknowingly to surrender money, property, rights or advantages without compensation.

Fraudulent: Deliberately false or deceptive.

G

Green Card: Resident identification document (not actually green) issued by the U.S. Citizenship and Immigration Services, in the form of either the I-551 or the older I-151 card.

Guardian: Person with the lawful power and duty to manage the affairs of another individual; conservator.

H

Hague Convention: *Hague Convention Abolishing the Requirement of Legalization for Foreign Public Documents*, a treaty signed by more than 90 nations, including the United States, that simplifies authentication of notarized documents sent between nations.

Hand: Signature.

Holographic: Handwritten.

I

Identification: Knowing who a person is without reasonable doubt or suspicion; positive identification.

Identification Document (ID Card): Document or card which establishes the bearer's identity. Examples include passports, drivers' licenses and nondriver IDs, among others.

Illiteracy: Inability to read and write.

Immigration: Entering a country to become a legal resident, permanent or temporary.

Immigration Consultant: One who advises and assists another in the legal process of immigrating to the United States, especially in preparing the necessary paperwork. Also called an immigration specialist, immigration expert and immigration counselor.

Immigration Document: Document used in the process of becoming a legal resident of the United States, such as the Affidavit of Support (I-134).

Impartial Witness: Observer without bias; one who has no financial or beneficial interest in the transaction at hand.

Impostor: Person with false identity.

Imposture: Pretending to have another identity.

Inking Seal: Device that imprints ink on paper to form a photocopiable notarial seal.

Interpreter: A person who explains or translates.

Instrument: Document.

Intellectual Disability: Mental condition resulting either from lack of education (illiteracy) or intellectual incapacity (low IQ), that can make signing or understanding a document impossible.

IQ: Intelligence quotient; measure of intelligence.

J

Journal, Notarial: Official record book of notarizations performed by a Notary Public.

Journal Entry: Information recorded in a journal describing a particular notarization.

Journal of Notarial Acts: Detailed, chronological record of the official acts of a Notary Public.

Judicial Official: Public officer who uses considerable judgment or discretion in the performance of official duties.

Jurat: Notarial act in which a Notary certifies having watched the signing of a document and administered an oath or affirmation.

Jurisdiction: Geographic area — a state or county — in which a Notary Public is authorized to perform notarial acts.

L

Lamination: Plastic, protective covering.

Layperson's Commonsense Judgment: Decision that would be reached by a person of reasonable intelligence but without extensive legal or medical training.

Legal Age: Age of majority.

Legal Disability: Legal status, including being under legal age or proven insanity, that can restrict or disqualify persons from signing on their own behalves.

Legalization: Authentication.

Liability: Obligation to suffer the penalties for misconduct.

Lineal Relatives: Family members of previous and subsequent generations in a direct line, such as parents, grandparents, great-grandparents and so on, and children, grandchildren, great-grandchildren and so on.

Living Will: Written statement of a person's wishes concerning medical treatment in the event the signer has an illness or injury and is unable to give instructions on his or her own behalf.

Long-Form Certificate: Standard or unabridged notarial certificate wording.

Loose Certificate: Notarial certificate wording on a separate sheet of paper that is attached to a document. Used when no wording is provided, when the provided certificate wording does not comply with state requirements, when there is no room for the seal on the document, or when a preprinted certificate has already been used by another Notary.

L.S.: Abbreviation of the Latin term *locus sigilli*, meaning "place of the seal." Traditional element indicating where the seal imprint is to be placed.

M

Marker: One who signs by mark.

Marriage: Act of uniting a couple as husband and wife. Performed by Notaries only in Maine, South Carolina, Florida and West Feliciana Parish, Louisiana.

Ministerial Function: Function performed according to statute, established procedure or instructions from an authority, without exercise of independent judgment.

Ministerial Official: Public officer who follows written rules without having to use significant judgment or discretion. A Notary is a ministerial official.

Minor: Person who has not reached the age of majority (usually 18) and therefore is not considered legally competent to handle his or her own affairs.

Moral Turpitude: Conduct contrary to expected standards of honesty, morality, justice or modesty; depravity.

N

N.A.: Not applicable. Also "NA" and "N/A."

Natural Guardian: Parent of a child.

Naturalization: Becoming a citizen.

NCR or No Carbon Required: Special duplication paper that does not require an intervening sheet of carbon paper.

Negligence: Failure to use a degree of care that is expected of a person of ordinary prudence and intelligence.

Negotiable Instrument: Document containing a promise to pay a certain sum of money to the document's bearer.

Nondriver's ID: Identification document similar to a driver's license issued by most states upon request to nondrivers, such as juveniles and the elderly.

Notarial Acts, Notarizations: Witnessing duties of a Notary that are specified by law. Most often, the Notary's duties involve signed documents and require the Notary to ensure a signer's identity and willingness to sign.

Notarial Ethics: Principles of conduct to guide Notaries when laws and regulations do not.

Notarial Misconduct: Notary's violation of a law, regulation, official directive or expected standard of honesty, care or good judgment, usually in executing a notarization.

Notary Public: Person of proven integrity appointed by a state government to serve the public as an impartial witness with duties specified by law. The Notary has the power to witness the signing of documents and to administer oaths.

Notary Public Code of Professional Responsibility: Code of conduct for Notaries developed by the National Notary Association. Printed in its entirety in Appendix 1.

O

Oath: Spoken, solemn promise to a Supreme Being that is made before a Notary in relation to a jurat or other Notarial act, or as a notarial act in its own right.

Oath of Office: Oath promising to faithfully discharge the duties of a particular office.

Oath-Taker: One who takes an oath.

Original: Any document of which a reproduction has been made.

Out-of-Court Settlement: Agreement between the two sides of a lawsuit to end the dispute without imposition of an official ruling.

P

Paralegal: Trained professional who, under the supervision of an attorney, prepares documents and performs certain other standard functions within a narrow area of discretion; legal assistant.

Partnership: Legal association of two or more persons — partners — who agree to share profits and losses in a business venture.

Party: Signer participating in a transaction; principal.

Perjury: Crime of making a false statement under oath or affirmation in an official proceeding.

Personal Appearance: Appearing in person, face to face, in the same room with the Notary at the time of the notarization — not before and not after.

Personal Honor: Individual conscience.

Personal Knowledge: Familiarity with an individual resulting from random interactions over a period of time sufficient to eliminate every reasonable doubt that the individual has the identity claimed.

Photocopy: Reproduction of a document made through exact photographic duplication of the original's image, rather than through approximation of its image by hand-copying or other methods.

Photographically Reproducible: Image that can be readily photocopied or microfilmed.

Physical Disability: Incapacitating physical condition that can prevent writing (paralysis or a broken arm, for example) or impair communication (blindness, deafness).

Plaintiff: Person or entity initiating a lawsuit to seek compensation for damages; the suer.

Positive Identification: Identification; knowing who a person is without reasonable doubt or suspicion.

Postdate: Deceptive and sometimes illegal act of dating a document with a time after that of the actual signing or execution.

Power of Attorney: Document granting authority for a person to act as attorney in fact for another.

Predate: Deceptive and sometimes illegal act of dating a document with a time prior to that of the actual signing or execution.

Principal: Person who is a signer of and party to a document.

Primary ID: Government issued identification document with at least a photograph of the bearer that may be the sole basis for identification by a Notary.

PKA: Abbreviation for "professionally known as"; name one uses for professional business purposes; professional alias.

Proof: Abbreviation for proof of execution by subscribing witness.

Proof of Execution by Subscribing Witness: Notarial act where a person (called the subscribing witness) states under oath or affirmation before a Notary that he or she either watched another individual (called the principal) sign a document or took that person's acknowledgment of an already signed document. The witness must affix a signature to the document in addition to the principal's.

Protest: Notarial act in which a Notary certifies that a signer did not receive payment for a negotiable instrument.

Prove: Authenticate the signature of a principal signer not appearing before a Notary.

Prothonotary: County clerk, in some states.

Publicly Recorded: Placed in the public record or filed with a county recorder as authentic.

Q

Quality of Officer: Term sometimes appearing on notarial certificates and meaning "title of official," such as "Notary Public."

R

Reasonable Care: Degree of concern and attentiveness that a person of normal intelligence and responsibility would exhibit.

Recordable Document: Document that may be filed with an official agency such as a County Recorder.

Representative Capacity: Status of signing or acting on behalf of another person or on behalf of a legal entity, such as a corporation, partnership or trust.

Representative Signer: Person with the legal authority to sign for another individual, organization or legal entity. Representative signing capacities include attorney in fact, trustee, corporate officer and partner.

Roman Alphabet: Characters of the alphabet used in English and other European languages.

Rules of Ethics: Widely accepted standards of honesty, fairness and common sense.

S

Satisfactory Evidence: Reliable identification documents; or the sworn or affirmed statement of a credible identifying witness that an individual has the identity claimed.

Seal of Notary: Inking or embossing device that imprints the Notary's name, title (Notary Public) and jurisdiction on a notarized document. Also may include such information as the county where the commission and bond are on file, commission number and date of commission expiration

Secretarial Service: Function of typing or otherwise transcribing another person's speech or writing verbatim, without altering, paraphrasing or advising.

Short-Form Certificate: Notarial certificate with abridged or condensed wording.

Shorthand Reporter: Person whose training in stenography qualifies him or her to transcribe spoken words into such form as a deposition. More often called a court reporter.

Signature by Mark: An "X" or other symbol made in place of a signature by a person unable to write and witnessed by a Notary and two other persons.

Signature by Proxy: Signature made on behalf of a principal by a Notary or third party. Notary signatures by proxy are allowed only in a few states.

Signature of Notary: Handwritten name of and by the Notary, matching exactly with the name on the Notary's commissioning paper.

Solicitation: Enticement; advertising with an offer.

SS. or SCT.: Abbreviations of the Latin word *scilicet*, meaning "in particular" or "namely." Traditional element appearing after or to the right of the venue in a notarial certificate.

Statement of Particulars: Wording in a notarial certificate that describes what the Notary has certified.

Statute of Limitations: Law setting a time limit on filing a lawsuit to recover damages or on prosecuting for criminal misconduct.

Statutory Fee: Charge prescribed by law for services.

Subscribe: Sign.

Subscribing Witness: Person who either watches another (the principal) sign a document or takes that person's acknowledgment of an already signed document and appears before the Notary on behalf of the principal. The subscribing witness must sign the document in addition to the principal, must be personally known by the Notary, and must take an oath or affirmation stating that he or she witnessed the principal sign or took the principal's acknowledgment.

Substantially Complies: In agreement, but not necessarily verbatim.

Supplemental ID: Identification document that, alone, does not provide positive identification of a signer due to its lack of a photograph, the ease with which it may be counterfeited, and the low level of security in its issuance.

Supreme Being: God.

Surety: Person or company obliged to pay money up to a limit in the event a bonded individual fails to do so; guarantor.

Swear: To make an oath; to state under oath. To make a solemn promise to a Supreme Being.

T

Testator, Testatrix: Maker of a will. Testator is male; testatrix is female.

Testimonial: Expression of praise; endorsement.

Testimonium Clause: Wording in a notarial certificate whereby the Notary formally attests to the facts. Typically phrased as, "Witness my hand and official seal."

Translation: Conversion of written or spoken statements from one language to another.

Translator's Declaration: Written statement that a translation is accurate, signed by the person, known as a translator, who has made the translation.

Trust: Arrangement under law in which one person — called the trustee — manages property for the benefit of another person.

Type Face: Style of printed letter characters.

U

Ultraviolet Light: Light source that produces radiation just short of visibility causing otherwise invisible markings to be seen. Also known as UV light or black light.

Unauthorized Practice of Law: Practice of law by a person who is not a legal professional. Illegal act of a nonattorney in helping another person to draft, prepare, complete, select or understand a document or transaction.

U.S. Citizenship and Immigration Services, USCIS: U.S. government agency having authority over immigration.

V

Venue: Wording in a notarial certificate that indicates the state and county where the notarization takes place.

Verification: Sworn or affirmed declaration that a statement or pleading is true.

Vital Record: Birth certificate, death certificate, marriage license or other public record of demographic data.

W

Will: Legal document containing a person's wishes about disposition of personal property after death; short for "last will and testament."

Willingness: State of acting freely without duress or undue influence.

Within: Attached or accompanying.

Witness: One who has personally seen something; to observe.

Index

B

S

The National Notary Association

Since 1957, The National Notary Association, a nonprofit educational organization, has served the nation's Notaries Public — today numbering over four and a half million — with a wide variety of instructional programs and services.

As the country's clearinghouse for information on notarial laws, customs and practices, the NNA educates Notaries through publications, seminars, annual conferences and a *Notary Information Service* that offers immediate answers to specific questions about notarization.

The Association is perhaps most widely known as the preeminent publisher of information for and about Notaries. NNA works include:

- *The National Notary*, a magazine for National Notary Association members featuring how-to articles with practical tips on notarizing.

- *Notary Bulletin*, keeping NNA members up to date on developments affecting Notaries, especially new state laws and regulations.

- *Notary Basics Made Easy*, a first-of-its-kind video instruction program that simplifies Notary practices and procedures.

- *Notary Home Study Course*, a work-at-your-own-speed course covering every facet of notarization.

- *Sorry, No Can Do!* series, four volumes that help Notaries explain to customers and bosses why some requests for notarizations are improper and cannot be accommodated.

- *U.S. Notary Reference Manual,* invaluable for any person relying on the authenticity and correctness of legal documents.

- *Notary Public Practices & Glossary*, widely hailed as the Notary's bible, a definitive reference book on notarial procedures.

- State *Notary Law Primers*, explaining a state's notarial statutes in easy-to-understand language.

- *Model Notary Act*, prototype legislation conceived in 1973 and updated in 1984 and 2002 by an NNA-recruited panel of secretaries of state, legislators and attorneys, and regularly used by state legislatures in revising their notarial laws.

- *Notary Law & Practice: Cases & Materials*, the definitive and one-of-a-kind text for teaching Notary law to students in law schools and to attorneys in Minimum Continuing Legal Education (MCLE) seminars, discussing every major judicial decision affecting the Notary's duties.

- The *Notary Signing Agent Certification Course*, invaluable for candidates preparing to complete the Notary Signing Agent Certification Exam developed by the National Notary Association.

• Public-service pamphlets informing the general public about the function of a Notary, including *What Is A Notary Public?*, printed in both English and Spanish.

In addition, the National Notary Association offers the highest quality professional supplies, including official seals and stamps, embossers, record-keeping journals, affidavit stamps, thumbprinting devices and notarial certificates.

Though dedicated primarily to educating and assisting Notaries, the National Notary Association devotes part of its resources to helping lawmakers draft effective notarial statutes and to informing the public about the Notary's vital role in modern society. ■

Instructions for the Course Examination

An extremely valuable component of the *Notary Home Study Course* is the take-at-home Comprehensive Examination issued and evaluated by the National Notary Association's Educational Services Group.

Students who complete the *Notary Home Study Course* may elect to take the Comprehensive Examination to test their mastery of the important concepts of notarization.

A passing score on the Comprehensive Examination demonstrates that the student has attained a high level of skill and is prepared to serve as a Notary Public.

HOW TO GET THE EXAM

To obtain a copy of the examination and complete instructions, the student simply completes, signs and mails the postage-paid card located at the back of this book. Only original cards will be accepted; students may not send photocopies. The exam will arrive within ten days.

EXAM TIME LIMIT

Once the Comprehensive Examination is received, the student has 30 days to complete it and return it to the NNA for scoring. Because of this time limit, we strongly suggest that students prepare adequately before mailing the Examination application.

CERTIFICATE OF EXCELLENCE

A passing score entitles the student to receive the National Notary Association's Certificate of Excellence, which is evidence of his or her uncommon degree of professional dedication.

Students who do not pass may take a follow-up examination, however there will be a fee assessed to cover the cost of the additional exam and scoring. Students who successfully complete the follow-up exam also will receive a Certificate of Excellence. ■

APPLYING FOR THE COMPREHENSIVE EXAMINATION

- Complete the card below.

- Sign and date it.

- Drop it in the mail; the postage is paid.

- The examination will arrive in approximately ten days.

Application for
Notary Home Study Course
Comprehensive Examination

I have completed the Notary Home Study Course and wish to take the Comprehensive Examination. Please forward the Examination to:

Name_____

Company Name _____

Address _____

City _____ State _____ Zip _____

Daytime Telephone _____ Fax _____

When was this Notary Home Study Course purchased? (month and year) _____

Who purchased it, if not yourself? _____

Signature: _____ Date: _____

BUSINESS REPLY MAIL

FIRST-CLASS MAIL   PERMIT NO. 393   CHATSWORTH, CA

POSTAGE WILL BE PAID BY ADDRESSEE

NATIONAL NOTARY ASSOCIATION
9350 DE SOTO AVE
PO BOX 2402
CHATSWORTH CA 91313-9965